SOCIETY, CULTURE, AND TECHNOLOGY IN AFRICA

MASCA Research Papers in Science and Archaeology

Series Editor,

Kathleen Ryan

MASCA Research Papers
in Science and Archaeology

Supplement to Volume 11, 1994

SOCIETY, CULTURE, AND TECHNOLOGY IN AFRICA

---

edited by

S. Terry Childs

MASCA, University of Pennsylvania Museum of Archaeology and Anthropology
Philadelphia, Pennsylvania
1994

Published by
Museum Applied Science Center for Archaeology (MASCA)
University of Pennsylvania Museum of Archaeology and Anthropology
33rd and Spruce Streets, Philadelphia, PA 19104-6324

ISSN 1048-5325

Printed by
Cushing-Malloy, Inc.
Ann Arbor, Michigan

Cover:
A traditional Toro Smith,
Mwenge district,
Uganda,1994.
Drawing by
Veronica Socha
from photo by
S. Terry Childs.

CONTENTS

1. Garenne-Marot et al. (Senegal)
2. LaViolette (Mali)
3. Gosselain (Cameroon)
4. Merrick et al. (Kenya)
5. Kusimba et al. (Kenya)
6. Bellomo (Kenya)
7. Miller (Zambia)

Fig. 1:
Map of Africa with the research areas of the volume contributors.

SOCIETY, CULTURE, AND TECHNOLOGY IN AFRICA: AN INTRODUCTION

S. Terry Childs

Conservation Analytical Laboratory, Smithsonian Institution, Washington, DC 20560

ABSTRACT   This essay introduces a group of papers that focus on the interaction of society, culture, and technology in Africa over the last two million years. The goal of the volume is to highlight some of the research being conducted in Africa on this broad topic and thereby facilitate communication between scholars of sociotechnical systems worldwide. The first two sections of the essay briefly discuss some of the theory and methods used by Africanist scholars in their research on sociotechnical systems. The last part introduces the seven papers in the volume in terms of the geographical region, time period, and technology explored by the authors.

Introduction

Africa is a continent rich in diversity. The technological systems that were devised, manipulated, and allowed to die out over the last two million years reflect this diversity, and are only beginning to be investigated.

There is growing interest within general anthropology and archaeology in examining technology as a complex social process integral to the construction and maintenance of meaningful social life. Concurrently, some archaeologists, historians, and anthropologists have begun to examine specific webs of non-technical factors involved in the past and present-day technological systems of Africa. Each group, unfortunately, has been working in relative isolation. While non-Africanist scholars can benefit from the practical, contextual insights elicited by Africanists on many technological systems through a wide range of research methods, Africanists can benefit from some of the general theory developed and discussed by non-Africanists.

It is the objective of this essay and this volume on African society and technology to facilitate and encourage communication between scholars of technological systems worldwide. The following papers present new research on a variety of African technologies using a number of different perspectives and methods. Much of this work has been inspired by the research of various Africanists over the last twenty years, so it is appropriate to preface the research papers with an overview of the principal theoretical and methodological orientations that have been and continue to be used.

This essay consists of three sections. The first examines the theoretical debate concerning the relationships between technology and the society in which it develops, as well as the position of many Africanist scholars in this discussion. The second section concerns the methods available to and used by Africanists in their study of technological systems. The final part briefly introduces the articles in this volume, particularly in terms of the geographical region, time period, and technology explored by each author. A sizable bibliography is also included, but one which provides only an inroad by which a rich literature can be explored.

The technological process

The definition of technology and its relation to society is a contested one and is often presented in one of two opposing ways.[1] One perspective, recently labeled the Standard View (Pfaffenberger 1992:493–494; see also Basalla 1988), identifies necessity as the driving force behind the creation of objects. Objects with particular forms and physical properties are produced to meet and adapt to specific functional, largely utilitarian, needs; stylistic attributes are seen to primarily embellish and adorn other, more critical characteristics of an object. The focus of attention is always on objects and materials; people are generally missing from the picture. The Standard View also incorporates technological determinism, the idea that technology is "a powerful and automonous agent that dictates the patterns of human social and cultural life" (Pfaffenberger 1988:239). Exaggerated by the blinding speed of modern-day technological innovation and change and its impact on Western life, this theory has been widely accepted as a force behind social action throughout the history of humankind. The central place, for example, of the "Stone" and the "Iron" in the archaeological reconstructions of past lifeways during the "Ages" of humankind are revealing testimonies to this notion.

The other general perspective on technology is that it is completely interactive with the sociocultural context in which it is developed and changes. Local social relations, economics, politics, and ideology impact and help structure the behavior involved in technological processes and vice versa. As this view has been elaborated, several conceptual labels with different emphases have been offered. These include "behavioral archaeology" (Schiffer 1976, 1992), "chaîne opératoire" (Lemonnier 1976, 1986), "technological style" (Lechtman 1977; Lechtman and Steinberg 1979; Childs 1991a), an "anthropology of technology" (Pfaffenberger 1988, 1992; Lemonnier 1992), and the "sociotechnical system" (Hughes 1990; Pfaffenberger 1992). The general notions that unite these ideas is that "human behavior fundamentally is the interaction of people and things" (Schiffer 1992:2), and that people actively make choices as they manipulate their social and natural environment to ensure the perpetuation and reproduction of their society.

Most of the scholars who have been studying the materials, objects, and technologies of Africa in recent years embrace the latter view of technology, but do so rather unconsciously (e.g., David and Hennig 1972; Schmidt 1978; de Maret 1980; Drewal 1980; Herbert 1984; Todd 1985; McNaughton 1988; Fowler 1989). Such scholars take it for granted that technology is a social process, centers on the relationships between people and objects, and is strongly influenced by worldviews and cultural values.

The relatively long-standing acceptance of the intimate relationship between African technology and society stems from at least two factors. The first is related to the nature of the ethnographic record that every student of Africa reads. There are many reports by explorers, missionaries, administrators, and anthropologists over the last century or so that describe the social and ideological complexities of traditional technological systems, such as iron smelting, copper casting, pottery making, and weaving (e.g., Wyckaert 1914; Rattray 1927; de Hemptinne 1926). These accounts defy any notion that necessity was a driving force behind the material and behavioral choices made during the technological operations observed, or that a technology dictated social life in Africa. The sociopolitical relationships between the participants, as well as the significance of taboos, control over technical and esoteric knowledge, scheduling of other activities, and ritual were much more evident than basic necessity.

The second factor relates to the opportunities that Africanist scholars[2] have had (and have often instigated) to witness and experience the operation of preindustrial technologies in their social and natural contexts. Contrary

to most situations in Europe and other parts of the world, it is still possible to engage practicing craftspeople in discussion about what factors—technical, social, economic, political, and the like—influence their decision-making during a technological activity. Negotiations over which resources to select and combine, or where to situate a work area can be witnessed firsthand. In such living contexts, it becomes perfectly clear that the relationships between people and the wide variety of information they control are just as critical, if not more so, to a successful technological process than the end product (i.e., van der Merwe and Avery 1987). These experiences also underscore the variety of other concerns that influence decision-making during production, such as politics, marking ethnic identity, structuring social status and age, or constructing and reinforcing cultural values (e.g., Larick 1986, 1991; Dilley 1987; David et al. 1988; Dietler and Herbich 1989; Sterner 1989; Berns 1990, 1993; Childs 1991a, 1991b; Herbert 1993).

It is unfortunate that many of the archaeologists and historians who have championed the documentation of African sociotechnical systems have not entered the general debate on the interaction between technology and society (for recent exceptions see Austen and Headrick 1983; Killick 1990; Gosselain 1992; Herbert 1993; Childs and Killick 1993). Two reasons may help explain this phenomenon. One is that many of the first scholars to investigate African technologies in depth simply have not read the writings of various historians of technology, engineers, and anthropologists whose work they perceive to be peripheral at best. Most take it for granted that technology is "simultaneously material, social and symbolic" (Pfaffenberger 1988:236); why, they might ask, should they spend the time to read that which states the obvious? As more scholars begin to examine the general implications of their research on African sociotechnical systems and present their observations to non-Africanist audiences, some may decide to enter this discussion with their compelling data.

The other reason that many Africanists have not argued the technology and society issue is that there are topics deemed to be much 'hotter' in anthropological archaeology. One such debate concerns the definition, functions, and sociocultural significance of style, both formal and technological, toward which some scholars have focused their work on African sociotechnical systems (e.g., Larick 1986; David et al. 1988; Dietler and Herbich 1989; Sterner 1989; Childs 1991a; Gosselain 1992). It is noteworthy that the Africanists writing on formal style (location and form of decoration, vessel shape, etc.) advocate its contextual study—the social, symbolic, and material factors that influence stylistic choices. These researchers, then, are actually involved in the theoretical discussion on the integration of technology and society, but in a backhanded way that focuses on the more fashionable issue of style.

Interdisciplinary research on African sociotechnical systems

It is useful to explore the methods used by scholars of African technology, such as ethnoarchaeology, film-making, replications, laboratory and field experiments, and various archaeological sciences, for several reasons. First, recognition of the multi-faceted nature of technological systems have encouraged Africanists to organize projects that involve a number of specialists (see Miller and van der Merwe 1994 for citations on recent metallurgical research). These projects tend to be more interdisciplinary than multidisciplinary and can provide non-Africanists with ideas on how to maximize specialist interaction and co-operation, a long-standing problem in archaeology (DeAtley and Bishop 1991). Second, some methods, particularly those involving ethnographic observations and participation, are available to Africanist scholars, but not to researchers in other parts of the world. The insights yielded from applying more than one method to a technological system, such as iron smelting, pottery making, or stone tool making, can be pooled for a more holistic understanding of the system and its variability. This knowledge base is then applicable to the study of and cross-cultural comparisons between preindustrial technologies worldwide (i.e., Killick 1991; Gordon and Killick 1993).

Survey and excavations of ancient production areas, particularly those involving lithic manufacture and metal working, are relatively commonplace for Africanist archaeologists (e.g., van der Merwe and Scully 1971; Bisson 1976; Isaac 1977; Schmidt and Childs 1985; de Barros 1986; Stiles 1991), but the integration of needed specialists from other disciplines into such projects is not. Gertrude Caton-Thompson (1931), the first professional archaeologist to excavate at Great Zimbabwe and related sites in the late 1920s, made a promising start at incorporating the contributions of specialists into the fabric of her project. Although she relegated specialist reports to the appendices, such as the metallurgical analyses of G. Stanley, she did discuss their general results in her text. This early interest in the use of outside expertise to augment the archaeological findings unfortunately languished until the 1970s when a very few individuals, such as J. Desmond Clark, Frank Willett, Clark Howell, Glynn Isaac, Peter Schmidt, and Nikolaas van der Merwe, revived integrated research. These and other researchers encouraged true interdisciplinary work that involved collaboration with other specialists (field archaeology is a specialty in itself) in order to solve a research problem well grounded in archaeological theory (DeAtley and Bishop 1991). Some, for example, have been interested in the ecological context of technology and sought the expertise of palynologists and wood experts (van Grunderbeek et al. 1983). Others have focused on the economics behind the selection of natural resources and collaborated with geologists, materials scientists, and engineers (e.g., Wenner and van der Merwe 1986; Merrick and Brown 1984).

The tendency toward interdisciplinary rather than multidisciplinary research among Africanist archaeologists seems to stem from several factors. One may relate to the fact that African archaeology is a relatively small field, the funding for projects in distant countries is difficult to get, and structured cooperation is recognized as being essential to the completion of a project. Relatedly, there is presently a general trend among archaeologists to be survivalists and Africanists are no exceptions. Some, including those mentioned above, have trained their students in a broad range of fields and provided them with a basic understanding of the capabilities and limitations of specialist studies for their efficient and productive use. A growing number of young Africanist scholars, both Africans and non-Africans, have been encouraged to master an archaeological science, such as archaeometallurgy, ceramic technology, lithic use wear, or archaeomagnetic dating.

Such individuals, including many contributors to this volume, are trained to approach a research problem by integrating the methods developed in other disciplines with archaeological theory. While they are contributing to a critical foundation of interdisciplinary activity, they are also confronting an unfortunate, but increasing problem— access to the laboratory or field equipment necessary for specialist pursuits. It benefits no one to expend the effort and money to train individuals in such methods if adequate research support does not exist beyond graduate school. Well-trained Africans returning to their universities are affected in particular because no funds exist to buy and maintain essential equipment, such as specialized microscopes (let alone film). This predicament may never be satisfactorily resolved during the present era of decreasing research money, but it does serve to promote and underscore one thing of global relevance: greater cooperation, communication, and understanding between individuals and international institutions.

What is always missing from archaeological studies of technological systems, despite various clues, is a complete picture of their sociocultural contexts and the social and symbolic factors influencing technical decisions. It is for this reason that a number of Africanist archaeologists and historians have also taken advantage of opportunities to recognize and explain prehistoric processes through ethnoarchaeology and direct analogy, as well as experiment. There are two common approaches. One is to observe the technical and social dynamics of an extant indigenous technology, while sometimes monitoring it with scientific equipment (e.g., Yellen 1977; Bisson 1976; Clark and Kurashina 1981; Agorsah 1985; Dilley 1987; Herbich 1987; Gifford-Gonzales 1989; Kanimba and Bellomo 1990; Gosselain 1992). The other strategy is to perform reconstructions of a technology by enlisting the expertise of local craftspeople, often those who have not practiced a craft for decades (e.g., Schmidt and Avery 1978; Nicklin and Salmons 1979; Todd 1985; van der Merwe and Avery 1987; David et al. 1989). Others, usually anthropologists and art historians, have become totally immersed in a sociotechnical system through apprenticeship (Coy 1982, 1989; McNaughton 1988) or have applied more standard ethnographic approaches (Balfet 1965; Darish 1989; Phillips 1989). Such ethnoarchaeological and ethnographic methods, whether or not interdisciplinary in nature, often involve some problems and biases (Herbert 1993), but also provide valuable insights that have broad relevance across Africa and the world.

Related to these latter approaches to African sociotechnical systems is the recognition and development of another important specialty with global application: film making. A number of important works (Echard 1968; David and LeBléis 1988; O'Neill et al. 1989; Saltman et al. 1986; David 1990; Dewey 1990; Belkin 1990; Oud 1991) reveal how film and video capture the complex social dynamics, along with the natural contexts, of technologies that are impossible to fully express in words. Film is also a flexible medium in which information produced by collaborating specialists can be incorporated into the drama in ways that are readily accessible to the non-specialist and lay audience.

A final method used by Africanist and non-Africanist archaeologists alike involves experimentation. Such work may be conducted for several reasons, although it is usually focused on the technical aspects of a process. The most common reason for experimental archaeology is to reproduce a process for which there is no known ethnographic analogy or homology. This is often needed for lithic manufacture and for technologies involving perishable materials (e.g., Jones 1980, 1981; Willoughby 1987). Another reason for experimentation is to determine the taphonomic processes that affect the physical attributes of objects produced by humans or that result in objects made by non-human means. Controlled experiments, either conducted in the field or designed to simulate field conditions, also provide ways to refine models concerning technical conditions that are otherwise difficult to measure or observe. This concern seems to be most relevant to pyrotechnical activities and taphonomic processes (e.g., Friede and Steel 1980; Gifford 1981; Friede et al. 1984; Blumenschine 1986; Childs 1986; Smith and Poggenpoel 1988; Bellomo 1991). Finally, experiments are used to test preliminary hypotheses to be examined and new procedures to be used during later field reconstructions with local elders (e.g., Childs and Schmidt 1985).

It should be reemphasized that the most complete understanding of a sociotechnical system, African or non-African, comes from long-term projects which build on the information yielded from more than one method and per-spective. A number of Africanist scholars have taken advantage of their ability to proceed from observations made during excavations, to laboratory analyses on the remains, to experimental work, and/or to ethnographic observations and field reconstructions (e.g., Schmidt 1983; David 1992). Although many authors in this volume have applied this research strategy to tackle their research interests, they focus on only one or two of these methods in the following articles.

The papers

The enormous size of the African continent, its ecological and topographical diversity, and the antiquity of its occupation by *Homo sapiens* and their bipedal predecessors make it impossible to represent adequately the tremendous range of sociotechnical systems devised and manipulated by Africans over time and across space. The papers presented here, therefore, can only provide a tiny glimpse of what has been accomplished by Africans over the last two to three million years. Some degree of representation is attempted, however, along the three dimensions of time, space, and material/technology.

Bellomo begins the coverage of a tremendous time depth by examining activities of early Hominids between one and two million years ago. Merrick et al. discuss the activities of Hominids in the Early Stone Age of East Africa, beginning about 1.5 million years ago, and compare them with those of *Homo sapiens* in the Middle Stone Age, some 100,000 years ago. Kusimba et al. and Garenne-Marot et al. focus on peoples who lived during the Iron Age (500 B.C.–A.D. 1900), while Gosselain, LaViolette, and Miller examine sociotechnical activities in the ethnographic present (last 100 years). The latter three articles certainly have implications for the prehistoric record that they examine.

The temporal gaps found in this volume, particularly during the Stone Ages and the Early Iron Age, do not reflect the sizeable amount of research that has been accomplished to date on these time periods. Many important use-wear, experimental, taphonomic, and laboratory studies have examined the production dynamics and variety of lithics, bone, and horn used and produced over the last hundreds of millennia. More attention, however, does need to be focused on documenting and then understanding the diversity of technologies used across Africa during all of the Stone and Iron Ages. Extensive work is also needed to determine the sociocultural and technical factors involved in the transition between different types of technologies within and between regions (i.e., the gradual shift from lithics to metals [Holl 1993]; the factors involved in the invention/adoption of ceramics in different ecosystems). The network of factors influencing changes over time in local technologies, such as food production, pottery making, iron working, and copper production, also needs to be explored more thoroughly (i.e., Bisson 1976; Okafor n.d.).

The second, spatial dimension of Africa (Fig. 1) is also only minimally covered in this group of papers. There are significant gaps in representation, especially in the Horn (Somalia, Ethiopia), along the northern coast, and along the southwestern coast into southern Africa. The best represented region is West Africa with the articles by Garenne-Marot et al. (Senegal), LaViolette (Mali), and Gosselain (Cameroon). Kusimba et al., Bellomo, and Merrick, all working in various parts of Kenya, represent East Africa. Miller's paper, focused on Zambia, is the sole representative for south-central Africa.

Again, the gaps found in these papers do not reflect the current distribution of work on African sociotechnical systems. They do highlight, however, two factors that have had some effect on research over the years. Ever since the British Punitive expeditions to Benin City (Nigeria) and to Kumasi (Ghana) in the late 1800s brought worldwide attention to the splendor and versatility of West African metal, ivory, textile, and wood carving technologies, they have been the subject of intense study (e.g., Dark 1973; Drewal 1980; Garrard 1989).

An attitude resulted, particularly among art historians, that the most interesting and sophisticated technologies for study were those of West Africa. Another bias, regional and international politics, also influenced where research has been conducted in Africa. The most effective research on sociotechnical systems involves long-term, multi-stage projects that are most easily accomplished in politically stable countries. Many of the West African countries have been relatively calm over the last two decades, as have Kenya, Zambia, South Africa, and parts of Zaire, where notable work has been accomplished.

The third dimension of representation in this volume, the various materials and technologies of Africa, is better distributed. Metallurgy is the best covered sociotechnical system, but several different metals and processes are explored. Miller discusses copper smelting, Kusimba et al. consider iron and copper forging, and Garenne-Marot et al. examine brass casting. Aspects of clay selection for pottery manufacture are studied by Gosselain, while LaViolette focuses on the earthen materials used in brick masonry. Although Bellomo's primary interest is on the early harnessing of fire, he also examines its effects on other materials. Finally, the importance of lithics to Africans over the millennia is represented by Merrick et al.'s work on the exploitation and use of obsidian.

Clearly, a large number of technologies could not be included in this volume, such as weaving, ivory working, bead making, shell working, and rock art painting, as well as those involving food production or many perishable materials. Although it is important to recognize and study these systems, there are also a number of related archaeological problems that demand closer scrutiny. These include the nature of interaction between the practitioners of different technologies in various sociocultural contexts (i.e., LaViolette 1987), the systemic effects of technological transfer between societies, why aspects (e.g., organization, raw materials, location) of some technologies are highly varied within a society (i.e., Monino 1983), and cross-cultural comparisons of sociotechnical systems (i.e., Kiriama 1993).

In closing, it will become apparent to the reader that all of the authors basically embrace the theory that technologies evolve through a dynamic interaction of social, ideological, and technical factors, and technologies must be examined in their sociocultural contexts. Given page constraints, it was impossible for each author to present all aspects of the sociotechnical system she or he examined. The papers as a group, however, provide insights into the different facets of these systems that can and should be studied worldwide, the variety of effective methods that can be used, and the exciting results that are yielded from cooperative, interdisciplinary research.

Acknowledgments

I want to thank Ronald Bishop and Lambertus van Zelst at the Conservation Analytical Laboratory, Smithsonian Institution for supporting all my undertakings, including this one, while I was a Post-doctoral Fellow of Materials Analysis. All the contributors to this volume, who were enthusiastic from start to finish, also deserve considerable thanks. David Killick, Duncan Miller, John Yellen, and an anonymous reviewer offered insightful comments on an early draft of this paper. Finally, I wish to acknowledge my profound debt to Nicholas David, Eugenia Herbert, Pierre de Maret, and Peter Schmidt, whose combined scholarship on African technology and society has been and continues to be an important source of inspiration to me.

Notes

1. The following is a simplified discussion of the arguments. There are a number of scholars who have explicated various nuances on both sides, but these cannot be addressed in this venue. For a recent review of the discussions, see Dobres and Hoffman (1994).

2. Many of these individuals are anthropological archaeologists, but historians, engineers, anthropologists, and art historians are also included.

References

Agorsah, K. 1985. Archaeological Implications of Traditional House Construction among the Nchumuru of Northern Ghana. *Current Anthropology* 26:103–115.

Austen, R., and D. Headrick. 1983. The Role of Technology in the African Past. *African Studies Review* 26(3/4):163–184.

Balfet, H. 1965. Ethnographical Observations in North Africa and Archaeological Interpretation: The Pottery of the Maghreb. In *Ceramics and Man*, ed. F. Matson, pp. 161–177. Aldine, Chicago.

Barros, P. de. 1986. Bassar: A Quantified, Chronologically Controlled, Regional Approach to a Traditional Iron Production Centre in West Africa. *Africa* 56:148–174.

Basalla, G. 1988. *The Evolution of Technology*. Cambridge University Press, Cambridge.

Belkin, T. 1990. *The Potters of Buur Heybe, Somalia*. Video. Filmmakers Library, New York.

Bellomo, R. 1991. Identifying Traces of Natural and Humanly-controlled Fire in the Archaeological Record: The Role of Actualistic Studies. *Archaeology in Montana* 32(2):75–93.

Berns, M. 1990. Pots as People. Yungur Ancestral Portraits. *African Arts* 23(3):50–60, 102.

‾‾‾‾‾‾ 1993. Art, History, and Gender: Women and Clay in West Africa. *The African Archaeological Review* 11:129–148.

Bisson, M. S. 1976. *The Prehistoric Copper Mines of Zambia*. Unpublished Ph.D. dissertation, Department of Anthropology, University of California, Santa Barbara.

Blumenschine, R. J. 1986. *Early Hominid Scavenging Opportunities: Implications of Carcass Availability in the Serengeti and Ngorongoro Ecosystems*. BAR International Series 283. British Archaeological Reports, Oxford.

Caton-Thompson, G. 1931. *The Zimbabwe Culture*. Oxford University Press, Oxford.

Childs, S. T. 1986. *Style in Technology: A View of African Early Iron Age Iron Smelting through its Refractory Ceramics*. Unpublished Ph.D. dissertation, Department of Anthropology, Boston University.

‾‾‾‾‾‾ 1991a. Style, Technology and Iron-smelting Furnaces in Bantu-speaking Africa. *Journal of Anthropological Archaeology* 10:332–359.

‾‾‾‾‾‾ 1991b. Transformations: Iron and Copper Production in Central Africa. In *Recent Advances in Archaeometallurgical Research*, ed. P. Glumac, pp. 33–46. MASCA Research Papers in Science and Archaeology 8, part 1. University of Pennsylvania Museum, Philadelphia.

Childs, S. T., and D. Killick. 1993. Indigenous African Metallurgy: Nature and Culture. *Annual Review of Anthropology* 22:317–337.

Childs, S. T., and P. Schmidt. 1985. Experimental Iron Smelting: The Genesis of a Hypothesis with Implications for African Prehistory and History. In *African Iron Working*, ed. R. Haaland and P. Shinnie, pp. 121–141. Norwegian University Press, Oslo.

Clark, J. D., and H. I. Kurashina. 1981. A Study of a Modern Tannery in Ethiopia and its Relevance for Archaeological Interpretation. In *Modern Material Culture: The Archaeology of Us,* ed. R. Gould and M. Schiffer, pp. 303–321. Academic Press, New York.

Coy, M. 1982. *The Social and Economic Relations of Blacksmiths among Kalenjin-speaking Peoples of the Rift Valley, Kenya*. Unpublished Ph.D. dissertation, Department of Anthropology, University of Pittsburgh.

‾‾‾‾‾‾ 1989. Being What We Pretend to Be: The Usefulness of Apprenticeship as a Field Method. In *Apprenticeship: From Theory to Method and Back Again*, ed. M. Coy, pp. 115–135. State University of New York Press, Albany.

Darish, P. 1989. Dressing for the Next Life. Raffia Textile Production and Use among the Kuba of Zaire. In *Cloth and Human Experience*, ed. A. Weiner and J. Schneider, pp. 117–140. Smithsonian Institution Press, Washington, DC.

Dark, P. J. 1973. *An Introduction to Benin Art and Technology*. Clarendon Press, London.

David, N. 1990. *Vessels of the Spirits. Pots and People in North Cameroon*. Video (50 mins.). Dept. of Communications Media, University of Calgary, Alberta.

‾‾‾‾‾‾ 1992. Integrating Ethnoarchaeology: A Subtle Realist Perspective. *Journal of Anthropological Archaeology* 11:330–359.

David, N., R. Heimann, D. Killick, and M. L. Wayman. 1989. Between Bloomery and Blast Furnace: Mafa Iron-smelting Technology in North Cameroon. *The African Archaeological Review* 7:185–210.

David, N., and H. Hennig. 1972. *The Ethnography of Pottery: A Fulani Case Seen in Archaeological Perspective*. McCaleb Module: Addison-Wesley, #21.

David, N., and Y. LeBléis. 1988. *Dokwaza, Last of the African Iron Masters*. Video. Dept. of Communications Media, University of Calgary, Alberta.

David, N., J. Sterner, and K. Gavua. 1988. Why are Pots Decorated? *Current Anthropology* 29:365–389.

DeAtley, S., and R. Bishop. 1991. Toward an Integrated Interface for Archaeology and Archaeometry. In *The Ceramic Legacy of Anna O. Shepard*, ed. R. Bishop and F. Lange, pp. 358–380. University of Colorado Press, Niwot, CO.

Dewey, W. 1990. *Weapons for the Ancestors*. Video. University of Iowa Video Production Unit, Iowa City.

Dietler, M., and I. Herbich. 1989. Tich Matek: The Technology of Luo Pottery Production and the Definition of Ceramic Style. *World Archaeology* 21(1):148–164.

Dilley, R. 1987. Myth and Meaning and the Tukolor Loom. *Man* (n.s.) 22(2):256–266.

Dobres, M-A., and C. Hoffman. 1994. Social Agency and the Dynamics of Prehistoric Technology. *Journal of Archaeological Method and Theory* 1(3):211–258.

Drewal, H. 1980. *African Artistry: Technique and Aesthetics in Yoruba Sculpture.* High Museum of Art, Atlanta.

Echard, N. 1968. *Noces de feu.* 16 mm. film. Musée de l'Homme, Paris.

Fowler, I. 1989. *Babungo: A Study of Iron Production, Trade and Power in a Nineteenth Century Ndop Plain Chiefdom (Cameroon).* Unpublished Ph.D. dissertation, Department of Anthropology, London University.

Friede, H., A. Hejja, A. Koursaris, and R. Steel. 1984. Thermal Aspects of the Smelting of Iron-ore in Reconstructed South African Iron Age Furnaces. *Journal of the South African Institute of Mining and Metallurgy* 84:285–297.

Friede, H., and R. Steel. 1980. Experimental Burning of Traditional Nguni Huts. *African Studies* 39(2):175–181.

Garrard, T. F. 1989. *Gold of Africa.* Prestel-Verlag, Munich.

Gifford, D. 1981. Taphonomy and Paleoecology: A Critical Review of Archeology's Sister Discipline. In *Advances in Archaeological Method and Theory*, Vol. 4, ed. M. Schiffer, pp. 365–438. Academic Press, New York.

Gifford-Gonzales, D. 1989. Ethnographic Analogues for Interpreting Modified Bones: Some Cases from East Africa. In *Bone Modification*, ed. R. Bonnichsen and M. Sorg, pp. 179–246. Center for the Study of the First Americans, Orono, ME.

Gordon, R., and D. Killick. 1993. Adaptation of Technology to Culture and Environment: Bloomery Iron Smelting in America and Africa. *Technology and Culture* 34(2):243–270.

Gosselain, O. 1992. Technology and Style: Potters and Pottery among Bafia of Cameroon. *Man* 27(3):559–586.

Hemptinne, Msgr. de. 1926. Les 'mangeurs de cuivre' du Katanga. Extract from *Congo* 7:371–403.

Herbert, E. W. 1984. *Red Gold of Africa.* University of Wisconsin Press, Madison.

——— 1993. *Iron, Gender and Power: Rituals of Transformation in African Societies.* Indiana University Press, Bloomington.

Herbich, I. 1987. Learning Patterns, Potter Interaction and Ceramic Style among the Luo of Kenya. *The African Archaeological Review* 5:193–204.

Holl, A. 1993. Transition from Late Stone Age to Iron Age in the Sudano-Sahelian Zone: A Case Study from the Perichadian Plain. In *The Archaeology of Africa. Food, Metals and Towns,* ed. T. Shaw, P. Sinclair, B. Andah, and A. Okpoko, pp. 330–343. Routledge, London.

Hughes, T. 1990. From Deterministic Dynamos to Seamless-web Systems. In *Engineering as a Social Enterprise*, ed. H. Sladovich, pp. 7–25. National Academy Press, Washington, DC.

Isaac, G. 1977. *Olorgesailie.* University of Chicago Press, Chicago.

Kanimba Misago, and R. Bellomo. 1990. Methods of Pottery Construction and Firing Techniques Observed in the Village of Bukokoma II, Zaire. *Virginia Museum of Natural History Memoir* 1:339–356.

Killick, D. J. 1990. *Technology in its Social Setting: Bloomery Iron-working at Kasungu, Malawi, 1860–1940.* Ph.D. dissertation, Department of Anthropology, Yale University.

——— 1991. The Relevance of Recent African Iron-smelting Practice to Reconstructions of Prehistoric Smelting Technology. In *Recent Advances in Archaeometallurgical Research*, ed. P. Glumac, pp. 47–54. MASCA Research Papers in Science and Archaeology 8, part 1. University of Pennsylvania Museum, Philadelphia.

Kiriama, H. 1993. The Iron-using Communities in Kenya. In *The Archaeology of Africa. Food, Metals and Towns*, ed. T. Shaw, P. Sinclair, B. Andah, and A. Okpoko, pp. 484–498. Routledge, London.

Jones, P. R. 1980. Experimental Butchery with Modern Stone Tools and its Relevance for Palaeolithic Archaeology. *World Archaeology* 12:153–165.

——— 1981. Experimental Implement Manufacture and Use: A Case Study from Olduvai Gorge. *Philosophical Transactions, Royal Society of London B* 292:189–195.

Larick, R. 1986. Iron Smelting and Interethnic Conflict among Precolonial Maa-speaking Pastoralists of North-central Kenya. *The African Archaeological Review* 4:165–176.

——— 1991. Warriors and Blacksmiths: Mediating Ethnicity in East African Spears. *Journal of Anthropological Archaeology* 10:299–331.

LaViolette, A. 1987. *An Archaeological Ethnography of Blacksmiths, Potters and Masons in Jenne, Mali, West Africa.* Unpublished Ph.D. dissertation, Department of Anthropology, Washington University.

Lechtman, H. 1977. Style in Technology—Some Early Thoughts. In *Material Culture—Styles, Organization and Dynamics of Technology*, ed. H. Lechtman and R. Merrill, pp. 3–20. West Publishing, St. Paul, MN.

Lechtman, H., and A. Steinberg. 1979. The History of Technology: An Anthropological Point of View. In *The History and Philosophy of Technology*, ed. G. Bulliarello and D. Doner, pp. 135–160. University of Illinois Press, Chicago.

Lemonnier, P. 1976. La decription des chaînes opératoires: Contribution à l'analyse des systemes

13

techniques. *Techniques et Culture* 1:100–151.

_____ 1986. The Study of Material Culture Today: Towards an Anthropology of Technical Systems. *Journal of Anthropological Archaeology* 5:147–186.

_____ 1992. *Elements for an Anthropology of Technology*. Museum of Anthropology, University of Michigan Anthropological Papers 88. Ann Arbor.

Maret, P. de. 1980. Ceux qui jouent avec le feu: la place du forgeron en Afrique Centrale. *Africa* 50:263–279.

McNaughton, P. 1988. *The Mande Blacksmiths: Knowledge, Power, and Art in West Africa*. Indiana University Press, Bloomington.

Merrick, H., and F. H. Brown. 1984. Obsidian Sources and Patterns of Source Utilization in Kenya and Northern Tanzania: Some Initial Findings. *The African Archaeological Review* 2:129–152.

Miller, D., and N. van der Merwe. 1994. Early Metal Working in Sub-Saharan Africa: A Review of Recent Research. *Journal of African History* 34:1–23.

Monino, Y. 1983. Accoucher du fer: la métallurgie Gbaya (Centrafrique). In *Métallurgies Africaines: Nouvelles Contributions*, ed. N. Echard, pp. 281–310. Société des Africanistes, Paris.

Nicklin, K., and J. Salmons. 1979. Bokyi Barkcloth: An Ethnographic Retrieval Study in S. E. Nigeria. *Baessler-Archiv, Neue Folge* Band 27:367–387.

Okafor, E. n.d. Economy and Politics: Factors of Technological Change in Nsukka, Nigeria Bloomery Iron Smelting. Unpublished manuscript.

O'Neill, P., F. Mulhy, and W. Lambrecht. 1989. *Tree of Iron*. Film. Foundation of African Prehistory and Archaeology, Gainesville, FL.

Oud, P. 1991. *Nagayati: Arts and Architecture among the Gabra Nomads of Kenya*. Video (50 mins.). Loaned by the Dept. of Education, National Museum of African Art, Smithsonian Institution, Washington, DC.

Pfaffenberger, B. 1988. Fetished Objects and Humanised Nature: Towards an Anthropology of Technology. *Man* 23:236–252.

_____ 1992 Social Anthropology of Technology. *Annual Review of Anthropology* 21:491–516.

Phillips, R. 1989. "So That People Will See I am Skilled in Carving." The Role of the Woodcarver among the Mende. In *Man Does Not Go Naked*, ed. B. Englebrecht and B. Gardi, pp. 235–252. Wepf, Basel.

Rattray, R. S. 1927. *Religion and Art in Ashanti*. Clarendon Press, Oxford.

Saltman, C., C. Goucher, and E. W. Herbert. 1986. *The Blooms of Banjeli: Technology and Gender in African Ironmaking*. Film. Documentary Educational Resources, Boston.

Schiffer, M. 1976. *Behavioral Archaeology*. Academic Press, New York.

_____ 1992. *Technological Perspectives on Behavioral Change*. University of Arizona Press, Tucson and London.

Schmidt, P. R. 1978. *Historical Archaeology: A Structural Approach in an African Culture*. Greenwood, Westport, CT.

_____ 1983. An Alternative to a Strictly Materialist Perspective: A Review of Historical Archaeology, Ethnoarchaeology and Symbolic Approaches in African Archaeology. *American Antiquity* 48(1):62–79.

Schmidt, P. R., and D. Avery. 1978. Complex Iron Smelting and Prehistoric Culture in Tanzania. *Science* 201:1085–1089.

Schmidt, P. R., and S. T. Childs. 1985. Innovation and Industry during the Early Iron Age in East Africa: The KM2 and KM3 Sites of Northwestern Tanzania. *African Archaeological Review* 3:53–94.

Smith, A., and C. Poggenpoel. 1988. The Technology of Bone Tool Fabrication in the South-western Cape, South Africa. *World Archaeology* 20:103–115.

Sterner, J. 1989. Who is Signalling Whom? Ceramic Style, Ethnicity and Taphonomy among the Sirak Bulahay. *Antiquity* 63:451–459.

Stiles, D. 1991. Early Hominid Behavior and Culture Tradition. *The African Archaeological Review* 9:1–19.

Todd, J. 1985. Iron Production by the Dimi of Ethiopia. In *African Iron Working*, ed. R. Haaland and P. Shinnie, pp. 88–101. Norwegian University Press, Oslo.

van der Merwe, N. J., and D. H. Avery. 1987. Science and Magic in African Technology: Traditional Iron Smelting in Malawi. *Africa* 57(2):143–172.

van der Merwe, N. J., and R. Scully. 1971. The Phalaborwa Story: Archaeological and Ethnographic Investigation of a South African Iron Age Group. *World Archaeology* 3:178–196.

van Grunderbeek, M.-C., E. Roche, and H. Doutrelepont. 1983. *Le premier age du fer au Rwanda et au Burundi. Archéologie et environnement*. I.F.A.Q., Brussels.

Wenner, D. B., and N. van der Merwe. 1986. Mining for the Lowest Grade Ore: Traditional Iron Production in Malawi. *Geoarchaeology* 2:199–216.

Willoughby, P. 1987. *Spheroids and Battered Stones in the African Early and Middle Stone Age*. BAR International Series 321. British Archaeological Reports, Oxford.

Wyckaert, R. P. 1914. Forgerons païens et forgerons chrétiens au Tanganyika. *Anthropos* 9:371–380.

Yellen, J. E. 1977. *Archaeological Approaches to the Present: Models for Reconstructing the Past*. Academic Press, New York.

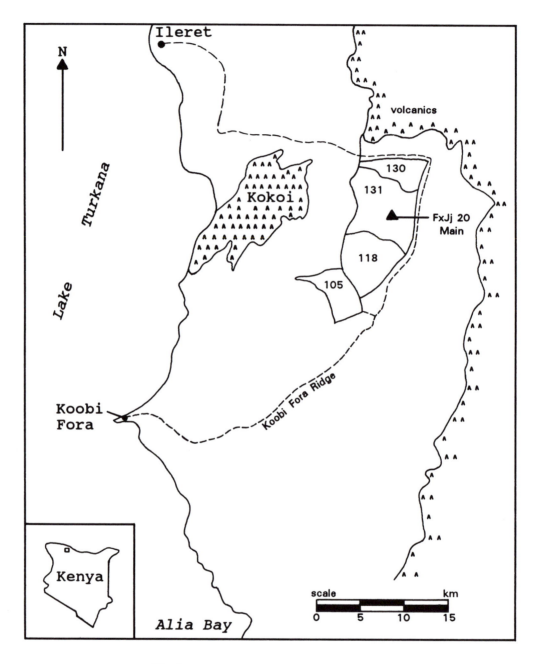

Fig. 1:
Location of FxJj 20 Main, Koobi Fora, Kenya.

EARLY PLEISTOCENE FIRE TECHNOLOGY IN NORTHERN KENYA

Randy V. Bellomo

Department of Anthropology, University of South Florida, Tampa, FL 33620-8100

ABSTRACT A methodological approach involving several analytical techniques has recently been used to identify evidence of hominid-controlled fire at FxJj 20 Main, an early Pleistocene archaeological site near Koobi Fora, Kenya. The evidence of fire at the site consists of highly localized, fully oxidized sediment features found near the base of the archaeological horizon, dated to approximately 1.6 Mya. Similar features are preserved at the nearby sites of FxJj 20 East and FxJj 20 AB, but evidence of hominid-controlled fire has not yet been confirmed at those sites.

The use and control of fire is regarded as a major technological breakthrough, since fire was the first external source of energy harnessed by hominids. The controlled use of fire would have provided hominids with a number of adaptive advantages that have important evolutionary implications. It is assumed that the early Pleistocene hominids at Koobi Fora captured fire from sources ignited by lightning strikes or spontaneous combustion, since (1) natural fires are believed to have been a regular occurrence in African savanna ecosystems, (2) there was a total lack of volcanic activity in the Turkana basin between 3.7 and approximately 0.5 Mya, and (3) convincing archaeological evidence of fire making dates to the Upper Paleolithic. Archaeological evidence from FxJj 20 Main, derived from examinations of the extent and three-dimensional configurations of the oxidized features, of the stone artifacts and bones for evidence of thermal alteration, and of the observed spatial patterning of the artifacts in relation to the features, suggest that the early hominids at Koobi Fora primarily used fire as protection against predators, as a source of light, and/or as a source of heat.

Introduction

Unequivocal evidence of hominid-controlled fire has recently been reported from the site of FxJj 20 Main, Koobi Fora, Kenya (Fig. 1), dated at 1.6 Mya (Bellomo 1990; Bellomo and Kean 1993). The evidence was confirmed using a methodological approach which can distinguish between traces of fire resulting from natural processes (e.g., grass fires, brush fires, tree stump fires, and forest fires) and traces of fire resulting from human activities (e.g., multiple-burn campfires, hearths, ovens, etc.) based on macroscopic, magnetic, and archaeomagnetic techniques of analysis (Bellomo 1990, 1991, 1993). The localized features at FxJj 20 Main contained fully oxidized sediments to a depth of at least 5 cm and exhibited diagnostic magnetic anomalies, while samples collected from the features displayed dramatic increases in magnetic susceptibility, highly stable to very highly stable responses to alternating field demagnetization, dramatic differences in

IRM acquisition and coercivity of remanence responses, and diagnostic paleointensity results, when compared with the responses of adjacent unfired control samples. The observed characteristics of the FxJj 20 Main features and samples were consistent with those from multiple-burn campfires and archaeological hearths and ovens, and were mutually exclusive from the results exhibited by features and samples from grass fire, isolated tree stump fire, and forest fire contexts. The characteristics of the FxJj 20 Main features and samples suggest that individual campfire sites were used on more than three or four occasions, or that the fires at those sites were maintained for a duration of at least a few days.

In addition to the evidence from the FxJj 20 Site Complex near Koobi Fora, Kenya (Harris 1978; Bellomo 1990; Bellomo and Kean 1993), evidence of fire has previously been reported from four other early Pleistocene archaeological sites in Africa, including Chesowanja, Kenya

(Gowlett et al. 1981), Gadeb (Clark and Kurashina 1979) and the Middle Awash (Clark and Harris (1985) in Ethiopia, and Swartkrans, South Africa (Brain 1985; Brain and Sillen 1988). The evidence from these sites was represented in the form of oxidized features (Koobi Fora, Chesowanja, and the Middle Awash), thermally altered stone artifacts (Gadeb), or burned bones (Swartkrans).

This paper will focus on the sources of fire in antiquity, the adaptive advantages of fire, and methods of determining the behavioral activities associated with the use of controlled fire at FxJj 20 Main. Identification of the available sources of fire in antiquity was derived from paleoenvironmental and ecological data, while discussions of the adaptive advantages of fire are based on a synthesis of published information. The methods of determining the behavioral activities associated with the use of fire at FxJj 20 Main include (1) the analysis and classification of fire types and associated activities, (2) examinations of stone artifacts and bones for evidence of thermal alteration, (3) observations regarding the spatial patterning of the stone artifacts in relation to the oxidized features, and (4) analyses of stone artifact frequencies by type, and by size and depth.

Sources of fire in antiquity

The natural ignition of vegetation can result from lightning strikes, volcanic eruptions, spontaneous combustion from the admixture of volatile compounds and/or gases, sparks produced by direct percussion resulting from rock falls, and friction between dry tree branches (Clark and Harris 1985; Daubenmire 1968; Harrison 1954; Oakley 1955, 1956, 1961a, 1961b; Phillips 1974). Evidence of natural fires preserved in petrified wood and coal deposits dating to the Carboniferous period of the Paleozoic era (Kemp 1981; Komarek 1972; and Pyne 1982), indicates that fire has been a component of the natural environment for at least 345 million years. Dechamps (1984) has documented evidence of Plio-Pleistocene bush fires preserved in fossilized wood recovered from the Omo and Sahabi areas of Africa, suggesting that the early hominids would have at least been familiar with the presence of fire on the African landscape.

Studies of the frequency of modern lightning-induced fire (Arnold 1964; Despain and Sellers 1977; Fuquay et al. 1979; Komarek 1964, 1968a, 1968b, 1972; Rowe 1969) suggest that lightning could have been a regular source of fire in the past, just as it is today. Data compiled from studies of lightning storms (e.g., Sparrow and Ney 1971) indicate that more strikes occur over equatorial land masses than anywhere else in the world. The common occurrence of charcoal remains dated to the mid Holocene, contained within the soils of mature rain forests in the Amazon basin (Sanford et al. 1985), may provide evidence of lightning-generated fires in the tropics. However, de Golia (1989:9) reports that while lightning is more common in the tropics,

natural fires are less common due to the climate and vegetation. Still, lightning-generated fire is a frequent event in grassland ecosystems (de Golia 1989:9).

The early Pleistocene fire-using hominids probably did not know how to make fire. Although fire can be produced by direct percussion, wood-friction, or use of a fire-piston (see Harrison 1954 for a detailed discussion), it is much more likely that early Pleistocene hominids acquired or captured fire from existing sources (Clark and Harris 1985; Harrison 1954; Oakley 1955, 1956, 1961a, 1961b). This assumption is based on the fact that convincing archaeological evidence for fire making is scant, and none dates prior to the Upper Paleolithic (e.g., Campbell 1988:460; Oakley 1975:85). Flint strikers provide the earliest widely accepted evidence that humans had the technological capability to produce fire. However, it is quite possible that earlier humans used a wood-based technology to produce fire (e.g., friction), but the evidence has not been preserved in the archaeological record. Regardless, it is likely that hominids used fire long before they acquired the skills to make it.

According to Clark and Harris (1985), the most likely available sources of fire in East Africa during the early Pleistocene would have been areas ignited by lightning strikes, spontaneous combustion, or active lava flows. Their assumption is supported by four types of ecological data:

1. Savanna habitats began to expand in Africa at the expense of tropical rain forests following the general reduction of global temperatures during the Miocene, and its associated changes in rainfall (Behrensmeyer 1982; Brain 1981; Laporte and Zihlman 1983).

2. Fire probably has always been a common and widespread phenomenon in grassland ecosystems throughout history (e.g., Tainton and Mentis 1984; Vogl 1974; Wright and Bailey 1982). Some scientists (e.g., Glover 1968), however, argue that grassland fires would only have occurred occasionally under natural conditions, and that they did not become common and widespread until after humans learned to use fire as a tool.

3. Without recurrent fires, woody species will recolonize areas dominated by grasslands (Sauer 1950; Wright and Bailey 1982). The continuing dominance of grasslands in Plio-Pleistocene East Africa implies that a recolonization of woody species did not occur, and suggests that natural fires were active during that time.

4. Volcanism, associated with the dynamics of the African Rift system, was a common component of the East African ecosystem from Plio-Pleistocene to recent times (King 1978).

Within the Turkana basin, however, geological evidence indicates that there was a total lack of volcanic activity between 3.7 Mya and approximately 0.5 Mya (Feibel 1988). Thus, the early Pleistocene hominids that inhabited the Koobi Fora area most likely acquired fire from sources ignited by lightning strikes or spontaneous combustion.

The adaptive advantages of fire

Modern humans are known to use fire for a variety of purposes. The uses of fire by modern humans will be used as a guide to explore the possible uses of fire at FxJj 20 Main.

The use of fire could have provided hominids with a number of adaptive advantages (Fig. 2) that have important evolutionary implications. As a source of light, fire could have allowed activities to continue after nightfall, or could have made habitation in the interiors of caves possible (Oakley 1955, 1961b; Perles 1981). Fire could also have provided the warmth and protection necessary to exploit environments occurring at higher elevations and latitudes, and may have facilitated the movements of hominid populations out of the African continent by making it possible for hominids to cope with colder ambient temperatures (Bordes and Thibault 1977; Eiseley 1954; Oakley 1961b; Pfeiffer 1971; and Sauer 1961).

As a hunting strategy, fires set under the right conditions by an organized group of hominids could have resulted in increased hunting returns since animals fleeing from the advancing fire line or those which suffocated in burrows could have become easy prey (Oakley 1961b; Stewart 1958). Recently burned areas also attract grazing animals once new grass shoots become available (Stewart 1958). Knowledge of this could have provided the hominids with additional hunting opportunities.

Fire could also have been employed by hominids to clear vegetation from habitation areas to facilitate intrasite mobility, and to reduce the danger of contact with smaller harmful animals which can easily hide in vegetated areas (Stewart 1958). This practice could also have functioned as a form of pest control, by reducing insect populations (Stewart 1958). In addition, the frequent occurrence of fire results in the gradual selection of certain plant species, some of which may have been nutritionally desired by early hominids (Stewart 1958).

Cooking could have played a premier role in rendering meats more tender and palatable, as well as making it possible to exploit tuberous foods which contain natural toxins in the uncooked state (Leopold and Ardrey 1972; Oakley 1955, 1961b; Pfeiffer 1971; Stahl 1984). Fire could also have been employed as a food preservative, because cooked meats can be stored for longer periods of time before turning rancid than uncooked meats can (Perles 1981). Fire could also have been used for hardening the tips of wooden tools (such as spears), and for enhancing the flaking properties of stone materials (Oakley 1955; Perles 1981; Pfeiffer 1971; Whittaker 1994).

Sauer (1975) and Perles (1981) have suggested that the possession of fire by hominids could have allowed increased exploitation and dominance of the surrounding environ-

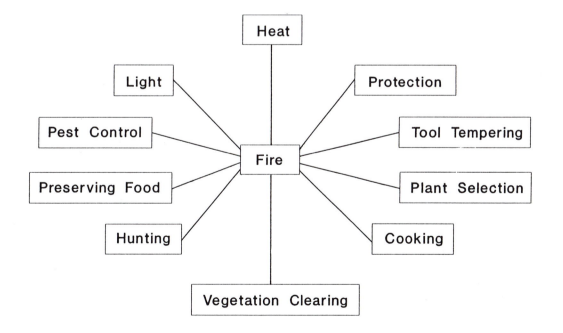

Fig. 2:
The adaptive advantages of fire.

Table 1. Fire-type categories and associated activities

Activity*	Fire-type categories		
	Camp-fires	Stump fires	Grass/ Brush fires
Source of heat	x	x	
Source of light	x	x	
Protection	x		
Tool tempering	x		
Cooking	x	x	
Preserving food	x		
Vegetation clearing			x
Pest control			x
Plant selection			x
Hunting			x

* Excluding metal smelting and pottery firing

ments, thereby permitting hominids to enlarge their ecological range. Regular, controlled use of fire could have facilitated hominid movements into new, more open habitats, since it could have provided the necessary protection against the larger carnivorous predators which may have preyed on the smaller-bodied hominids (Clark and Harris 1985; Oakley 1956, 1961b; Pfeiffer 1971).

Thus, the adaptive advantages offered by the controlled use of fire could have provided early hominids with the technological potential for increasing their chances of survival, and for significantly and efficiently exploiting and dominating the surrounding environment. These potentials, which were not available to any other species, may have contributed to the evolutionary success of the hominids.

Hominid use of fire at Koobi Fora

The archaeological record from FxJj 20 Main contains evidence which can be used to determine what activities the controlled use of fire may have been associated with. Various lines of evidence from the site are discussed in the following sections.

Fire types and associated activities

The controlled use of fire is associated with a number of different activities (see Bellomo 1990; Clark and Harris 1985). Based on considerations of task requirements and overall efficiency, these activities are associated with three categories of fire types (Table 1), including campfires, tree stump fires, and grass and brush fires. Grass and brush fires are set to efficiently clear vegetated areas, to control pest populations, as a hunting strategy, and for purposes of plant selection (Stewart 1958). Campfires are lit and maintained to provide an efficient source of heat for personal comfort, cooking, preserving food, and for hardening wooden tools

and improving the flaking characteristics of stone materials, as well as to provide a source of light, and protection from large carnivores and other dangerous animals (Clark and Harris 1985; Oakley 1955, 1961b; Pfeiffer 1971). Although burning stumps can be used as a source of light, heat, and possibly for cooking, it is unlikely that stumps were purposefully ignited for these reasons because burning stumps produce a soft glow, and lower relative temperatures (see Bellomo 1990, 1993). However, stumps ignited by natural processes were probably used opportunistically as a source of fire, and as a temporary focal point while traveling across the landscape.

A specific methodological approach (Bellomo 1990, 1993) has shown that each of the three fire-type categories produces mutually exclusive feature configurations and sample responses that allow the types to be identified and distinguished in the archaeological record as long as the sites are found in primary context. The methodological approach utilizes several parameters of investigation, including: (1) macroscopic examinations of fire feature surfaces and profiles, (2) analyses of magnetometer data, (3) magnetic susceptibility studies, (4) analyses of alternating field demagnetization characteristics, (5) studies of isothermal remanent magnetization (IRM) acquisition, (6) analyses of coercivity of remanence characteristics, and (7) paleointensity studies (Bellomo 1993). Comparisons of the results from analyses of features and samples from grass fire experiment sites, isolated tree-stump fire experiment sites, multiple-burn campfire experiment sites, modern forest fire sites, known archaeological hearths from Modoc Rock Shelter, Illinois, and known archaeological clay ovens from Tell Ashkelon, Israel revealed that multiple-burn campfire sites and known archaeological fire features exhibit basin-shaped three-dimensional configurations of oxidized sediments and diagnostic magnetic anomalies, while multiple-burn campfire samples and samples from known archaeological fire features display dramatic increases in magnetic susceptibility, highly stable to very highly stable responses to alternating field demagnetization, dramatic differences in IRM acquisition and coercivity of remanence responses, and diagnostic paleointensity results when compared with the responses of adjacent unfired control samples.

This methodological approach (Bellomo 1990, 1993) has been used to demonstrate that one of two oxidized features at FxJj 20 Main was produced by either a multiple-burn campfire or a campfire that was kept burning for a relatively long period of time (Bellomo 1990; Bellomo and Kean 1993). Although unequivocal evidence of fire was not confirmed for the second oxidized feature because some of the results fell just below the minimum level of acceptability (see Bellomo and Kean 1993), the consistency of the results suggests that the second feature was probably also produced by a campfire.

The identification of a campfire feature, characterized by a highly localized basin-shaped configuration of fully oxidized sediments, indicates that hominid fire use at FxJj 20 Main was not associated with vegetation clearing, pest control, plant selection, or hunting (see Table 1). Although campfire use is known to be associated with at least six behavioral activities, archaeological evidence from FxJj 20 Main provides important clues regarding the specific use of fire at that site. The evidence is presented in the following sections.

Examinations of the stone artifacts and bones

Over 4,000 stone artifacts and nearly 3,000 bone specimens were recovered from the site of FxJj 20 Main during the original excavations at the site (Harris 1978). All of the stone artifacts and bones recovered from excavation units located within two meters of the oxidized features were examined in 1986 and 1989 at the National Museum of Kenya in Nairobi to determine if evidence of thermal alteration could be identified using published criteria and direct comparisons with specimens recovered from campfire experiments as a guide.

Previous research has shown that thermally altered stones can often be recognized by changes in color, differential luster, pot-lidding, cracking, and crazing (e.g., Purdy and Brooks 1971; Mandeville 1971), and that thermally altered bones can usually be recognized by changes in color, changes in structure, and degree of calcination (e.g., Knight 1985; Shipman et al. 1984; Buikstra and Swegle 1989). A sample of stone artifacts and bones from FxJj 20 Main were specifically examined to determine if any of these characteristics were present.

Less than one percent of the 335 stone artifacts examined from the site of FxJj 20 Main are believed to contain evidence of thermal alteration. These specimens include two chert artifacts which exhibit reddish and yellowish spot discolorations (artifact nos. 1461a and 20311), and one basalt artifact (no. 1255) which appears to contain evidence of pot-lidding. Over 90% of the stone artifacts recovered from FxJj 20 Main are made of volcanic lava (see Harris 1978), a raw material that I observed to explode within two minutes after being placed in experimental campfires. Since the majority of stone artifacts from FxJj 20 Main are made of lava, and evidence of thermal alteration is scant, it can be concluded that the use of fire at FxJj 20 Main was not associated with activities designed to improve the flaking characteristics of lithic raw materials.

The examination of approximately 250 fossilized bones recovered from FxJj 20 Main revealed that all of the bones generally exhibited white exterior surfaces and bluish gray to black interiors. These color ranges are comparable to those observed on burned bones from experimental contexts (Bellomo 1990:286; Shipman et al. 1984; Buikstra and Swegle 1989). However, the fact that all of the bones

examined exhibited the same range of colors and color distribution patterns suggests that the bones from FxJj 20 Main were not altered by thermal processes. This assumption is supported by the observation that bones burned in experimental campfires exhibit highly variable changes in color and display mosaic color patterns (Bellomo 1990:182). Thus, the consistency of color ranges and the lack of mosaic color patterns on bones recovered from FxJj 20 Main indicate that the observed colors and patterns did not result from thermal processes; the observed colors and patterns most likely formed during the fossilization process.

A specific pattern of thermal alteration results when meat containing bone is cooked or smoked over (i.e., above) an open fire. From roasting experiments, I have observed that bone segments which were not covered with flesh became thermally altered (usually smoked) from exposure to direct heat and/or flames, while bone segments surrounded by meat were often only minimally affected because those segments were apparently insulated from direct heat. This resulted in a differential pattern characterized by one or more segments of a single bone which exhibited evidence of thermal alteration (e.g., smoke damage, color changes, partial calcination, etc.) and other segments on the same bone which appeared virtually unchanged. This pattern is quite different from that produced when fleshed bone is actually placed within a fire for purposes of cremation (see Buikstra and Swegle 1989). Regardless, none of the bones examined from FxJj 20 Main displayed a roasting type of pattern, or any other convincing evidence of thermal alteration. The combined data suggest that the use of fire at FxJj 20 Main was not associated with cooking or food preservation activities.

Observed spatial patterning of features and stone artifacts

The locations of two of the oxidized features from FxJj 20 Main are shown in Fig. 3. Both of these features were investigated, although only the easternmost feature (B) was confirmed to have been produced by a hominid-controlled campfire (Bellomo 1990; Bellomo and Kean 1993).

Two separate stone artifact distribution plots were generated for the easternmost feature at FxJj 20 Main to explore whether or not the artifacts were behaviorally associated with the campfire feature. The first plot includes all of the stone artifacts recovered from the same elevation as the top of the feature (Fig. 4), and the second plot includes all of the stone artifacts recovered between the top of the feature and a depth of 5 cm below the top of the feature (Fig. 5). The latter plot was generated because archaeological sites are the product of complex patterns of behavior, and trampling and other post-depositional processes result in the vertical dispersion and size sorting of artifacts (see Gifford-Gonzalez et al. 1985; Schiffer 1983;

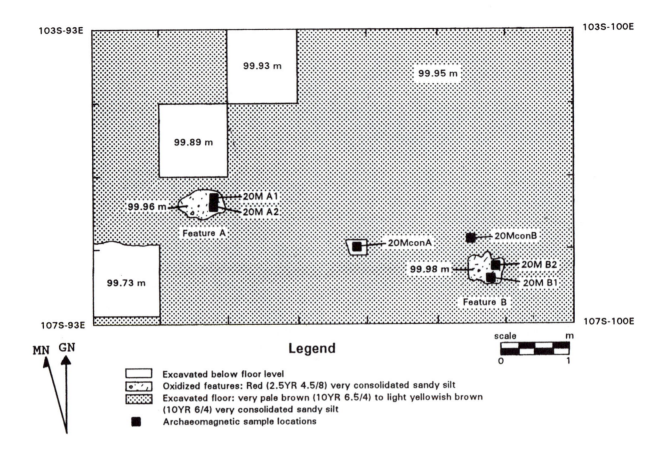

Fig. 3:
The locations of two of the oxidized features at FxJj 20 Main.

Stevenson 1985, 1991; and Villa 1982). This 5 cm range of elevations is considered to be a conservative estimate of vertical dispersion (e.g., see Stockton 1973). Two additional artifact distribution plots were generated to determine if evidence of size sorting was apparent (Figs. 6 and 7).

The artifact distribution plots show that six different categories of artifacts are included in levels associated with the oxidized feature, including unmodified cobbles, whole flakes, proximal flakes, medial/distal flake fragments, non-orientable fragments, and tools. At first glance, the spatial association of the different artifact categories relative to the feature (Figs. 4 and 5) suggests that unintensive lithic reduction activities involving tool production and/or maintenance were performed near the oxidized features (see Harris 1978:377). However, the apparent spatial associations require more rigorous analyses, since the site probably records a palimpsest of occupations through time, and numerous hominid activities (e.g., tool manufacture, animal butchery, site cleaning, tool sharpening, etc.) and post-depositional processes (e.g., water transport, burrowing of animals, soil movement, trampling by animals, etc.) are known to affect the distribution of artifacts within

archaeological contexts (see Gifford-Gonzalez et al. 1985; Schiffer 1983; Stevenson 1985, 1991; and Villa 1982). More rigorous spatial analyses are beyond the scope of this paper, but will be undertaken in the future.

Artifact size distribution plots (Figs. 6 and 7) were generated to examine if evidence of size sorting and/or vertical dispersion could be identified. Three different artifact size categories (based on maximum dimensions) were utilized for this purpose. Figure 6 shows that the majority of artifacts are in the smallest size category (i.e., less than 3 cm). Although the number of artifacts greater than 6 cm in maximum dimension is low, the relative locations of these larger artifacts could be an indication that intentional size sorting was periodically practiced to keep the central site area somewhat clear to facilitate intrasite movement, or that larger artifacts were usually further reduced in size at the site or were transported to another location for later reduction (see Schick and Toth 1994:127–128). In addition, Fig. 7 shows that the largest size categories are found vertically dispersed throughout the oxidized feature horizon, which may be an indication that separate episodes of site occupation are represented (see Stern

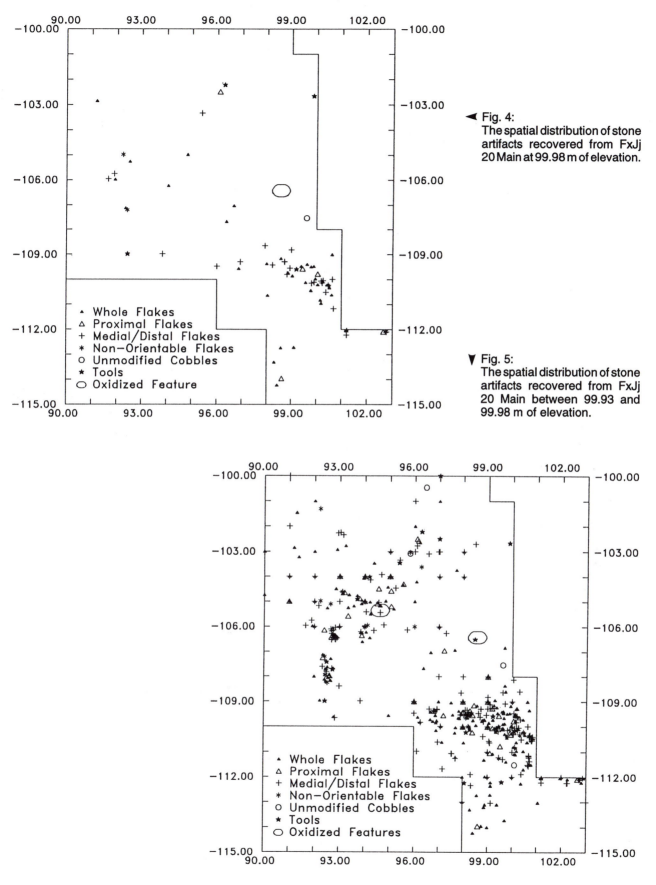

◄ Fig. 4:
The spatial distribution of stone artifacts recovered from FxJj 20 Main at 99.98 m of elevation.

▼ Fig. 5:
The spatial distribution of stone artifacts recovered from FxJj 20 Main between 99.93 and 99.98 m of elevation.

Legend (both figures):
▲ Whole Flakes
△ Proximal Flakes
+ Medial/Distal Flakes
* Non−Orientable Flakes
○ Unmodified Cobbles
★ Tools
⬭ Oxidized Feature

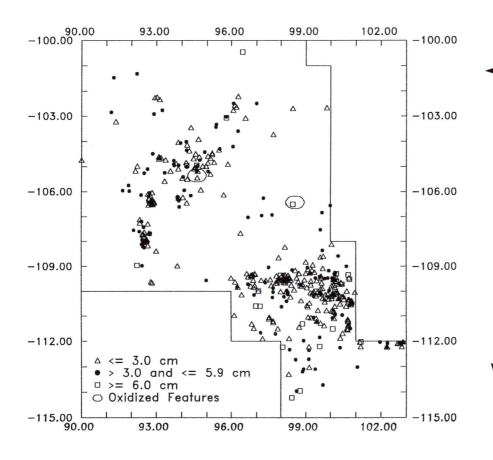

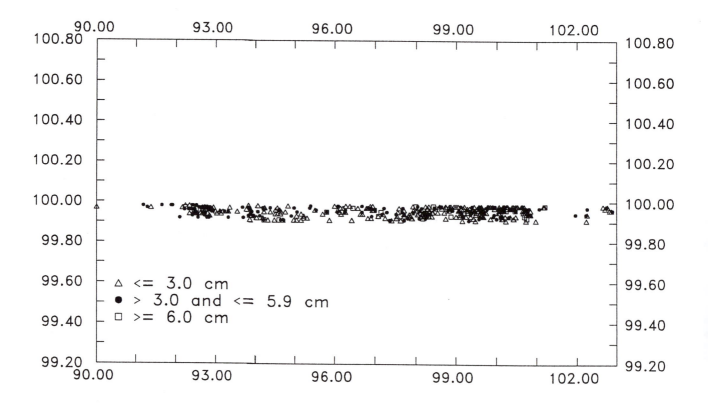

◀ Fig. 6:
The horizontal distribution of stone-artifact size categories recovered from FxJj 20 Main between 99.91 and 99.98 m of elevation.

▽ <= 3.0 cm
● > 3.0 and <= 5.9 cm
□ >= 6.0 cm
○ Oxidized Features

▼ Fig. 7:
The vertical distribution of stone-artifact size categories recovered from FxJj 20 Main between 99.91 and 99.98 m of elevation.

△ <= 3.0 cm
● > 3.0 and <= 5.9 cm
□ >= 6.0 cm

1993). However, it is just as likely that the artifact distributions represented in Fig. 7 resulted from a single occupational event because the vertical dispersion of artifacts can result from numerous post-depositional processes that can make single occupational episodes difficult to recognize. To explore whether or not the observed spatial associations could be linked to specific hominid activities, analyses of the relative frequencies of stone artifact types and size distributions were undertaken.

Stone artifact frequencies by type, and by size and depth

To assess whether or not the stone artifacts and features may have been behaviorally associated, lithic data were analyzed using the approach developed by Sullivan and Rozen (1985), to determine what technological activities were undertaken based on the relative frequencies of stone artifact and debitage categories (Table 2). Sullivan and Rozen's (1985) interpretations are based on comparisons with experimentally produced assemblages and assemblages recovered from New World archaeological sites, so their approach may not be entirely valid for Karari Industry assemblages.

Based on Sullivan and Rozen (1985) the relative percentages of the FxJj 20 Main artifact types associated with the oxidized feature horizon suggest that the hominids were involved in core reduction and tool manufacturing activities. This interpretation is consistent with the observed spatial distributions of the stone artifact type categories presented in Figs. 4 and 5. The combined spatial and artifact type frequency data suggest that hominid lithic manufacturing and maintenance activities were undertaken in more peripheral site areas that were still in close relative proximity to the campfire location.

Lithic size data were also analyzed in relation to depth to determine if evidence of size sorting or site maintenance could be identified. Table 3 presents the relative frequencies of artifacts by size categories and elevation. As shown in Table 3, the majority of artifacts are less than or equal to 4 cm in maximum dimension, suggesting that larger arti-

Table 2. FxJj 20 Main artifact category percentages (after Sullivan and Rozen 1985)

| | Elevation | |
| | 99.98 m | 99.93– |
		99.98 m
Artifact category		
Whole flakes	48.0%	44.1%
Proximal flakes	6.7	6.2
Medial/Distal flakes	34.7	45.2
Non-orientable fragments	3.9	2.1
Tools	6.7	2.4

Table 3. FxJj 20 Main artifact frequencies by size categories and elevation

| | Elevation | | |
| | 99.97– | 99.95– | 99.93– |
	99.98 m	99.96 m	99.94 m
Maximum dimension			
≤ 1.0 cm	5	82	3
> 1.0 and ≤2.0 cm	43	306	32
> 2.0 and ≤ 3.0 cm	50	85	27
> 3.0 and ≤ 4.0 cm	38	39	23
> 4.0 and ≤ 5.0 cm	15	11	8
> 5.0 and ≤ 6.0 cm	9	6	5
> 6.0 and ≤ 7.0 cm	4	3	3
> 7.0 and ≤ 8.0 cm	5	1	1
> 8.0 and ≤ 9.0 cm	0	3	0

facts may have been intentionally removed to facilitate intrasite movement, transported to another location for later reduction (see Schick and Toth 1994:127–128), or further reduced in size at the site. The vertical dispersion and size sorting of artifacts are implied, but not confirmed, using this simplistic method of analysis. The identification of these processes at FxJj 20 Main would require more detailed analyses, which are beyond the scope of this study. More rigorous methods of spatial analysis will be undertaken in the future in an attempt to determine if the site represents a single or multiple occupation episode(s), and if vertical dispersion and size sorting can be demonstrated.

Conclusions

Ecological data suggest that fire was probably a regular occurrence in the savanna ecosystems of Africa where the hominids were known to have ranged. Evidence of campfires at the site of FxJj 20 Main indicates that early Pleistocene hominids used and controlled fire. Early hominids probably captured fire from sources ignited by lightning strikes, spontaneous combustion, or lava flows long before they had the technological capabilities to make fire. Since volcanic activity was absent in the Turkana basin between 3.7 Mya and approximately 0.5 Mya, early Pleistocene hominids at FxJj 20 Main most likely captured fire from sources ignited by lightning strikes or spontaneous combustion.

The controlled use of fire provided a number of adaptive advantages that may have contributed to the evolutionary success of the hominids. Elsewhere (Bellomo 1990; Bellomo and Kean 1993), I have reported that the evidence of fire at FxJj 20 Main was the result of controlled campfires. In this paper, archaeological data from FxJj 20 Main were analyzed to determine the possible uses of controlled fire by early hominids. I have also assumed that the possible uses of fire presented in Fig. 2 is exhaustive,

25

excluding, of course, metal smelting and ceramic firing. Therefore, based on a process of elimination, hominid fire use at FxJj 20 Main could not have been associated with hunting, plant selection, vegetation clearing, or pest control. In addition, the lack of thermally altered stone artifacts and bones suggests that fire use was not associated with activities designed to improve the flaking characteristics of stone raw materials, for cooking, or for preserving food. It is most likely that fire was used to provide protection from predators, as a source of light, and as a source of heat. The observed spatial patterning of the stone artifacts relative to the fire features suggests that the campfires provided a central focus of activities, including the production and maintenance of stone tools and the consumption of food. This evidence for the controlled use of fire by early Pleistocene hominids at FxJj 20 Main, along with the observed spatial patterning of artifacts and bones relative to the fire features, may provide the most important evidence to date in support of the home base model[1] presented by Isaac (1971, 1978) and others.

Acknowledgments

This research was funded by grants from the National Science Foundation, the L. S. B. Leakey Foundation, the Boise Fund, Sigma Xi, and the NATO Advanced Study Institute. The assistance provided by these organizations is gratefully appreciated. I would also like to express thanks to the governments of Zaire and Kenya, members of the Semliki Research Expedition, and the U. S. National Park Service, without whose assistance this research project would not have been possible.

Note

1. The home base is a central location in space at any given time where individuals in a group join up after completion of tasks (such as hunting, scavenging, or foraging) undertaken elsewhere on the landscape.

References

Arnold, K. 1964. Project Skyfire Lightning Research. *Proceedings of the Third Annual Tall Timbers Fire Ecology Conference* 3:121–130. Tall Timbers Research Station, Tallahassee, FL.

Behrensmeyer, A. K. 1982. The Geological Context of Human Evolution. *Annual Review of Earth and Planetary Sciences* 10:39–60.

Bellomo, R. V. 1990. *Methods for Documenting Unequivocal Evidence of Humanly Controlled Fire at Early Pleistocene Archaeological Sites in Africa: The Role of Actualistic Studies.* Ph.D. dissertation, Department of Anthropology, University of Wisconsin-Milwaukee. University Microfilms International, Ann Arbor.

_____ 1991. Identifying Traces of Natural and Humanly-Controlled Fire in the Archaeological Record: The Role of Actualistic Studies. *Archaeology in Montana* 32(2):75–93.

_____ 1993. A Methodological Approach for Identifying Archaeological Evidence of Fire Resulting From Human Activities. *Journal of Archaeological Science* 20(5):525–553.

Bellomo, R. V., and W. F. Kean. 1993. Evidence of Hominid-controlled Fire at the FxJj 20 Site Complex, Karari Escarpment, Koobi Fora, Kenya. Accepted for publication in *Koobi Fora Research Project Monograph Series.* Vol. 3: *Archaeology*, ed. G. L. Isaac and B. Isaac. Clarendon Press, Oxford.

Bordes, F., and C. Thibault. 1977. Thoughts on the Initial Adaptation of Hominids to European Glacial Climates. *Quaternary Research* 8:115–127.

Brain, C. K. 1981. The Evolution of Man in Africa: Was It a Consequence of Cainozoic Cooling? *The Geological Society of South Africa* 84:1–19.

_____ 1985. Cultural and Taphonomic Comparisons of Hominids from Swartkrans and Sterkfontein. In *Ancestors: The Hard Evidence*, ed. Eric Delson, pp. 72–75. Alan R. Liss, New York.

Brain, C. K., and A. Sillen. 1988. Evidence From the Swartkrans Cave for the Earliest Use of Fire. *Nature* 336:464–466.

Buikstra, J. E., and M. Swegle. 1989. Bone Modification Due to Burning: Experimental Evidence. In *Bone Modification*, ed. R. Bonnichsen and M. H. Sorg, pp. 247–258. Center for the Study of the First Americans, University of Maine, Orono.

Campbell, B. G. 1988. *Humankind Emerging*, 5th ed. Scott Foresman, Glenview, IL.

Clark, J. D., and J. W. K. Harris. 1985. Fire and Its Roles in Early Hominid Lifeways. *African Archaeological Review* 3:3–27.

Clark, J. D., and H. Kurashina. 1979. Hominid Occupation of the East-central Highlands of Ethiopia in the Plio-Pleistocene. *Nature* 282(5734):33–39.

Daubenmire, R. 1968. Ecology of Fire in Grasslands. In *Advances in Ecological Research*, vol. 5, ed. J. B. Cragg, pp. 209–266. Academic Press, London.

Dechamps, R. 1984. Evidence of Bush Fires During the Plio-Pleistocene in Africa (Omo and Sahabi) with the Aid of Fossil Woods. In *Palaeoecology of Africa and the Surrounding Islands*, vol. 16, ed. J. A. Coetzee and E. M. Van Zinderen Bakker, Sr., pp. 291–296. A. A. Balkema, Rotterdam.

Despain, D. G., and R. E. Sellers. 1977. Natural Fire in Yellowstone National Park. *Western Wildlands* 4:20–24.

Eiseley, L. C. 1954. Man the Fire-maker. *Scientific American* 191(3):52–57.

Feibel, C. S. 1988. *Paleoenvironments of the Koobi Fora Formation, Turkana Basin, Northern Kenya.* Ph.D. dissertation, University of Utah. University Microfilms International, Ann Arbor.

Fuquay, D. M., R. G. Baughman, and D. J. Latham. 1979. A Model for Predicting Lightning-fire Ignition in Wildland Fuels. *U.S.D.A. Forest Service Research Paper* INT-217.

Gifford-Gonzalez, D. P., D. B. Damrosch, D. R. Damrosch, J. Pryor, and R. L. Thunen. 1985. The Third Dimension in Site Structure: An Experiment in Trampling and Vertical Dispersal. *American Antiquity* 50(4):803–818.

Glover, P. E. 1968. The Role of Fire and Other Influences on the Savanna Habitat, With Suggestions for Further Research. *East African Wildlife Journal* 6:131–137.

Golia, J. de. 1989. *Fire: The Story Behind A Force of Nature.* K. C. Publications, Las Vegas.

Gowlett, J. A. J., J. W. K. Harris, D. A. Walton, and B. A. Wood. 1981. Early Archaeological Sites, Hominid Remains, and Traces of Fire from Chesowanja, Kenya. *Nature* 294(5837):125–129.

Harris, J. W. K. 1978. *The Karari Industry: Its Place in East African Prehistory.* Ph.D. dissertation, Department of Anthropology, University of California-Berkeley. University Microfilms International, Ann Arbor.

Harrison, H. S. 1954. Fire–making, Fuel, and Lightning. In *A History of Technology*, vol. 1, ed. Charles Singer, E. J. Holmyard, and A. R. Hall, pp. 216–237. Clarendon Press, Oxford.

Isaac, G. 1971. The Diet of Early Man: Aspects of Archaeological Evidence from Lower and Middle Pleistocene Sites in Africa. *World Archaeology* 2:278–299.

————— 1978. The Food-sharing Behavior of Protohuman Hominids. *Scientific American* 238(4):90–108.

Kemp, E. M. 1981 Pre-Quaternary Fire in Australia. In *Fire in the Australian Biota*, ed. A. M. Gill, R. M. Groves, and J. R. Noble, pp. 3–21. Australian Academy of Science, Canberra.

King, B. C. 1978. Structural and Volcanic Evolution of the Gregory Rift Valley. In *Geological Background to Fossil Man: Recent Research in the Gregory Rift Valley, East Africa*, ed. W. W. Bishop, pp. 29–54. University of Toronto Press, Toronto.

Knight, J. A. 1985. Differential Preservation of Calcined Bone at the Hirundo Site, Alton, Maine. M.S. thesis, Quaternary Studies, University of Maine at Orono.

Komarek, E. V., Sr. 1964. The Natural History of Lightning. *Proceedings of the Third Annual Tall Timbers Fire Ecology Conference* 3:139–183. Tall Timbers Research Station, Tallahassee, FL.

————— 1968a. The Nature of Lightning Fires. *Proceedings of the Seventh Annual Tall Timbers Fire Ecology Conference* 7:5–41. Tall Timbers Research Station, Tallahassee, FL.

————— 1968b. Lightning and Lightning Fires as Ecological Forces. *Proceedings of the Eighth Annual Tall Timbers Fire Ecology Conference* 8:169–197. Tall Timbers Research Station, Tallahassee, Florida.

————— 1972. Lightning and Fire Ecology in Africa. *Proceedings of the Eleventh Annual Tall Timbers Fire Ecology Conference* 11:473–511. Tall Timbers Research Station, Tallahassee, Florida.

Laporte, L. F., and A. Zihlman. 1983. Plates, Climate and Hominid Evolution. *South African Journal of Science* 79:96–110.

Leopold, A. C., and R. Ardrey. 1972. Toxic Substances in Plants and the Food Habits of Early Man. *Science* 176:512–513.

Mandeville, M. 1971. The Baked and the Half Baked: A Consideration of the Thermal Pretreatment of Chert. M.S. thesis, Department of Anthropology, University of Missouri, Columbia.

Oakley, K. P. 1955. Fire as a Palaeolithic Tool and Weapon. *Proceedings of the Prehistoric Society for 1955* 21:36–48.

————— 1956. The Earliest Fire-makers. *Antiquity* 30:102–107.

————— 1961a. Possible Origins of the Use of Fire. *Man* 61:244.

————— 1961b. On Man's Use of Fire, With Comments on Tool-making and Hunting. In *Social Life of Early Man*, ed. S. L. Washburn, pp. 176–193. Aldine, Chicago.

————— 1975. *Man the Tool-maker*, 6th ed. British Museum of Natural History, London.

Perles, C. 1981. Hearth and Home in the Old Stone Age. *Natural History* 90(10):38–41.

Pfeiffer, J. 1971. When *Homo erectus* Tamed Fire, He Tamed Himself. In *Human Variation: Readings in Physical Anthropology*, ed. H. R. Bleibtreu and J. F. Downs, pp. 193–203. Glencoe Press, CA.

Phillips, J. 1974. Effects of Fire in Forest and Savanna Ecosystems of Sub-Saharan Africa. In *Fire and Ecosystems*, ed. T. T. Kozlowski and C. E. Ahlgren, pp. 435–481. Academic Press, New York.

Purdy, B. A., and H. K. Brooks. 1971. Thermal Alteration of Silica Minerals: An Archaeological Approach. *Science* 173:322–325.

Pyne, S. J. 1982. *Fire in America: A Cultural History of Wildland and Rural Fire.* Princeton University Press, Princeton, NJ.

Rowe, J. S. 1969. Lightning Fires in Saskatchewan Grassland. *Canadian Field Naturalist* 83:317–324.

Sanford, R. L., Jr., J. Saldarriaga, K. E. Clark, C. Uhl,

and R. Herrera. 1985. Amazon Rain-forest Fires. *Science* 227:53–55.

Sauer, C. O. 1950. Grassland Climax, Fire, and Man. *Journal of Range Management* 3(1):16–21.

———— 1961. Fire and Early Man. *Paideuma Mitteilungen zur Kulturkunde*, Band 7 (November), Heft 8.

———— 1975. Man's Dominance by Use of Fire. *Geoscience and Man* 10:1–13.

Schick, K. D., and N. Toth. 1994. *Making Silent Stones Speak: Human Evolution and the Dawn of Technology*. Simon and Schuster, New York.

Schiffer, M. B. 1983. Toward the Identification of Formation Processes. *American Antiquity* 48(4):675–706.

Shipman, P., G. Foster, and M. Schoeninger. 1984. Burnt Bones and Teeth: An Experimental Study of Color, Morphology, Crystal Structure and Shrinkage. *Journal of Archaeological Science* 11:307–325.

Sparrow, J. G., and E. P. Ney. 1971. Lightning Observations by Satellite. *Nature* 232:540–541.

Stahl, A. B. 1984. Hominid Dietary Selection Before Fire. *Current Anthropology* 25(2):151–168.

Stern, N. 1993. The Structure of the Lower Pleistocene Archaeological Record: A Case Study from the Koobi Fora Formation. *Current Anthropology* 34(3):201–225.

Stevenson, M. G. 1985. The Formation of Artifact Assemblages at Workshop/Habitation Sites: Models From Peace Point in Northern Alberta. *American Antiquity* 50(1):63–81.

———— 1991. Beyond the Formation of Hearth-associated Artifact Assemblages. In *The Interpretation of Archaeological Spatial Patterning*, ed. E. M. Kroll and T. D. Price, pp. 269–299. Plenum Press, New York.

Stewart, O. C. 1958. Fire as the First Great Force Employed by Man. In *Man's Role in Changing the Face of the Earth*, ed. W. L. Thomas, Jr., pp. 115–133. University of Chicago Press, Chicago.

Stockton, E. D. 1973. Shaw's Creek Shelter: Human Displacement of Artifacts and its Significance. *Mankind* 9:112–117.

Sullivan, A. P., III., and K. C. Rozen. 1985. Debitage Analysis and Archaeological Interpretation. *American Antiquity* 50(4):755–779.

Tainton, N. M., and M. T. Mentis. 1984. Fire in Grassland. In *Ecological Effects of Fire in South African Ecosystems*, ed. P. de V. Booysen and N. M. Tainton, pp. 115–147. Springer-Verlag, Berlin.

Villa, P. 1982. Conjoinable Pieces and Site Formation Processes. *American Antiquity* 47(2):276–290.

Vogl, R. J. 1974. Effects of Fire on Grasslands. In *Fire and Ecosystems*, ed. T. T. Kozlowski and C. E. Ahlgren, pp. 139–194. Academic Press, New York.

Whittaker, J. C. 1994. *Flintknapping: Making and Understanding Stone Tools*. University of Texas Press, Austin.

Wright, H. A., and A. W. Bailey. 1982. Temperature and Heat Effects. In *Fire and Ecology: United States and Southern Canada*, pp. 8–23. J. Wiley and Sons, New York.

USE AND MOVEMENT OF OBSIDIAN IN THE EARLY AND MIDDLE STONE AGES OF KENYA AND NORTHERN TANZANIA

Harry V. Merrick

Anthropology Program, Massachusetts Institute of Technology, Cambridge, MA 02139

Francis H. Brown

Department of Geology and Geophysics, University of Utah, Salt Lake City, UT 84112

William P. Nash

Department of Geology and Geophysics, University of Utah, Salt Lake City, UT 84112

ABSTRACT Obsidian use for artifact manufacture has a very long history in eastern Africa. The study of its frequency of use and the distances it has moved from sources to sites offers the potential for examining long-term changes in patterns of resource use and socio-territorial organization. Limited use and movement of obsidian is documented for Early Stone Age times while patterns of the distribution and use of obsidian in some subsequent Middle Stone Age sites display a combination of features, some antecedent to, and others typical of, but less well developed than, those of the recent modern *H. sapiens* hunter/gatherers in the region.

Introduction

Characterization studies of source materials and their archaeological distributions have long been noted for offering the potential for examining distances traveled by prehistoric peoples and/or intergroup interactions. Recently Ambrose and Lorenz (1990) significantly expanded the potential use of such studies, at least in the case of Subsaharan African paleolithic studies, with the presentation of an elegant model relating regional resource structure and the socio-territorial organization of hunter/gatherers with their potential archaeological correlates (see table 1.1 in Ambrose and Lorenz 1990). In their study of the southern African Middle Stone Age (MSA) record they examined ratios of local to non-local stone materials, changes in lithic technology, and patterns of faunal utilization to evaluate the territorial and hunting and gathering behaviors of the Middle Stone Age folk in that region. One of their ultimate goals was to determine how early the behavioral features characterizing modern *Homo sapiens* hunter/gatherers could be recognized in MSA times. Their

successful demonstration that headway on this question can be made for the southern African MSA when adequate data on raw materials, lithic technology, fauna, and site distributions are available is very encouraging.

The application of their integrated approach to the study of subsistence practices and resource utilization in other regions of Subsaharan Africa, including eastern Africa where microlithic LSA technologies may appear surprisingly early (Ambrose n.d.), clearly offers a tantalizing prospect. However, at present the MSA archaeological record for almost all other regions of Subsaharan Africa is far less complete than the record for southern Africa. In eastern Africa the small number of sites that have been studied heretofore, their small or non-existent faunal assemblages, and the scant interest paid to patterns of raw material use make the immediate prospects for defining changes in patterns in socio-territorial behaviors fairly dim. Nonetheless, one integral component of this study, the examination of patterns of source use, does currently offer considerable promise for establishing a baseline to begin the study of long term changes in socio-territorial organization of Pleistocene hunter/gatherers in eastern Africa.

In the first study of regional patterning of obsidian use in Kenya and northern Tanzania, two of us (Merrick and Brown 1984) noted and briefly commented on several apparent changing patterns of obsidian use through time. We observed that the use of obsidian as a material for flaked stone artifact manufacture increased gradually, but dramatically over the past one million years, and that over time obsidian artifacts appeared in sites increasingly distant from the sources of obsidian. The observed patterning suggested that the use of obsidian in Early Stone Age (ESA) times at all archaeological sites, with one exception, was very infrequent and we suggested the distance of movement of obsidian from source to site was likely to be very small. The popularity of obsidian use and the distance of its movement from source to site increased through Middle Stone Age and Later Stone Age (LSA) times to the point where its use was nearly total at most sites located within 50 km of a major obsidian source. More recently in Pastoral Neolithic times both long-distance movement and the exclusive use of obsidian were not uncommon in sites up to 250 km from source areas.

We also noted limited evidence suggesting a pattern wherein the number of obsidian sources represented at the MSA and LSA sites occupied by hunter/gatherers and at the 'LSA with pottery' sites occupied by presumed hunter/gatherers, especially in areas outside the immediate Rift Valley, were more numerous and eclectic than in subsequent Pastoral Neolithic times. We subsequently added additional support for this observation by demonstrating that in many Pastoral Neolithic sites obsidian use became even more widespread but was marked by heavy reliance on fewer sources (Merrick et al. 1990). This latter change very likely reflects the basic differences between the hunter/gatherer and pastoral subsistence adaptations and the concomitant differences in the nature of group interactions among and between hunter/gatherers and pastoralists. In this paper we will examine the patterns of obsidian use in the earlier portions of the Stone Age record in central Kenya and northern Tanzania as the first step in determining whether significant changes between the ESA, MSA, and LSA hunting and gathering adaptations can be recognized.

When we made our initial observations on regional patterning of obsidian use we had been unable to analyze any ESA artifacts to document the actual distances any materials had moved from source to sites, nor did we have a very large sample of MSA assemblages to strongly support the emerging pattern outlined above (Merrick and Brown 1984). In the following presentation we provide analyses of a small series of ESA artifacts and a much larger series of MSA artifacts from several sites in Kenya and northern Tanzania which reinforce our preliminary observations and indicate that additional technological

study of assemblages and further chemical analyses of ESA and MSA artifacts will be profitable.

Obsidian sources and their chemistry

Our present knowledge of the distribution of obsidian sources in the southern half of Kenya is slightly improved from the previously published summaries available in Merrick and Brown (1984) and Merrick et al. (1990). We have now sampled over eighty outcrops in the region, and based on a combination of X-ray fluorescence (XRF) and electron probe microanalysis (EPMA) for ten to thirteen major, minor and trace elements, we currently recognize some thirty distinctive petrological groups of obsidian. As our knowledge of outcrops and source chemistries increases it is clear that some of the distinctive groups of obsidian we previously recognized were almost certainly produced by successive flows from single sources whose magma compositions were evolving gradually over time. That is, some of the groups reflect our arbitrary divisions, defined by the vagaries of outcrops and exposure, superimposed over the continuous geochemical evolution of a single volcanic source area. The consequence is that, especially on Mt. Eburru where there were many closely spaced eruptions which produced obsidian, the allocation of one or another outcrop to a particular petrological group becomes very difficult, even using eight to ten elements for characterizing the obsidian glasses. In four instances we decided to handle this problem by lumping two or more of our petrological groups into larger composite groups. This was done for Groups *20* and *25*; *30* and *32*; *29*, *31*, and *40*; and *27* and *35*. Each of these composite groups still represents a geographically discrete entity and while this presents some loss of precision in assignment to specific outcrops, for purposes of evaluating long-distance movement of obsidian, it makes essentially no difference. Figure 1 presents the distribution of sources and sites for southern central Kenya and northern Tanzania, while Fig. 2 provides the distribution of sources, petrological groups, and sites around the Lake Naivasha basin.

Analytical methods, artifact characterization, and assignment to sources

The chemical analysis of the majority of artifacts discussed below was undertaken by electron probe microanalysis (EPMA), although some artifacts were analyzed by X-ray fluorescence (XRF). The analytical methods for electron probe microanalysis of natural glasses are described in Nash (1992). Analytical precision on our primary obsidian standard (MM3) and comparative analyses for two natural glasses are provided in Table 1. X-ray fluorescence analyses were performed by the methods and using the standards described in Brown and Cerling (1982). The characterization of obsidian source types for the artifacts discussed below is based primarily on electron probe

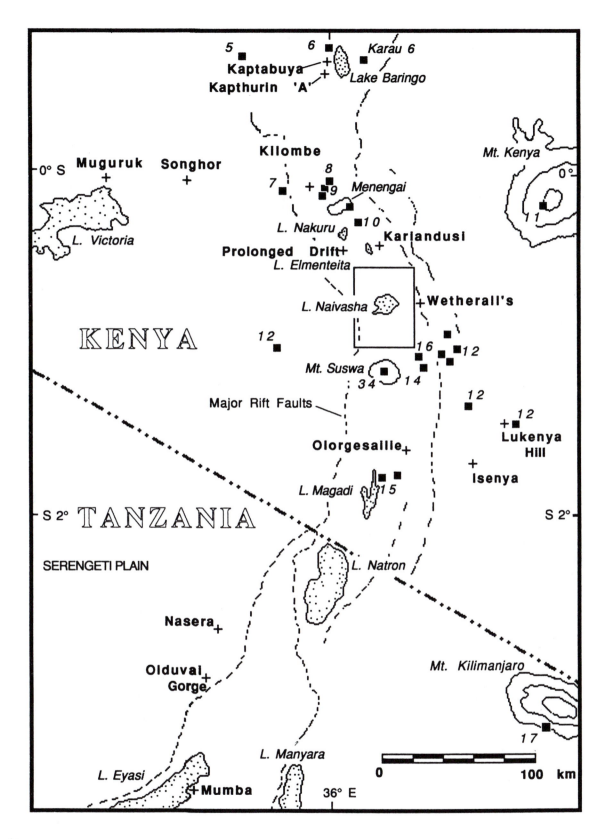

Fig. 1:
Known sources of obsidian in southern central Kenya and northern Tanzania and the ESA and MSA sites discussed in the text. (See Fig. 2 for inset of the Lake Naivasha area.)

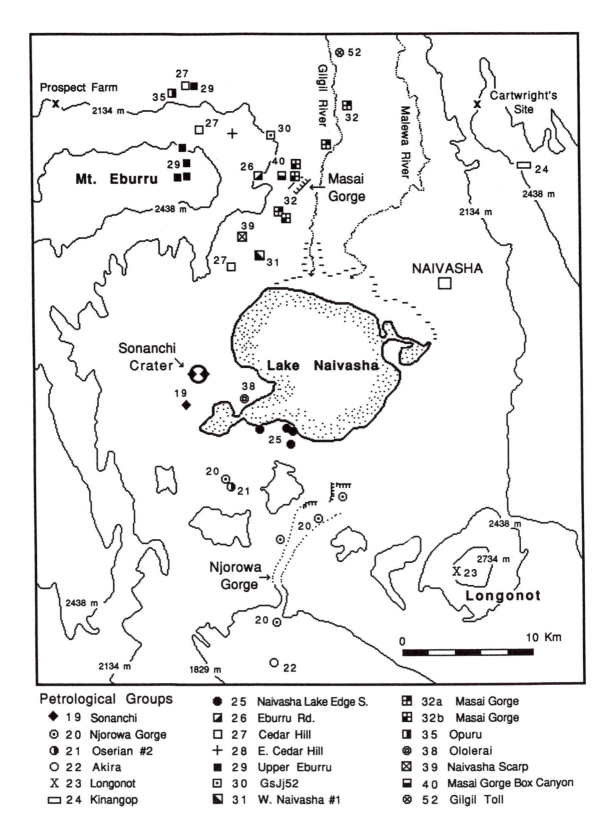

Fig. 2:
Outcrops of analyzed obsidian and the distribution of source areas in the Lake Naivasha area.

Petrological Groups

- ◆ 19 Sonanchi
- ⊙ 20 Njorowa Gorge
- ◑ 21 Oserian #2
- ○ 22 Akira
- X 23 Longonot
- ▭ 24 Kinangop
- ● 25 Naivasha Lake Edge S.
- ◪ 26 Eburru Rd.
- □ 27 Cedar Hill
- + 28 E. Cedar Hill
- ■ 29 Upper Eburru
- ▣ 30 GsJj52
- ◣ 31 W. Naivasha #1
- ▦ 32a Masai Gorge
- ▦ 32b Masai Gorge
- ▯ 35 Opuru
- ◉ 38 Ololerai
- ⊠ 39 Naivasha Scarp
- ▱ 40 Masai Gorge Box Canyon
- ⊗ 52 Gilgil Toll

Table 1. Electron probe microanalyses of standard and comparative glasses

				Sample			
	MM3 Utah EPMA		RLS-132 Utah EPMA	wet chem.*	Lava Creek B Utah EPMA	USGS EPMA**
	n=394	s.d.	n=34			
Composition						
SiO_2	76.4	0.7	75.8	75.7	73.7	72.2
TiO_2	0.08	0.03	0.20	0.21	0.10	0.10
Al_2O_3	12.3	0.1	11.2	11.44	11.6	11.7
Fe_2O_3	0.73	0.09	2.38	2.36	1.46	1.48
MnO	0.05	0.02	0.14	0.15	0.03	0.03
MgO	O.06	0.02	0.06	0.05	0.03	0.03
CaO	0.55	0.03	0.11	0.12	0.50	0.51
Na_2O	3.53	0.15	4.95	5.25	3.49	3.37
K_2O	5.24	0.08	4.64	4.53	4.87	4.86
Cl	0.07	0.01	0.19	0.18	0.17	-
F	0.13	0.05	0.26	0.23	0.01	-
H_2O	0.6†	0.1	-	0.07	4.5†	-
Sum	99.14		99.9	100.29	100.46	-
less O=F, Cl	0.08		0.15	0.13	0.04	
Total	99.1	0.42	99.8	100.16	100.4	94.3

* MacDonald et al. 1992:analysis no. 150
** Sarna-Wojcicki et al. 1987:table 1
† H_2O calculated from difference between measured and stoichiometric oxygen (Nash 1992)

microanalysis for Fe, Ti, and Ca supplemented by EPMA and XRF analyses for a limited number of additional elements. We have previously argued (Merrick and Brown 1984, but see the limitations noted in Merrick et al. 1990) that using these three elements provides excellent discrimination between sources with lower Fe_2O_3 values and reasonable discrimination for most of the higher Fe_2O_3 sources in the region. Figures 3a and b provide illustration of the variation in the Fe_2O_3, TiO_2, and CaO compositions for the sources with greater than 5% Fe_2O_3. In many cases, but not all, where these elements have not provided completely unambiguous characterization for individual artifacts, subsequent supplemental XRF or electron probe microanalyses for additional elements were undertaken. We have found that Zr, F, Mn, and Na are the most useful in this regard. While we feel the assignments presented here are all reasonably secure in view of our knowledge of the area's sources, the discovery of additional petrological groups is likely—witness the number of unknown sources represented in both the ESA and MSA artifact samples discussed here—and the possibility exists that some of the source assignments presented here may need to be reevaluated in future.

Several other difficulties in conducting source and artifact distribution studies for ESA and MSA sites in central Kenya and northern Tanzania should be mentioned. A fair number of the obsidian artifacts in the ESA and MSA assemblages discussed below are made on obsidian from currently unknown and unlocated geological sources. This adds an unavoidable imprecision to the study of the distances which materials have moved from source to site. This observation should not be surprising given the considerable age of the sites and the active volcanic and tectonic history of the central Rift area. Because the central Rift region has been so active geologically over the past several million years, it is logical that a number of sources of obsidian available to early humans in the Middle and early Upper Pleistocene might no longer be exposed and accessible, and thus remain unknown to us as potential sources. Indeed, the obsidians most commonly used in the late Pleistocene and Holocene and those most readily available and accessible today (including many outcrops from the Njorowa Gorge, Sonanchi Crater, and upper elevation Mt. Eburru areas) are all likely to be less than 250,000 years in age on both geological grounds and potassium-argon (K-Ar) dating evidence. In fact the presence and/or the first appearance of the Njorowa Gorge (20–25) and Sonanchi (19) obsidian types in a site sequence is very likely an excellent *maximum* age limit for that assemblage.

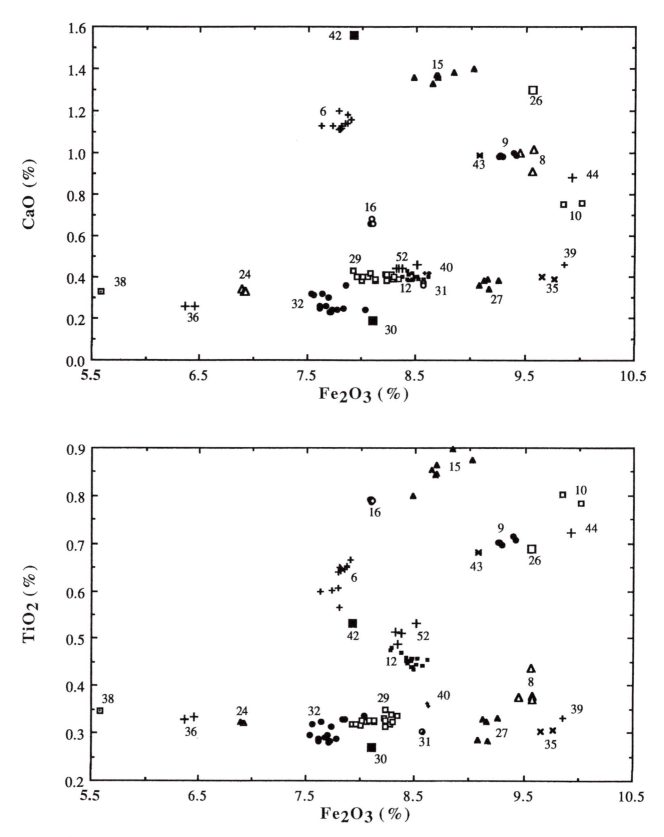

Fig. 3a and b:
Scatter-plots of (a) the total iron as (Fe$_2$O$_3$) versus calcium (as CaO) values and (b) the total iron as (Fe$_2$O$_3$) versus titanium (as TiO$_2$) values for analyses of source materials from source localities with >5.5 Fe$_2$O$_3$.

Table 2. Obsidian source assignments for artifacts in ESA assemblages. Straight line distances over land to the nearest known outcrops of the source group are given in parentheses

	Source areas						
	Karau group	Kedong	Kinangop	Masai Gorge	Gilgil Toll		
Petrological Group	*6*	*14*	*24*	*30/32*	*52*	*Unknowns*	
Site	n (km)	n (km)	n (km)	n (km)	n (km)	n	Totals
Kariandusi	-	-	2 (30)	2 (20)	7 (15)	-	11
Kilombe	-	-	-	-	-	1 "a"	1
Isenya	-	1 (60)	-	-	-	-	1
Kaptabuya (GnJi 16)	1 (10)	-	-	-	-	-	1
Kapthurin 'A' (GnJh 15)	-	-	-	-	-	1 "b"	1

A further difficulty in evaluating patterns of obsidian use at these early sites in terms of long distance and local interactions is that longer distance movement and hence rarer interactions are likely to be represented by only a very few specimens of obsidian. While this is not a major sampling problem for sites like those at Lukenya Hill which have modest obsidian use and are located some distance from obsidian sources, in sites whose assemblages are completely dominated by obsidian, this becomes a very significant sampling problem. In addition when any significant number of unknown sources is represented in an assemblage, as at Prospect Farm, it is usually not possible to confidently predict whether or not the use of these sources may represent significant long distance interactions. This remains a serious problem for both ESA and MSA sites in the region because our knowledge of the totality of sources available during Middle Pleistocene and early Upper Pleistocene times still remains limited.

Obsidian use in the ESA

In almost all cases obsidian seems to have been very infrequently used as a material for artifact manufacture during ESA times in Kenya and northern Tanzania. There is no evidence of its use in Oldowan times either at Olduvai (M. D. Leakey 1971) or at Koobi Fora (Isaac and Harris 1978), and with the single exception of Kariandusi (Gowlett 1980) all of the better known and documented Acheulian sites in Kenya and northern Tanzania, including Olorgesailie (Isaac 1977), Isenya (Roche et al. 1988), Kilombe (Gowlett 1978), Lewa (Kibunjia 1987), the Kapthurin sites (M. Leakey 1969; Cornelissen et al. 1990), Peninj (Isaac 1967) and Olduvai (M. D. Leakey 1974) either lack obsidian artifacts entirely or contain less than 1% obsidian artifacts in their assemblages, as near as can be determined from the literature. At all of these sites lava artifacts predominate, while small numbers of chert and quartz artifacts are

occasionally encountered. Whether the absence of obsidian artifacts at most ESA sites is simply a function of the proximity to obsidian sources, or a preference for other raw materials is probably not a resolvable question now, given our small sample of sites, but it is nonetheless worthy of some consideration.

Obsidian sources represented at ESA sites

We have analyzed fifteen obsidian artifacts from five ESA sites in southern central Kenya. These include artifacts from the well known sites of Kariandusi, Kilombe, and Isenya, and from two lesser known Lake Baringo area sites, Kaptabuya (GnJi 16) (Merrick, unpub. notes) and Kapthurin 'A' (GnJh 15) (Cornelissen et. al. 1990). The Kariandusi and Kilombe assemblages are probably more than 700,000 years in age (Gowlett 1980) and the assemblage from Isenya, although as yet undated, typologically resembles these two. The two Baringo area sites have assemblages with typological features that suggest probable later or final Acheulian ages. Table 2 presents a summary of the source assignments and distances between the sources and sites for the identified sources. Figures 4a and b illustrate the Fe, Ca, and Ti compositions of the artifacts from the four ESA sites which exhibit high Fe (>6%) compositions. A discussion of the specifics of the source assignments for each site follows.

Obsidians at Kariandusi

Eleven artifacts (eight bifaces, one chopper, one core, and one unmodified flake fragment) from the Upper Site at Kariandusi were analyzed by electron microprobe (seven specimens) and XRF (four specimens) analysis. The microprobe analyses for Fe, Ca, and Ti undertaken on the seven artifacts are compared in Figs. 4a and b with the analyses of the other sampled Acheulian artifacts. At least three different sources are represented in the Kariandusi

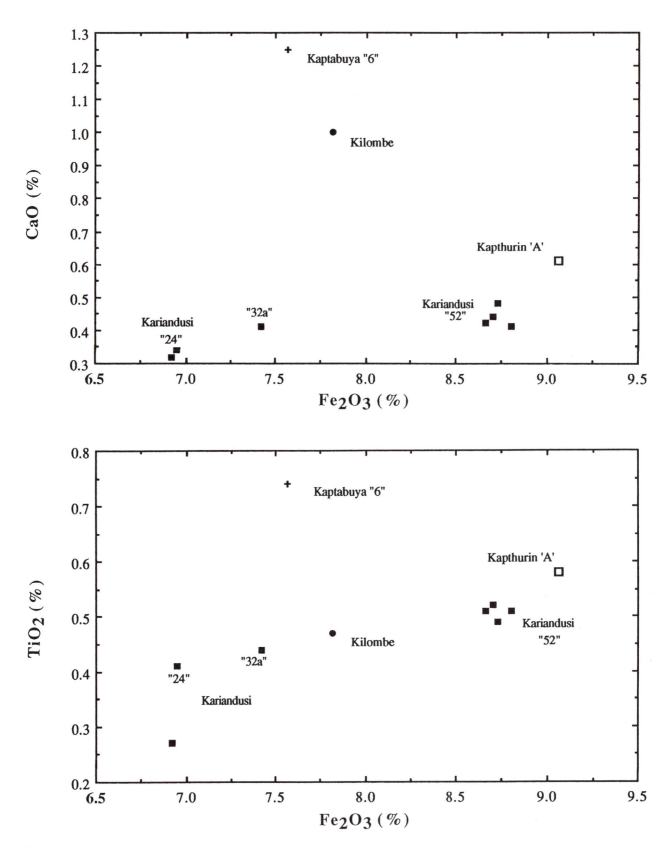

Fig. 4a and b:
Scatter-plots of microprobe values for (a) CaO versus Fe_2O_3 and (b) TiO_2 versus Fe_2O_3 for the ESA artifacts from the Kariandusi, Kilombe, Kaptabuya, and Kapthurin 'A' sites. The assigned source groups are indicated when known.

assemblage. Characterization on these three elements suggests that the Kinangop (Group *24*), Masai Gorge (Group *32*), and Gilgil Toll Station (Group *52*) source areas are probably represented. The assignments to the Kinangop and Gilgil groups seem reasonably secure; however, both the TiO_2 and the CaO values for the piece tentatively assigned to the Masai Gorge group appear a bit higher than is usual for that petrological group. XRF analyses for eleven elements were also conducted on an additional four artifacts. The analytical results are presented in Table 3 which also presents the chemistries typical of source groups with generally similar characteristics. These analyses support the assignments of the artifacts to the Gilgil and Masai Gorge obsidian sources. Three of the four artifacts have compositions which best match that of the Gilgil Toll source (*52*). The fourth artifact's composition best matches that of the "a" subgroup of Masai Gorge obsidians (*32a*). In all three cases the distances between site and nearest known outcrops of the sources identified at Kariandusi do not exceed 30 km.

Unfortunately, beyond the observations that obsidian comprised about 15% of the raw material present at the Upper Site, that at least three sources were represented and that the obsidian may have moved upwards of 15 to 30 km from source to site, it is difficult to deduce any further palaeoanthropological significance from these findings because of the site's context and our obviously non-random sampling. The Kariandusi Upper Site assemblage comes from a stream channel and is clearly a disturbed secondary context occurrence (Gowlett 1980). The visual impression one receives viewing the site (it is preserved as a public museum display) strongly suggests that the artifacts were sorted by size by water action prior to burial. Large bifacial tools and cores of both lava and obsidian far exceed smaller flakes and debitage. Such a context makes it impossible to determine both the forms in which the obsidian (blocks, blanks, or finished artifacts) may have arrived at the site, and the extent to which flaking of obsidian actually occurred in the vicinity of the site.

Obsidians at Isenya, Kaptabuya, Kilombe, and Kapthurin

The single piece of obsidian, a fragmentary flake, recovered from the Isenya excavation (H. Roche, pers. comm.) is confidently assignable to the Kedong obsidian type (Group *14*) (see Table 4 for analytical results). The nearest known outcrops of this obsidian group are about 60 km distant although it is not impossible that closer outcrops, now buried by more recent volcanics, may have been available in the past. The Kaptabuya Acheulian site is located just northwest of Kampi ya Samaki near Lake Baringo. Test excavations supervised by the senior author in 1983 revealed an Acheulian assemblage dominated by smallish lava bifaces and unmodified lava flakes and

fragments. A fragment of a single obsidian biface was also recovered. Chemical analysis indicates the Karau source (*6*) is the probable source of obsidian. The main Karau source localities are currently some 30 km away by land traveling around modern Lake Baringo, but would be only 17 km in straight line distance in the absence of the lake. Pyroclastic tuffs in the Lokoritabim area just 10 km north of Kaptabuya also contain pebble and small cobble size obsidian lapilli of Karau type.

The sources of obsidian used for the single obsidian biface recovered from the Kilombe site and a flake fragment from the Kapthurin 'A' site cannot be identified at present. Comparison of the Fe_2O_3, TiO_2, and CaO compositions in Figs. 3 and 4 illustrates that neither the Kilombe nor the Kapthurin 'A' obsidians closely match any currently known sources. Kilombe is near known sources of obsidian on Mt. Londiani to the west; near Kisanana to the northeast and to the south are Menengai volcanics which contain obsidian. These outcrops are all with 25 km of the site, however, the Kilombe obsidian does not appear to closely match the chemistry of the Londiani source based on Jones' (1981) published analysis, nor does it match Kisanana or any of the Menengai area volcanic glasses we have analyzed. The nearest known obsidian source to the Kapthurin 'A' site is Karau, but the Kapthurin 'A' obsidian is clearly not from a Karau (*6*) group outcrop.

Discussion

The single obsidian artifact encountered at Isenya potentially documents the movement of obsidian 60 km in an ESA assemblage. However, although similar long-distance movement of the unprovenanced obsidians at the Kilombe and Kapthurin 'A' sites cannot be excluded, all of the obsidians whose sources can be documented at Kariandusi and the Kaptabuya sites are available within 30 km of the sites. Moreover the overall rarity of obsidian in all ESA assemblages and the frequent presence of obsidian artifacts as finished retouched pieces, rather than debris suggests that the movement of finished tools to sites, rather than raw material to site is the most frequent pattern. Overall the patterning suggests limited use and movement of obsidian in ESA times and by implication that obsidian's utility or desirability was limited, and/or that group territories or interaction networks were very limited.

There are obviously a number of permutations for the interplay of these factors, but a brief consideration of the factors may help in evaluating the possibilities. The general rarity of obsidian use in central Kenyan and northern Tanzanian Acheulian ESA sites may be simply attributable to differential transport costs associated with using obsidian instead of lavas. Most of the major Acheulian site complexes are not within 25 to 30 km of major obsidian sources which we believe would have been contemporary and accessible when the sites were inhabited. In all instances

Table 3. XRF analyses of source samples and Kariandusi artifacts

Petro. Group	Sample no.		Location	Fe$_2$O$_3$ %	CaO %	K$_2$O %	Mn ppm	Nb ppm	Rb ppm	Sr ppm	TiO$_2$ %	Y ppm	Zn ppm	Zr ppm
Source samples:														
6	MER	60	Karau	7.80	1.11	5.1	2585	214	142	1	0.56	86	202	776
12	MER	44	Mangu	8.42	0.39	4.3	2226	298	194	5	0.46	119	343	1607
16	MER	51	Gacharage	8.08	0.66	4.8	2600	294	161	1	0.79	93	278	1424
29	MER	117	GsJj 50 locality	8.13	0.39	4.5	1959	316	190	5	0.33	196	295	1589
30	MER	24	GsJj52 locality	8.10	0.19	4.2	1880	539	401	2	0.27	327	509	2988
31	MER	5	W. Naivasha #1	8.56	0.37	4.5	1956	270	230	6	0.30	167	348	1304
32a	MER	71	Ilkek	7.56	0.31	4.4	1600	425	358	5	0.32	263	396	2770
32b	MER	90	Masai G. Rockshelter	7.72	0.23	4.3	1706	502	401	4	0.28	313	422	3267
40	CMN	10	Masai G. Box Canyon	8.61	0.42	4.4	2010	278	219	8	0.36	189	338	1387
52	MER	110	Gilgil Toll Station	8.51	0.46	4.6	1976	349	278	1	0.53	207	369	2142
Artifacts:														
32a	MER	501	Kariandusi - Acheulian	7.83	0.36	4.2	1673	411	337	<5	0.32	246	373	2582
52	MER	508	Kariandusi - Acheulian	8.32	0.44	4.6	1870	356	284	<5	0.51	210	360	2142
52	MER	509	Kariandusi - Acheulian	8.34	0.44	4.7	1844	365	294	1	0.49	218	360	2229
52	KAR RIV 7/84		Kariandusi - Acheulian	8.37	0.44	4.6	1870	363	277	5	0.51	203	351	2130

Table 4. Comparison of electron probe microanalyses of the Isenya Acheulian artifact and Group *14* source material

Composition	Petro. Group *14* MER 1* Kedong Escarp. source	Petro. Group *14* Acheulian artifact* Isenya
	%	%
SiO_2	71.7	69.7
TiO_2	0.49	0.54
ZrO_2	0.14	0.15
Al_2O_3	13.8	13.6
Fe_2O_3	3.43	3.33
MnO	0.15	0.13
MgO	0.30	0.37
CaO	0.73	0.84
Na_2O	4.86	5.09
K_2O	5.45	5.06
F	0.29	0.29
Cl	0.10	0.10
Sum	101.5	99.2
less O	0.14	0.14
Total	101.3	99.1

* average of 5 microanalyses

alternative raw materials, principally lavas, are available within 10 to 15 km of each of the sites. Additionally, it is possible that behaviors involving longer distance movement of any raw materials and/or 'curating' of artifacts may simply not have been well developed. Obsidian may have also not proved a particularly suitable material for the functions usually performed by large bifacial tools which are the most common formal Acheulian tools. Clearly the edges of obsidian bifaces are more brittle and markedly less durable than those of lava. It may be noteworthy in this light that many of the Kariandusi bifaces are made on a very tough phenocryst-rich obsidian (which proved in six of eight biface specimens to be Group *52* obsidian) whose flaking characteristics more closely resemble lava than the glassier obsidian from the other sources represented at Kariandusi. A possible, but perhaps more speculative explanation for the rarity of obsidian use, is the suggestion that obsidian may have been intentionally avoided by early hominids because of the greater likelihood (in comparison with knapping lavas and cherts) of being cut or injured during its flaking. One can easily envision very strong selection pressures to avoid being cut or injured during stone tool manufacture in earlier times. Finally the options remain that Acheulian groups had more limited mobility and smaller range sizes than succeeding hunter/gatherers in the region because of the nature of their subsistence

practices, and/or that exchange and interaction between groups was more limited. Clearly the future resolution of these issues, if indeed ever resolvable, will require greater geological knowledge of the availability of contemporary obsidian sources, a larger sample of sites, broad scale integration of site location data with raw material source information and the additional study of the artifactual and faunal assemblages. Suffice to say the pattern of obsidian utilization is not the same as displayed by more recent archaic and modern *Homo sapiens* groups inhabiting the region.

Obsidian use in the MSA

In our first paper on Kenyan obsidian sources and their use we examined a small number of artifacts from five MSA sites, including Cartwright's, Wetherall's, Lukenya Hill (GvJm 16), Muguruk, and Songhor (Merrick and Brown 1984). This study provided definite evidence of movement of modest quantities of obsidian beyond 50 km and up to 190 km from source to site. We have now enlarged our sample of sites and artifacts to include a greater number of artifacts from the GvJm 16 site at Lukenya Hill, as well as artifacts from four additional sites. These include Nasera (Mehlman 1977) and Mumba-Höhle (Mehlman 1979), Prospect Farm (Anthony 1978), and Prolonged Drift (GrJi 11) (Merrick 1975). The artifacts from the first two sites in northern Tanzania, provided by the courtesy of M. Mehlman, now document movement of central Kenyan obsidian up to 305 km from source to site. The results of this recent work are consistent with the initial patterning observed and confirm that the frequency of obsidian use in MSA times and its movement from source to site offer a marked contrast to the general pattern presented in the preceding ESA. Obsidian artifacts occur in very high frequencies in many sites within 50 km of major sources, and in significant, but increasingly declining frequencies in sites up to at least 305 km from these sources. Table 5 inventories the MSA assemblages examined, the sources identified and the distances from sources to sites. Discussion of the assignments and their significance for the specific sites follow.

Northern Tanzanian MSA sites

The obsidians from the two northern Tanzanian rockshelter sites merit brief comment. Obsidian forms a very small percentage of the flaked stone material present at these sites. The fourteen artifacts sampled from Mumba, (twelve pieces of debitage and two retouched pieces) all come from Bed VI which contains an MSA assemblage which may be dated as early as 100,000 to 130,000 years ago (Mehlman 1987). The absence of any sources besides the Njorowa Gorge group (although it is the closest major source by 40 km) is mildly surprising considering the sample size and the generally eclectic assortment of sources

Table 5. Obsidian source assignments for artifacts from MSA sites. Straight line distances over land to the nearest known outcrops of the source are given in parentheses

Source	Petro. group	Muguruk @ n(km)	Songhor @ n(km)	Mumba-Höhle @ n(km)	Nasera @ n(km)	Lukenya Hill* X₁ - 98.10–97.90 n	Lukenya Hill* X₁ - 98.50–98.45 n	Lukenya Hill* (km)	Prospect Farm* Spits 22–23 n	Prospect Farm* Spits 16–18 n	Prospect Farm* Spits 9–10 n	Prospect Farm* (km)	Prolonged Drift* n(km)	Cartwright's @ n(km)	Wetherall's @ n(km)
Kisanana	*8*	-	-	-	-	26	-	(6)	2	1	1	(75)	-	-	-
Highlands	*12*	-	-	-	-	8	15	-	-	-	-	-	-	-	1 (45)
Kedong	*14*	-	-	-	-	3	3	(65)	-	-	-	-	-	-	-
Sonanchi	*19*	1 (190)	1 (145)	14 (305)	6 (230)	3	-	(125)	-	-	56	(30)	41 (40)	-	5 (38)
Njorowa Gorgo	*20/25*	-	-	-	-	1	23	(105)	2	25	1	(40)	45 (50)	20 (35)	16 (24)
Oserian #2	*21*	-	-	-	-	-	1	(115)	1	-	-	(40)	-	-	-
Kinangop	*24*	-	-	-	-	-	1	(125)	2	6	1	(30)	-	2 (5)	3 (12)
Cedar Hill/Opuru	*27/35*	-	-	-	-	3	1	(135)	10	-	1	(10)	+ (33)	-	1 (35)
Upper Eburru	*29/31/40*	1 (185)	-	-	1 (240)	5	1	(130)	5	24	9	(15)	4 (30)	-	5 (34)
Masai Gorge	*30/32*	-	-	-	2 (240)	-	2	(135)	60	49	24	(15)	-	28 (16)	16 (25)
Ololerai	*38*	-	-	-	-	-	-	-	-	14	-	(30)	-	-	-
Unknowns															
PF unkn-1									26	15	18		6		
PF unkn-2									6	-	-		-		
PF unkn-3									2	-	1		-		
PF unkn-4									-	2	-		-		
PF unkn-5									-	-	3		-		
TOTAL PIECES		2	1	14	9	49	47		116	136	115		96	50	47

* indicates artifacts were drawn from the assemblage by systematic sampling
+ appears in artifacts selected for analysis on the basis of optical criteria to identify the presence of rarer types
@ non-random samples

represented at other MSA occupied rockshelters located at considerable distances from sources. The absence of Sonanchi (*19*) obsidian, which is very frequent in most southern Kenyan and northern Tanzania sites in later times, may be understandable if, as we increasingly suspect on archaeological and geological grounds, the Sonanchi volcanic source is no older than Upper Pleistocene in age. The nine pieces of debitage drawn from the MSA assemblages in Levels 14 to 22 at the Nasera rockshelter include examples of Sonanchi (*19*), Masai Gorge area (*30/32*), and Upper Eburru (*29/31/40*) glasses and document obsidian movement up to 240 km.

Lukenya Hill

The GvJm 16 rockshelter on Lukenya Hill contained a small but nearly 2 m thick deposit of MSA-bearing sediments. The site remains undated. Artifact densities were generally low and faunal remains sparse, probably due in part to poor conditions for bone preservation. If the excavator were pressed, he would suggest sporadic short-term occupations, rather than longer term regular occupation to account for the debris accumulated at the site. While the industrial affiliation of the assemblage has never been formalized, in general technological features the assemblage is similar to the Prospect Industry as represented by the assemblages from Spits 16–18 and 22–23 of the Prospect Farm sequence (Merrick 1975).

The analysis of the larger number of artifacts from GvJm 16, a sample which includes both debitage and retouched pieces in their representative proportions, does not greatly alter the patterning previously observed. However, it does allow us greater confidence in the results (Table 5). At GvJm 16 obsidian artifacts comprise between 5% and 8% of the artifacts in the MSA levels, both quartz and cherts being more frequent (Merrick 1975). For the earliest MSA level (98.10–97.90) locally available obsidian (*12*) forms the majority (53%) of the assemblage, with the next nearest source, Kedong (*14*) some 65 km away, being represented by another 16%. The remaining 31% come from five different source areas between 105 and 135 km distant. These exotics form about 2% of the total of all raw material present in the level. The overlying MSA level (98.50–98.45) exhibits a somewhat different pattern. Local (*12*) and Kedong (*14*) obsidians represent 32% and 6% of the total obsidian and exotic obsidians from six sources, dominated by Njorowa Gorge obsidian (*20/25*), form 62% of the total obsidian. This shift might be interpreted as either the appearance of a subsistence system involving more mobility or alternatively more interaction between groups which facilitates the exchange of obsidian. The choice between these alternatives remains problematic. Although the total number of retouched pieces in each level is small (6%–8%) compared to the quantity of debitage, both retouched pieces and debitage appear on local and non-local obsidians in the same proportions. This suggests working of all materials at the site with no particular evidence of a preference for non-local obsidian for retouched tool production, nor evidence for the import of finished obsidian artifacts.

Lake Nakuru basin sites

The final two sites we examined are Prospect Farm and Prolonged Drift which are located in the Lake Nakuru basin. Both of these open air sites are located within 50 km of most of the known major obsidian sources which were widely used in late Pleistocene and Holocene times. At both sites between 90% and 99% of all the material used for artifact manufacture is obsidian. For these two sites our interest centers around the choices of sources, given the number available and that their proximity probably made them reasonably accessible to the inhabitants of both sites. The artifact samples from the Prolonged Drift and Prospect Farm sites were drawn by systematic sampling from the entire assemblages, and thus include both debitage and retouched artifacts in approximately their respective proportions in each assemblage. As was the finding for the GvJm 16 site there is no strong evidence for intentional selection of obsidian from specific sources for the manufacture of retouched pieces, nor is there strong evidence for the import of finished tools to the sites, based on the proportions of obsidian types among retouched pieces and debitage.

Prospect Farm

The Prospect Farm site is an open air site located on the northern slopes of Mt. Eburru, overlooking the Lake Nakuru basin from an elevation of about 2150 m. Today it is situated in a grassland/bushland zone below the forest margin. The MSA sequence spanning nearly 15 m of deposits at the site has been described and analyzed by Anthony (1978) and additional evidence on the technology and dating of the industry is available in Merrick (1975) and Michels et al. (1983). Little is definitely known of the paleoenvironmental setting of the site during the MSA occupation although it is reasonable to assume it was probably near the ecotonal boundary between the evergreen forest and the bushland/grassland boundary as it is today. The site has no preserved fauna and although it has high densities of artifacts in some levels the functional type(s) of the site (long- or short-term occupations) over time is problematic.

Obsidian artifacts from three MSA levels in the Prospect Farm Locality 1 sequence (base, Spits 22/23; middle, Spits 16/18; and top, Spits 9/10) were sampled. These levels perhaps span the period from >120,000 to just less than 50,000 years ago (Michels et al. 1983). On typological grounds the material from the lower two levels represents the local MSA Prospect Industry (Anthony 1978) while the upper material can be described as late MSA (Merrick

1975) or transitional MSA/LSA (Michels et al. 1983). It is of note that all of the assemblages sampled are heavily dominated by debitage. Well-finished tools, predominately scraper and point forms, are very rare. Obsidian is the preferred material representing 90% of all materials used in the earliest level, 96.9% in the middle level, and 99.5% in the latest MSA level. Table 5 tabulates the sources identified in each level and the distances to sources.

Prospect Farm Spits 22–23

Of the 116 pieces examined, we have analyzed 25% of the sample for 13 elements, but for the remaining 75% we have only analyses for Fe, Ti, and Ca. Consequently our resolution for making assignments to many of the Eburru/ Masai Gorge area sources is not highly refined. Nonetheless the overall patterning is clear. The earliest MSA levels at Prospect Farm are dominated by Mt. Eburru area sources. The most distant source represented in the level, Kisanana (*8*) some 75 km away, is represented by two specimens. Southern Naivasha area sources (*20/25* and *21*) some 40 km distant are represented by only three pieces (2.5%). The Kinangop source (*24*) is likely represented by two pieces as well. Additional elements will need to be analyzed to confirm these preliminary assignments to the various Masai Gorge area localities and sources, but tentatively 52% of the total can be assigned to Group *30/32* and 4% to Group *29/31/40* localities although the latter must be derived from the localities assigned to Groups *31* and *40*, rather than the uppermost Eburru (Holocene) outcrops. Ten artifacts (8.6%) probably represent Group *27/35* obsidian from nearby outcrops (10 km) at Cedar Hill or Opuru. However, this assignment may present some problems on geological grounds as the Cedar Hill volcanics are generally regarded as very recent in age (see Thompson and Dodson 1963).

Unfortunately, a significant percentage of the artifacts are made on obsidian from sources whose locations are not currently known. At least three unknown sources are represented. Just over 22% (n=26) come from an unknown high Fe_2O_3 (10–11%), high TiO_2 (0.4–0.6%) source (PF unkn-1) whose closest similarity is with some of the Menengai area volcanics to the north and east of Lake Nakuru. Five percent of our sample was represented by a high Fe_2O_3 (6%), moderate TiO_2 (0.38–0.45%) obsidian (PF unkn-2) with similarities to the Kinangop source group (*24*). The remaining unknown source was represented by two pieces. While long-distance movement for the pieces of unknown source provenance cannot be excluded, their frequency and composition, albeit on the limited data available, generally suggest probable origins in the Lake Naivasha and Lake Nakuru basins.

Prospect Farm Spits 16–18

More of the obsidians from the Spits 16–18 sample come from known sources and are seemingly less domi- nated by the immediate Mt. Eburru area sources than in the underlying MSA levels. Again, the most distant source recognized was Kisanana with one specimen. Southern Naivasha obsidians (*20/25*) formed some 18.5% of the obsidian. An obsidian type which we have tentatively identified as from the Ololerai source (*38*) at the south- western edge of Lake Naivasha appears in use for the first time, forming 10% of the obsidian. Its appearance, which is restricted to this one level in our Prospect Farm samples, is especially noteworthy because we have never observed its use in any other MSA, LSA, or Pastoral Neolithic site which we have sampled. Masai Gorge area obsidians from the *30/32* and *31/40* groups form 36% and 18% of the obsidians, respectively. The PF unkn-1 source is repre- sented by 11% of the sample.

Prospect Farm Spits 9–10

The obsidian sources used in the most recent MSA levels contrast in some important respects with earlier levels. The most notable changes are the first appearance and very frequent use (49%) of Sonanchi obsidian (*19*) in the sequence and the marked decline (<1%) of southern Naivasha area obsidians (*20/25*) as well as the disappear- ance of the Ololerai type (*38*). Masai Gorge area obsidians (*30/32*) are well represented, as are Upper Eburru sources (*29/31/40*) although the latter presumably again must be derived from the Group *31/40* localities, rather than up- permost Eburru (Holocene) outcrops. Some 10% of the sampled obsidian came from the unknown source, PF unkn-1, whose close chemical similarity to some of the Menengai area volcanics to the north and east of Lake Nakuru was noted above. A continued northward contact is also indicated by the presence of a single example of Kisanana obsidian (*8*) whose source is 75 km distant. There are also probably three pieces from another unknown source (PF unkn-5) with Fe_2O_3 values around 8.5% and CaO values around 1%. It is very probable that these come from a local Eburru source as a number of small (<1 gm) unmodified obsidian lapilli recovered in the same strati- graphic level have a similar composition.

Prospect Farm discussion

Several observations can be made on the patterns of obsidian used at Prospect Farm over time. Although a considerable number of unknown sources are represented, particularly in the earliest levels, to the extent we can identify the sources the earliest levels seem to contain higher frequencies of obsidians from the immediate vicin- ity of the site. The earliest levels also have a greater diversity of minor sources present. The two more recent levels tend to have more of the distant (but still local) obsidians present, but in all levels demonstrated exotic obsidian from more than 50 km away is rare. However, the regular presence of these exotics (Kisanana) is very interesting for the evidence of long distance trekking or exchange they provide, given that the Prospect Farm site is situated so close to numerous major sources. In all cases the exotics are debitage rather than retouched pieces. Whether obtained by exchange or during occasional visits to the source area is unknown, but once the material reaches the site it is apparently being used in the same manner as the other local obsidians.

GrJi 11

The Prolonged Drift Middle Stone Age site (GrJi 11) (Merrick 1975) is located along the west side of the Enderit River about 10 km south of the modern edge of Lake Nakuru. Although MSA artifacts were principally found concentrated in three separate horizons in a 5 m sequence of fluvial sediments, all the artifacts analyzed here come from the 15 cm thick "upper feature" horizon where a discrete low-density scatter of late MSA artifacts and faunal material was recovered in a context that suggested minimal disturbance during burial. The horizon was interpreted as the remains of a short-term camp site where a small amount of tool making and equipment outfitting probably occurred (Merrick 1975).

The pattern of obsidian source use at GrJi 11 is in marked contrast to the uppermost level (Spits 9–10) of the Prospect Farm site (see Table 5), which is probably the most nearly contemporaneous artifact sample. At the GrJi 11 site obsidian from the Njorowa Gorge (*20/25*) and Sonanchi Crater (*19*) groups are about equally represented and form nearly 90% of the obsidian. Almost certainly neither of these sources was the geographically nearest available contemporary obsidian sources. Both of these sources are lower elevation Lake Naivasha area sources some 55 km and 45 km distant if one does not travel directly over Mt. Eburru. Only a few specimens from Masai Gorge outcrops (*30/32*) represent the much nearer Mt. Eburru area sources. This is all the more noteworthy because the shortest route at lower elevations between GrJi 11 and the southern Lake Naivasha sources would take one close to or directly past the Masai Gorge sources. About 6% of the pieces exhibit compositions typical of the PF unkn-1 source, whose similarity to Menengai volcanics some 20 km to the north has been noted. The overall patterning of obsidian procurement here is consistent with either a very mobile subsistence strategy and/or a marked preference for particular sources of raw material for tool manufacture. This represents a marked departure from the pattern characterizing all of the earlier MSA assemblages studied.

Concluding comments

Although our sample of sites is still very small several patterns of obsidian use in the ESA and MSA are emerging more clearly. Obsidian use at ESA sites is rare and documented distances of movement between sources and sites are usually less than 30 km. The maximum distance of 60 km documented for a single case is not so great that direct access to the sources by the site's occupants is improbable. Consequently, the potential of using obsidian movement in ESA times to evaluate territorial ranges, subsistence and land use patterns, and interaction networks appears very limited at present. The study of obsidian use at MSA sites in the region offers far greater potential for examining these issues. Movement of obsidian for long distances (>300 km) as documented for the Tanzania MSA sites makes it very unlikely that individuals were making direct collection trips to sources. The movement of obsidian in the 100 to 130 km range as documented for Lukenya Hill is perhaps within the range of very mobile hunting and gathering groups. However, on balance we suspect that the increasing movement of obsidian over these intermediate distances is just as likely to represent increased interaction between groups. There is also perhaps some evidence of this increased interaction developing over the course of MSA time as well. In the two cases where we have examined patterning within single sequences, both the earlier assemblages at Prospect Farm and Lukenya Hill display greater reliance on the closest obsidian sources. Over time at both sites greater reliance develops on more distant (and possibly more plentiful and better quality) source localities. That obsidian may be becoming a more desirable raw material is also suggested by the observation that in both sequences, the proportion of obsidian to alternative raw materials increases gradually through time, a pattern which continues through the LSA in the region (Merrick and Brown 1984). In sum, many of the patterns, including increasing frequency of use, and long-distance movement of obsidian between sources and sites which came to characterize obsidian use by modern *Homo sapiens* hunting and gathering groups in the region have clear antecedents in the Middle Stone Age.

Acknowledgments

This research was conducted as part of the research program of the Division of Archaeology of the National Museums of Kenya. The support of the Kenya Museum Society and the Kenneth and Harle Montgomery Foundation for the collection of source samples is gratefully acknowledged. Support for the chemical analyses was provided by the National Science Foundation (U.S.A.), under grant BNS 8210735 and by the University of Utah, Department of Geology and Geophysics. The senior author thanks M. Mehlman and H. Roche for making artifacts from their respective excavations at Nasera, Mumba, and Isenya available for study. He also wishes to thank S. H. Ambrose, C. M. Nelson, and R. Soper for sharing their knowledge of Kenyan obsidian sources and for their help in collecting and in contributing source samples.

References

Ambrose, S. H. n.d. Chronology of the Later Stone Age in East Africa. Unpublished manuscript.

Ambrose, S. H., and K. G. Lorenz. 1990. Social and Ecological Models for the Middle Stone Age in Southern Africa. In *The Emergence of Modern Humans*, ed. P. Mellars, pp. 3–33. Edinburgh University Press, Edinburgh.

Anthony, B. W. 1978. *The Prospect Industry—A Definition*. Ph.D. dissertation, Harvard University.

Brown, F. H., and T. E. Cerling. 1982. Stratigraphic Significance of Tulu Bor Tuff. *Nature* 299:212–215.

Cornelissen, E., A. Boven, A. Dabi, J. Hus, K. Ju Yong, E. Keppens, R. Langohr, J. Moeyersons, P. Pasteels, M. Pieters, H. Uytterschaut, F. Van Noten, and H. Workineh. 1990. The Kapthurin Formation Revisited. *African Archaeological Reveiw* 8:23–75.

Gowlett, J. A. J. 1978. Kilombe—An Acheulian Site Complex in Kenya. In *Geological Background to Fossil Man*, ed. W. W. Bishop, pp. 337–360. Geological Society of London, Special Publication 6. Scottish Academic Press, Edinburgh.

——— 1980. Acheulean Sites in the Central Rift Valley, Kenya. In *Proceedings of the 8th Panafrican Congress of Prehistory and Quaternary Studies*, ed R. E. F. Leakey and B. A. Ogot, pp. 213–217. The International Louis Leakey Memorial Institute for African Prehistory, Nairobi.

Isaac, G. 1967. The Stratigraphy of the Peninj Group—Early Middle Pleistocene Formations West of Lake Natron, Tanzania. In *Background to Evolution in Africa*, ed. W. W. Bishop and J. D. Clark, pp. 229–257. Chicago University Press, Chicago.

———, assisted by B. Isaac. 1977. *Olorgesailie, Archaeological Studies of a Middle Pleistocene Lake Basin in Kenya*. Chicago: University of Chicago Press.

Isaac, G., and J. W. K. Harris. 1978. Archaeology. In *Koobi Fora Research Project*. Vol. 1: *The Fossil Hominids and Introduction to their Context 1968–74*, ed. M. G. Leakey and R. E. Leakey, pp. 64–85. Clarendon Press, Oxford.

Jones, W. B. 1981. Chemical Effects of Deutric Alteration in Some Kenyan Trachyte Lavas. *Mineralogical Magazine* 44:279–285.

Kibunjia, N. M. 1987. Lewa Downs Palaeolithic Site. *Nyame Akuma* no. 29:31–32.

Leakey, M., with contributions from P. V. Tobias, J. E. Martyn, and R. E. F. Leakey. 1969. An Acheulean Industry with Prepared Core Technique and the Discovery of a Contemporary Hominid Mandible at Lake Baringo, Kenya. *Proceedings of the Prehistoric Society* 35:8–76.

Leakey, M. D. 1971. *Olduvai Gorge*. Vol. 3: *Excavations in Beds I and II 1960–1963*. Cambridge University Press, Cambridge.

——— 1974. Cultural Patterns in the Olduvai Sequence. In *After the Australopithecines*, ed. K. W. Butzer and G. Isaac, pp. 477–493. Mouton, The Hague.

Macdonald, R., R. L. Smith, and J. E. Thomas. 1992. Chemistry of the Subalkalic Silicic Obsidians. *U.S. Geological Survey Professional Paper* 1523, 214 pp.

Mehlman, M. 1977. Excavations at Nasera Rock, Tanzania. *Azania* 12:111–118.

——— 1979. Mumba-Höhle Revisited: The Relevance of a Forgotten Excavation to some Current Issues in East African Prehistory. *World Archaeology* 11(1):80–94.

——— 1987. Provenience, Age and Associations of Archaic *Homo sapiens* Crania from Lake Eyasi, Tanzania. *Journal of Archaeological Science* 14:133–62.

Merrick, H. V. 1975. *Change in Later Pleistocene Lithic Industries in Eastern Africa*. Ph.D. dissertation, University of California, Berkeley.

Merrick, H. V., and F. H. Brown. 1984. Obsidian Sources and Patterns of Source Utilization in Kenya and Northern Tanzania: Some Initial Findings. *The African Archaeological Review* 2:129–152.

Merrick, H. V., F. H. Brown, and M. Connelly. 1990. Sources of the Obsidian at Ngamuriak and Other South-western Kenyan Sites. In *Early Pastoralists of South-western Kenya*, ed. P. Robertshaw, pp. 173–182. British Institute in Eastern Africa, Nairobi.

Michels, J. W., I. S. T. Tsong, and C. M. Nelson. 1983. Obsidian Dating and East African Archaeology. *Science* 219:361–366.

Nash, W. P. 1992. Analysis of Oxygen with the Electron Microprobe: Applications to Hydrous Glass and Minerals. *American Mineralogist* 77:453–457.

Roche, H., J.-P. Brugal, D. Lefevre, S. Ploux, and P.-J. Texier. 1988. Isenya: état des recherches sur un vouveau site acheuléen d'Afrique orientale. *The African Archaeological Review* 6:27–55.

Sarna-Wojcicki, A. M., S. D. Morrison, C. E. Meyer, and J. W. Hillhouse. 1987. Correlation of Upper Cenozoic Tephra Layers between Sediments of the Western United States and Eastern Pacific Ocean and Comparison with Biostratigraphic and Magnetostratigraphic Age Data. *Geological Society of America Bulletin* 98:207–223.

Thompson, A. O., and R. G. Dodson. 1963. *Geology of the Naivasha Area*. Geological Survey of Kenya Report 55.

EARLY COPPER AND BRASS IN SENEGAL

Laurence Garenne-Marot

U.P.R. 311 (CNRS), 1 Place Aristide Briand, 92195 Meudon Cedex, France

Michael L. Wayman

Departments of Mining, Metallurgical and Petroleum Engineering and of Anthropology, University of Alberta, Edmonton, Alberta, Canada T6G 2G6

Vincent C. Pigott

MASCA, University of Pennsylvania Museum, Philadelphia, PA 19104, USA

ABSTRACT Elemental and metallurgical analyses have been carried out on a number of objects from tenth–thirteenth century A.D. sites in Senegal, the aims being to assess the production technologies and the sources of the materials. The focus has been on the analysis of brass bells and end-looped bars from the site of Sintiou Bara, where some production debris was found in association with finished metal artifacts. Metallographic analysis showed that all of the Sintiou Bara artifacts had been cast, then worked to a greater or lesser extent, and then annealed. In some cases, the annealed material had been subjected to localized surface working, abrasion, or wear. The elemental compositions, as determined by PIXE analysis, suggest affinities with brass imported from the north, although the possibility exists that the northern brass was being diluted with copper when remelted for local manufacturing operations. Selected bracelets and anklets from Senegal sites broadly contemporary with Sintiou Bara were found to be markedly different from the Sintiou Bara material, most notably in their low or negligible zinc contents. Re-analysis of a particularly ornate Sintiou Bara bell, for which an unorthodox solder-anneal fabrication technology had been suggested by previous investigators, was unable to confirm the earlier suggestion, and no differences in the production techniques between this bell and the other Sintiou Bara bells were apparent.

Introduction

This paper reports the results of an investigation of copper-based alloy objects from several sites in Senegal which date from the tenth to the thirteenth centuries A.D. The focus of the work is on a number of brass bells and end-looped bars from the site of Sintiou Bara, in the middle Senegal River valley; however, attention is also given to several bracelets and an anklet from broadly contemporary Senegalese sites. One objective of the research on the Sintiou Bara artifacts was an understanding of the production and decoration technologies and how these differed

from the technologies suggested for a previously examined object. The bracelets and anklet, although coming from different sites, are stylistically similar to one another and it was considered of interest to evaluate whether or not their similarities resulted from the use of comparable techniques. It was also hoped that the work would provide information concerning the possible origins of the materials involved, to add to our present understanding of West Africa at the end of the first millennium and in the first centuries of the second millennium A.D. where texts and archaeology provide some interesting comparative data.

The end of the first millennium A.D. saw major changes in West Africa, notably the rise of strong political units and centralized urban centers which created an appropriate setting for the gathering and flow of goods and craft workers (McIntosh and McIntosh 1986, 1988). Systems of exchange were certainly a crucial component of these developments. Important interregional trade within West Africa had significant impact, but what may have provided major impetus was the increase in trade relations with the north. Continuous northern demand for the gold of the "Sudan"[1] was the basis for the continuing and growing interest of the Arabs in this remote part of their known world (see Herbert 1984). As access to the south improved, trade increased in response. Arab texts of the eleventh–twelfth century A.D. mention regular contacts with sub-Saharan Africa; these textual references are supported by the marked presence of imported northern goods, for example at the site of Tegdaoust which has been interpreted as the ancient Sahelian trading city of Audaghust, a major stopping place in the trans-Saharan trade (Devisse and Robert-Chaleix 1982).

Contemporary records do not provide information concerning the quantities of goods that went north or of goods traded in return. The types of goods prized by southern peoples (e.g., the people of the "Sudan") are, however, recorded by Arab writers (see Levtzion and Hopkins 1981) and the archaeological record here again clearly corroborates the Arab texts. Copper is said to have been in great demand in sub-Saharan Africa. Herbert (1984:113–114) writes, with references to the Arab records: "The importance of copper in the trans-Saharan trade runs like a leitmotif through virtually all the written sources."

Situated in Senegal, in the middle Senegal River valley (Fig. 1), Sintiou Bara is one of the more than 300 urban sites that testify to the dynamism of the region in this era at the beginning of the second millennium A.D. It is one of the largest sites of the area, covering 67 ha, i.e., two-thirds of a square km, although less than one percent of the total area of the site has been excavated. The site itself consists of a succession of some hundred contiguous oval to circular areas scattered with sherds as well as both chippings and nodules of laterite. These are the remnants of mounds of anthropic origin which have largely eroded away, leaving behind the concentrations of stone and sherds. The objects described in this report were recovered by the partial excavation of one of the oval areas, which yielded altogether an impressive amount, nearly 8 kg, of worked copper-based objects.

Excavations of this area yielded radiocarbon dates ranging from the fourth to the fourteenth centuries A.D., which would suggest the manufacturing of copper-based objects as early as the mid-first millennium A.D. (Thilmans and Ravisé 1980). However, these dates have been subjected to discussion (McIntosh and McIntosh 1988). The portion of the site excavated by Thilmans and Ravisé is extensively disturbed, and the sequence of radiocarbon dates is not in accord with the stratigraphy. More recent work on other parts of the site, as well as at the middle Senegal River valley site of Tioubalel, "demonstrate[s] quite convincingly based on new C14 dates from both sites, that the advent of copper in the region and the exuberant use of it at Sintiou Bara does not antedate the 10th century, and may well date to the 11th or 12th" (Susan McIntosh, pers. comm., June 1992; published results in Bocoum et al. 1992). The confusion in the dates is explained by the intrusion of carbon from a lower occupational level into the level which yielded the eleventh–twelfth century assemblage. Analysis of the stratigraphy and the relationships among the objects can provide an explanation for the presence of skeletons and groupings of pottery, as well as copper-based artifacts mainly related to horse-trappings of a specially ornamented kind. This has led to a reappraisal of the true origin of this oval area. Rather than grouped living quarters, the former interpretation, this raised surface of 24 m by 27 m is now believed to be a burial mound, an earth tumulus built on an area previously devoted to iron smelting (Garenne-Marot 1993).

The economic or political importance of the deceased buried in this particular tomb is attested by the impressive burial goods. The presence of the ornamented horse-trappings recalls the text of the Arab writer al-Bakri on the importance of harnessed horses at the court of the king of Ghana (Levtzion and Hopkins 1981). Furthermore, nearly 8 kg of worked copper objects in a region devoid of copper resources points to the operation of important trade networks. In consideration of its extensive size and apparent importance, Thilmans and Ravisé (1980) identified the Sintiou Bara site with the capital city of the kingdom of Silla. According again to al-Bakri, in the eleventh century, the king of Silla was ruling a vast and populated kingdom that could almost compete with the kingdom of Ghana (Levtzion and Hopkins 1981). Direct evidence to confirm this identification is awaited.

Sintiou Bara is a site that can potentially yield much information on metalworking technology in this part of West Africa, an area which, for a long time, has been seen as lacking a long tradition of knowledge of metals and metalworking techniques. Clearly it is becoming apparent that this is due primarily to a lack of data, and sites such as Sintiou Bara yielding much new data are permitting revision of this former appraisal (see Grébenart 1988; McIntosh and McIntosh 1988). Excavations at Sintiou Bara have yielded both impressive finished artifacts and some production debris from local manufacturing operations. There is a long tradition of metallurgy, in the working of iron, at Sintiou Bara as evidenced by the

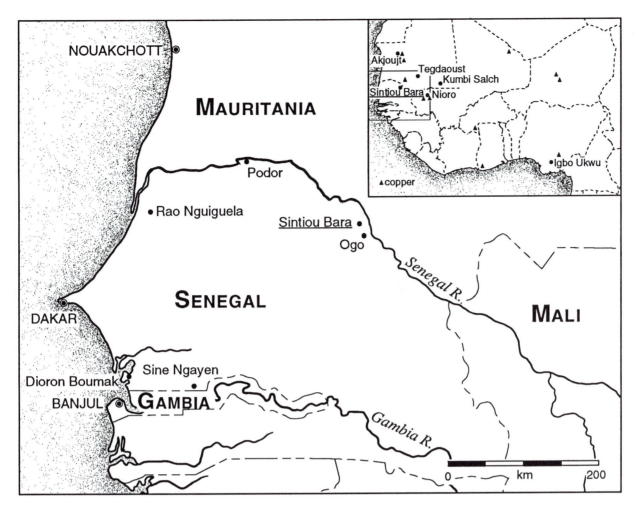

Fig. 1:
Map of the Senegal River area.

occurrence of iron smelting furnaces prior to the building of the tumulus. Among the horse trappings are many pieces fabricated from combinations of brass and iron in intricate association, with the functional components of the objects being iron and the decorative components, brass. The occurrence of such bimetallic artifacts may be related to this long tradition in the working of iron.

Sintiou Bara is impressive not only for the amount of copper metalwork unearthed there but also for the skill in the working of the metal as displayed in the artifacts (Thilmans and Ravisé 1980). Skill is also evident in the use of different alloys, including brasses of high zinc content and silver-zinc-copper alloys, and in the technology of manufacture, including lost wax casting, riveting, repoussé, and the use of multiple techniques in the same artifact (casting and sheet hammering, for example). Even if the excavations have inadvertently been carried out in a special use area that is not representative of the entire site, nevertheless it is clear that quality metalwork is present in quantity at Sintiou Bara.

For purposes of comparison, the study of the Sintiou

Bara material was extended to include analyses of four copper-based alloy artifacts, three bracelets and an anklet, from other sites in Senegal with dates similar to that of Sintiou Bara. These sites are Dioron Boumak, Sine Ngayen, and Rao-Nguiguela.

Dioron Boumak, situated on the Atlantic coast, is one of a number of funerary sites which are distinguished by being located in shell middens that are the result of local exploitation of shells and were subsequently used for funerary purposes. The site of Dioron Boumak, a massive shell midden, contains as many as 125 tumuli, each one of which is formed by an accumulation of tombs containing up to 69 inhumations each. The inhumations were accompanied by an important furniture set of pottery, weapons (in iron), and ornaments (in iron, shell, and copper). Most of the radiocarbon dates give, after calibration, a historical age between the ninth and the twelfth centuries A.D. (Thilmans and Descamps 1982).

Sine Ngayen is certainly the most important megalithic site of the Senegambia area, with up to 51 stone circles. Three stone circles have been excavated, all of

47

Fig. 2a:
Bells, with SB06 at extreme left and SB07 second from right. The metallographic samples from both bells were taken where the openwork wire joins the bell body. (Photo: A. Camara, IFAN, Dakar.)

which proved to be collective tombs. Ritual and funerary pottery vessels, as well as weapons (in iron) and ornaments (in iron and copper), were associated with the inhumations. The copper ornaments are mainly bracelets. A radiocarbon date for Sine Ngayen has given, after calibration, a historical age between the ninth and eleventh centuries A.D. (Thilmans et al. 1980).

Rao-Nguiguela is also a funerary site; it groups eleven sand tumuli which were excavated at the beginning of the century. Sixteen heavy anklets were found in tumulus H, amounting to about 13 kg of metal. In tumulus B, only one bracelet was found but it is of a form and color of metal identical to the larger anklets. A radiocarbon date places the tumulus between the twelfth and thirteenth centuries A.D. (Joire 1955).

Analysis

Eight metal artifacts from Sintiou Bara (six bells and two end-looped bars) were selected for metallographic and compositional analysis. The bells examined are here identified by the designations SB05, SB06, SB07, SB08, SB09b, SB12, while the bars are SB10 and SB11. A selection of the bells is shown in Fig. 2, and the end-looped bars in Fig. 3. The samples from the other three sites are identified as DB01 (anklet) and DB02 (bracelet) from Dioron Boumak, SNG03 (bracelet) from Sine Ngayen and RAO04 (bracelet) from Rao-Nguiguela. Each of these four objects had been made from a rod bent into a ring, with 3 deep parallel grooves running along the entire circumference. Samples were taken from the artifacts and prepared for metallographic examination using conventional sample preparation techniques. The polished

Fig. 2b:
Bell SB09b. The metallographic sample was taken on the decorated part of the rim, including both the ribbon border and the bell body. (Photo: A. Camara, IFAN, Dakar.)

Fig. 3:
End-looped bars. The large bar is SB11. (Photo: A. Camara, IFAN, Dakar.)

samples were examined unetched and etched in an optical microscope and in a scanning electron microscope which was equipped with an energy dispersive x-ray analysis (SEM-EDA) system. Compositional analysis was carried out by the PIXE technique (Fleming et al. 1990). The detection limits for the PIXE technique are typically of the order of 0.001–0.01%, whereas for the microanalysis carried out by SEM-EDA they are in the order of 0.1%.

Compositions

The PIXE analysis showed (Table 1) that all the Sintiou Bara bells and bars are brasses (copper-zinc alloys) with zinc contents in the 6–10% range except for one bell and one bar at 18% Zn. The arsenic and lead contents are noteworthy as well, ranging from 0.2 to 1.2%, and 0.3 to 0.7%, respectively.

The bracelets and the anklet from the other sites differ markedly in composition from the Sintiou Bara material as well as differing among themselves. First, all contain insufficient zinc contents for them to be considered as brasses with only DB01 containing more than 0.2% Zn. The bracelet DB02 stands out from all the other objects analyzed by its low content of impurity elements. The other three objects all contain small amounts of lead but differ markedly in their minor constituents, with DB01 containing 2% Zn and 0.4% As while SNG03 and RAO04 contain very low zinc but appreciable arsenic (2.2% and 1%, respectively). The implications of the compositional results are considered below, but first, attention is directed toward the microstructures of the bells and bars.

Table 1. Results of PIXE analyses of copper-based alloy objects from Sintiou Bara, Dioron Boumak, Sine Ngayen, and Rao-Nguiguela

		Elemental content (%, by weight)										
Analysis and inv. no.		Cu	Zn	As	Pb	Ni	Sb	Ag	Fe	S	Cl	Sn
Sintiou Bara bells												
SB05	SEN 75-41-8	88.8	9.7	0.44	0.57	0.048	≤0.039	0.043	0.17	0.059	0.0097	0.033
SB06	SEN 73-21-8	90.6	7.7	1.03	0.36	0.052	≤0.033	0.050	0.066	0.044	0.0077	≤0.009
SB07	SEN 73-21-9	90.7	7.1	1.19	0.64	0.045	≤0.035	0.042	0.10	0.045	0.0097	0.023
SB08	SEN 73-21-13	91.7	6.7	0.21	0.66	≤0.010	≤0.024	0.070	0.32	0.074	0.0120	0.12
SB09b	SEN 73-21-10	79.8	18.6	0.71	0.48	0.016	0.059	0.054	0.11	0.035	0.0067	0.014
SB12	SEN 73-21-11	91.9	6.1	0.79	0.57	≤0.011	0.085	0.056	0.21	0.065	0.0150	0.089
Sintiou Bara end-looped bars												
SB10	SEN 75-21-17	89.1	9.8	0.43	0.32	≤0.010	≤0.026	0.038	0.11	0.039	≤0.005	≤0.011
SB11	SEN 75-21-18	80.5	18.2	0.25	0.53	≤0.010	0.048	<0.016	0.18	0.035	0.0082	0.015
Dioron Boumak, Sine Ngayen, and Rao-Nguiguela anklet, bracelets												
DB01	SEN 71-16-11	96.5	2.1	0.39	0.40	0.120	0.110	0.072	0.079	0.025	≤0.003	0.067
DB02	SEN 71-16-11	99.4	≤0.060	0.065	0.07	0.029	0.065	0.046	0.045	0.020	0.0087	0.085
SNG03	SEN 75-56-11	96.8	≤0.066	2.2	0.50	≤0.019	0.074	0.130	0.048	0.053	0.0055	≤0.012
RAO04	SEN 41-35-P5	98.8	0.15	0.96	0.21	0.072	0.110	0.100	0.190	0.110	0.0096	0.035

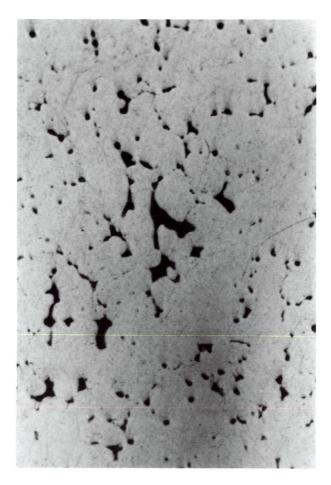

Fig. 4:
SB09b, unetched. Interdendritic pattern of inclusions and porosity. Magnification 60×.

Fig. 5:
SB09b, unetched. Interdendritic pattern of inclusions and porosity at higher magnification than Fig. 4. Magnification 210×.

Microstructures

In the cases of the bells and end-looped bars, metallographic samples were cut through the cross-sections of the artifacts in such a manner as to include both the body of the artifact and a particular aspect of its decoration. This permitted the assessment of the possibility that the decoration had been separately made and subsequently joined to the body in a fabrication operation. Such a process had previously been suggested for a uniquely decorated Sintiou Bara bell (Ravisé and Thilmans 1978); this bell is considered further in the discussion below. Metallographic samples were obtained from the bracelets and the anklet by cutting cross-sections close to the opening in the ring, i.e., close to the ends of the original rods from which these objects had been formed.

Bells. The similarities among the microstructures of the bells were striking. In all cases, the unetched microstructures showed arrays of non-metallic inclusions, in some cases associated with porosity. The distribution of the

inclusions and porosity displayed, sometimes very clearly (Figs. 4 and 5), the pattern created when the solidification of a casting occurs by the formation and growth of dendrites, with the inclusions and porosity being trapped between the arms of growing dendrites as the solidification proceeds. The inclusions were of two types. Very dark spheroidal particles were identified by SEM-EDA as being lead particles. Lead has a very low solubility in copper alloys and its occurrence as interdendritic spheroids after solidification is normal. The other type of inclusion appeared in the optical microscope as blue-gray particles, some of which were spheroidal while others were seen to be elongated. In some cases these inclusions appeared to be located on the boundaries of a network. SEM-EDA revealed that all of these blue-gray inclusions, regardless of their shape, contain sulfur, zinc, and possibly copper. EDA analysis using an ultra-thin window technique showed clearly that oxygen is not present in these inclusions, and they are therefore identified as sulfides, either zinc sulfides or zinc-copper sulfides.[2]

Fig. 6:
SB09b, ferric chloride etch. Dendritic solidification structure. Magnification 60×.

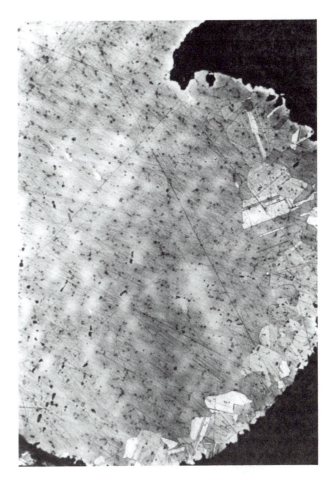

Fig. 7:
SB08, ferric chloride etch. Cast microstructure exhibiting diffuse coring, with recrystallized grains at periphery. Magnification 60×.

After etching, the cast nature of all the bells, which had been strongly suggested by the inclusion distribution, was clearly confirmed. The microstructures of some of the bells (SB06 and especially SB09b) showed strongly "cored" dendrites (Fig. 6), whose dark-light shading results from compositional differences between the solute-poor cores of the dendrites, the first solid alloy to form during solidification, and the solute-rich regions, which were the last to solidify. The sulfide inclusions, lead spheroids, and, when present, porosity were all located interdendritically, as expected. In other bells this coring was much more diffuse (Fig. 7), in the extreme being barely visible (SB12 and especially SB07). In all of the bells, most of the grains could be seen to be highly irregular in shape, consistent with the dendritic nature of the original solidification, and the boundaries between these grains were distinctly jagged (Fig. 6). Numerous sulfide and lead inclusions were located in the grain boundaries as well as inside the grains between the original dendrite arms. Intergranular and interdendritic shrinkage porosity was clearly observed in

some cases. The inclusions on the grain boundaries had shapes consistent with the equilibrium between the relative surface energies of the grain boundary and the inclusion-matrix interface.

No microstructural features were noted which gave any suggestion that the bells, at least at the sections examined, had been fabricated or decorated by the joining of several pieces of metal; rather they appeared to be one-piece integral castings such as would have been produced by the lost wax method.

Detailed examination of the etched microstructures revealed other features related to the thermal and mechanical histories of the bells. Although most of the microstructures consisted of cast grains with irregular boundaries, regions of smaller equiaxed grains were present to a greater or lesser extent in all six bells, as illustrated in Fig. 7. These equiaxed grains invariably exhibited annealing twins, showing that they were the result of recrystallization, which occurs when a mechanically worked structure is heated. The fact that the recrystallized grains are localized at specific regions of the surface shows that this mechanical working was carried out only at these particular locations, rather than throughout the entire bell or all over its entire surface. If the bell had been worked extensively, with deformation having occurred throughout the bulk of the material, then the entire cross-section would have recrystallized.

These microstructures are interpreted as meaning that at some point after casting the bells had been subjected to mechanical deformation, followed by (or perhaps accompanied by) annealing above a critical recrystallization temperature, which for these brasses would be in the range of 350–400°C (ASM 1990:296–300). In other words the castings could either have been hot worked or alternatively have been subjected to cycles of cold working followed by annealing. It is also conceivable that the working was carried out at a moderate temperature with the work-piece cycling above and below the recrystallization temperature as it was heated to soften it and then cooled during working, although the difficulty of performing delicate working operations on a hot small object must be acknowledged. Unfortunately, it is not possible by metallographic means to distinguish among these alternative thermo-mechanical treatments, all of which could lead to the observed microstructures.

In addition, it was noted that in some of the locally recrystallized regions, deformation bands and grain distortions are superimposed on the recrystallized grain structure, showing that some local deformation, either by deliberate working or by in-service use wear, had been carried out after the recrystallizing anneal. Specifically, three of the bells (SB05, SB06, SB07) show no evidence of post-anneal deformation, while bells SB08 and SB12 exhibit deformation markings localized close to the outer surface of the bell. Bell SB09b exhibits deeper deformation markings, most noticeably in a depression in the outer surface that corresponds to an incised feature of the decoration. The shallow depths of the deformation markings in bells SB08 and SB12 suggest that they are the result of abrasion (or use wear) whereas in SB09b the deeper markings are consistent with their having been formed when the decorative markings were incised. It may be significant that this evidence of post-anneal deformation was only observed in previously recrystallized regions, suggesting that the final working was in fact a continuation of the previous working, which had created the need for annealing and recrystallization.

Thus it can be suggested that the following technology was involved in the manufacture of these bells:
1. The bells were cast into molds (possibly made by the lost wax process) and allowed to solidify and cool.
2. After removal of the bells from the molds, some mechanical working was performed to accomplish shape changes, for example by forging or chasing. This

presumably was done to compensate for defects in the cast shape or in the surface condition, and/or to deliberately alter the shape from that produced by the mold geometry, by applying decoration, for example. This working would have work-hardened the bell locally.
3. The bells were then annealed, which recrystallized the worked regions and removed the work-hardening. The time and/or temperature of the annealing varied considerably from bell to bell. For example, bell SB06 was annealed under low temperature/short time conditions (e.g., 1 hour at about 400°C), a treatment which was sufficient to recrystallize the worked areas but not sufficient to homogenize the coring which remained from the casting (the homogenizing of bell SB09b, which has a much higher zinc content, would have required more severe annealing than the other bells). Bell SB07, on the other hand, was annealed under much higher temperature and/or longer time conditions (e.g., 800°C), which not only caused local recrystallization but also accomplished a near-complete homogenization of the solute concentrations. During the anneal any lead inclusions that had become elongated during the deformation would spheroidize, and those inclusions lying on boundaries would adjust their shapes toward equilibrium angles at phase junctions. Spheroidization of the elongated sulfides would require much higher annealing temperatures and longer times than would be the case for the lead inclusions.
3a. The possibility cannot be excluded that the working described above was performed at high or moderate temperatures in which case the deformation and the annealing would not have been distinct technological steps.
4. Some, but not all, of the bells have undergone some plastic deformation since this recrystallization. In one case, that of the bell SB09b, this final working appears to be associated with the forming of decorative features on the bell surface. In other cases this is more likely to have been caused by processes which deform only the near-surface regions of the metal, processes such as abrasion or possibly in-service use wear.

The production sequence postulated above explains the microstructural features, including the grain size and shape as well as the inclusion morphology and distribution. It might be considered surprising that a recrystallizing anneal was carried out. With a properly designed and prepared mold, it should be possible to cast an object to a shape very close to that desired so that little subsequent working would be required. It could therefore be suggested that the need to perform much working after casting reflects a lack of metalworking skills in casting procedures. But alternatively this may be a reflection of the Sintiou Bara technological inheritance, a long familiarity with hammering processes which, along with the existence of iron tools suitable for the reworking of the surfaces of copper or brass objects, could offer an alternative method to the casting practices. In the present case it appears that sufficient working was performed that a recrystallizing anneal was required to soften the worked areas so that further working or engraving could be carried out.

In interpreting these microstructures it is important to remember that only a small sample of each artifact was studied, and that the microstructure observed reflects only the working which was carried out locally, while on the other hand it reflects the heat treatment which was carried out on the entire object. It must also be noted that the amount of deformation which was carried out prior to the anneal was not sufficient (at the sections examined) for the subsequent annealing to have caused complete recrystallization through the entire thickness of the objects.

End-looped bars. Each of these artifacts consists of a brass bar terminating at each end in a loop to which iron chains were attached (remains of an iron link were present in some of the loops). One of the bars (SB11) can be clearly seen (Fig. 3) to be an assembly consisting of two brass components joined by an internal central, massive, square-sectioned iron piece. Heavy in-service use wear in bar SB10 has resulted in extreme thinning down of the external parts of the loops. These bars, which are certainly elements of horse harness as shown by the contextual set of artifacts, are too small to be interpreted as horse bridle bits or cheek pieces; they must have been elements of a bridle system which is not yet fully understood.

As with the bells, samples were cut from decorated parts of the bars, including both decoration and the underlying body. The microstructures of the bars were found in most respects to be similar to those of the bells, with lead spheroids as well as spheroidal and elongated zinc sulfide or zinc-copper sulfide inclusions present. The overall distribution of the inclusions in the unetched samples again suggested dendritic solidification; this was confirmed by etching, which showed that both samples have for the most part a cast grain structure, with irregular grain shapes as in the bells. Both bars had been mechanically worked, fairly heavily in the case of bar SB10, and subjected to a recrystallizing anneal. The annealing temperature/time conditions were relatively severe, as shown by the fact that only very diffuse coring was present in both bars. Again the amount of working was insufficient to cause full recrystallization of the entire bulk of the sections sampled. Following the recrystallization, these sections, that is, the decorated areas of both bars, had been subjected to further mechanical work, probably during the application of the decoration.

While the microstructures of the bars were in most respects similar to those of the bells, the morphologies of their sulfide inclusions were different. Here the sulfides are found within three-dimensional volumes, so that they appear to be arranged in clusters (Fig. 8) which are distributed on an interdendritic network (Fig. 9). In many cases one edge of the cluster is a grain boundary. This is consistent with the formation of sulfides in the last regions to solidify, between the dendrite arms and between the dendrites. In bar SB11 some of the sulfides formed in the three-dimensional regions are markedly elongated, both within grains and on grain boundaries and some occur in clusters of multiple orientation where they display a star-like appearance.

This particular sulfide morphology is a manifestation of the presence of a larger volume of interdendritic material than is the case for the bells. However, it is not clear why this should be so. The sulfur contents of the bars are not higher than those of the bells. Furthermore the inclusions in both bells and bars do not contain oxygen or any other element detectable by ultra-thin window SEM-EDA that would distinguish their sulfide compositions. Although the inclusion distribution would be affected by the solidification conditions, the spacing of the secondary dendrite arms is comparable to that of the bells, suggesting similar

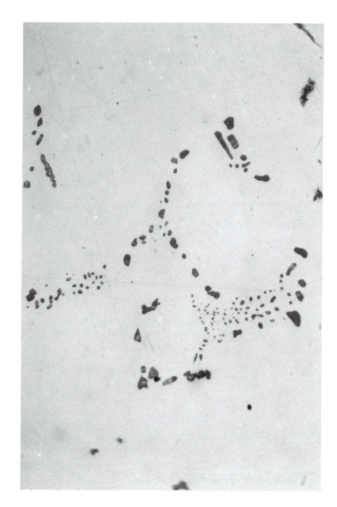

Fig. 8:
SB10, unetched. Inclusion clusters. Magnification 500×.

53

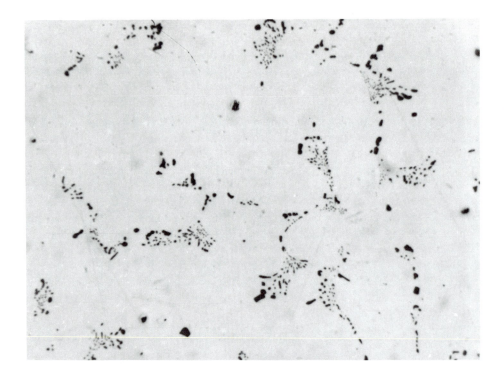

Fig. 9:
SB10, unetched. Interden-
dritic pattern of inclusion clusters at lower magnification.
Magnification 200×.

Fig. 10:
RAO04, ferric chloride etch. Recrystallized microstructure.
Magnification 60×.

solidification rates. It may be worth noting that SB11, at least, is bimetallic, having been assembled from brass and iron component parts; this assembly process may have involved specific conditions of thermal processing that could conceivably have affected the sulfide morphology.

Anklet and bracelets. Examination showed that the microstructures of the anklet and bracelets are markedly different from those of the Sintiou Bara bells and end-looped bars described above, and furthermore that the four artifacts differ significantly among themselves. Bracelet DB02 is the most different in that it is much the cleanest of all the pieces analyzed in terms of nonmetallic inclusions and has clearly been forged to shape, rather than directly cast. It contains numerous forging laminations and a microstructure that has fully recrystallized throughout its bulk, with a small amount of final deformation. The other three artifacts are castings which have subsequently been either cold worked and then annealed, or alternatively hot or warm worked as discussed above for the bells and bars. However, in these cases, unlike the bells and bars, the combination of working and annealing has been sufficient to fully recrystallize the materials throughout their volumes (Fig. 10). The basically cast nature of the three objects is revealed by their inclusion distributions, which display a distorted interdendritic nature. Correspondingly, the microstructures of anklet DB01 and bracelet SNG03, although fully recrystallized, show remnant coring patterns which are also distorted by deformation. These observations indicate that the three objects were more heavily worked prior to annealing than were the bells or the end-looped bars (although the amount of deformation necessary to cause full recrystallization would be less in these artifacts because of their much lower zinc contents). The recrystallized grain sizes are consistently smaller near the outer edges of these artifacts, reflecting higher deformation levels there.

In all four of these anklet/bracelets additional working has been carried out after the recrystallization, with DB01 being the most heavily worked after recrystallization and DB02 the least.

The inclusions present in these microstructures also differ markedly. Anklet DB01 contains lead inclusions as well as two-phase sulfides, one phase being copper sulfide and the other zinc (or zinc-copper) sulfide. Bracelet DB02 has very few inclusions; they are small lead particles, copper sulfides, and what appear to be iron oxides. Bracelet SNG03 contains two types of inclusion which are present both as individual particles and also in association as two-phase inclusions. One of these inclusion phases is copper sulfide, the other a lead compound, probably lead oxide or carbonate. RAO04 contains lead spheroids and large copper-iron sulfides.

Discussion

Consideration of the levels of zinc as well as of the minor and trace elements present in brass can in some cases have potential for addressing questions of material origin and processing technology; however, several factors can seriously complicate the interpretation. The brass would originally have been produced by the cementation of metallic copper with zinc oxide or carbonate, and the brass product would thus reflect the composition of both the copper and the zinc ore.[3] Remelting of brass stock prior to casting can result in a loss of some elements, including zinc, from the liquid brass, the effect multiplying with the number of times the brass is remelted. It is also possible that imported brass could have been mixed with copper, either local or imported, diluting the zinc content and causing the overall elemental composition to reflect the compositions both of the diluent copper and of the imported brass. Furthermore, the possibility of some scrap remelting and mixing cannot be discounted, nor can the possibility of the pick-up of impurities from crucibles, slags, or fluxes during melting. The complexity of interpreting elemental compositions to obtain information about the origin of the brass or its production technology becomes obvious, nevertheless some discussion can be worthwhile.

The elemental compositions of the Sintiou Bara brasses are not unusual for European or Islamic brass artifacts of the period (Craddock 1985; Craddock et al. 1990). The zinc contents fall within the range expected, bearing in mind the above factors. The arsenic contents of the brasses are high, but they are not high enough to be indicative of deliberate addition, although the observed levels of both arsenic and lead would be beneficial to the casting properties. It is worthy of note that the thousands of rod-shaped brass ingots that were found at Ma'den Ijâfen in the Mauritanian desert where a caravan came to grief about A.D. 1200 (Monod 1969) contain comparable levels of arsenic and lead (Table 2). In medieval Islamic and European cultures, silver would almost certainly have been removed for economic reasons, unlike the situation at Igbo Ukwu (Nigeria), where high levels of silver in the copper have been used to lend credence to the idea of an indigenous industry (Craddock 1985:36; Chikwendu et al. 1989). Sintiou Bara material has much lower silver contents, ranging from 0.02% to 0.07%. These are too low to be suggestive of a local product or one from elsewhere in West Africa. The iron contents, ranging from 0.07 to 0.32%, although slightly higher than most of the values reported from the Ma'den Ijâfen brass (Table 2), fall in line with medieval Islamic brasses (Craddock et al. 1990), suggestive of sphaleritic zinc ores. The tin contents of the Sintiou Bara material are noticeably low in comparison with most medieval brasses, although once again they are not inconsistent with the Ma'den Ijâfen brass.

Table 2. Elemental analysis of brass ingots from Ma'den Ijâfen*

| | Elemental content (%, by weight) | | | | | | | | | |
	Zn	As	Pb	Fe	Sn	Sb	Ag	Ni	Bi	Au
Bar 10	21.0	1.12	0.47	0.04	n.d.†	0.058	ca. 0.10	0.12	0.008	n.d.
Bar 10 projection	20.8	1.20	0.50	0.04	n.d.	0.060	ca. 0.10	0.13	0.008	n.d.
Bar 18	20.0	1.12	0.30	0.05	n.d.	0.075	ca. 0.10	0.13	0.007	n.d.
Bar 17	19.23**	0.87	0.61	0.17	tr.†	0.080	ca. 0.05	0.20	tr.	n.d.

* Analyses of Bar 10 and Bar 18 from Werner and Willett (1975:151, table 7); analysis of Bar 17 by Smith from Monod (1969:304)

† n.d. = not detected; tr. = trace

** In Bar 17, Cu analysis gave 78.84% and the Zn content was obtained by difference. Traces of Mn, Mg, Cd, and Co were also detected in Bar 17

In summary, the Sintiou Bara brass is similar in its elemental makeup to the Ma'den Ijâfen brass, except for its zinc content which is in many cases considerably lower. Furthermore, it is also comparable in the character of its sulfide inclusions (Castro 1974; Wayman, unpubl. research, 1992) with the Ma'den Ijâfen brass ingots. There is no evidence to suggest that zinc ore or zinc metal, one or the other of which would be necessary for local brass production, was being mined or produced locally. Thus all indications are that the brass in the Sintiou Bara artifacts is material which was imported into West Africa, and possibly diluted later by the addition of copper.

In order to understand what is going on at Sintiou Bara in terms of metal imports, it is first necessary to place the site in its context, that is, westernmost sub-Saharan Africa at the end of the first millennium A.D. A major site in this part of western Africa at this time is Tegdaoust, first because of its importance in the trans-Saharan trade, and secondly because it is one of the rare sites from which we have the elemental analyses of metallic artifacts from well-dated contexts. As mentioned above, Tegdaoust (Audaghust) was an important stopping place on the great caravan route across the Sahara. It was also in the center of the Empire of Ghana at its maximum expansion. Copper objects were present early at the site, and copper working was an important aspect of the place in the mid tenth–eleventh centuries A.D. as shown by workshops with the presence of molds and ingots (Vanacker 1979, 1983).

Whereas the analysis of the copper-based artifacts from Sintiou Bara has revealed a metal which has close affinities with the brass ingots of Ma'den Ijâfen, the metal composition (Vanacker 1983:99) of the ingots discovered at Tegdaoust is quite different. High (percentage level) iron contents are present in the Tegdaoust material, a marked difference and an important factor. Another difference is seen in the lead contents, which vary in most of the Tegdaoust brasses between 1.5% and 2.5%, with one at 20%. Ingots were being cast at Tegdaoust and some alloying may have been involved in this process. The presence of high iron levels in both the copper and the brass ingots (Vanacker 1983:99) has raised the possibility of a common origin for both metals.

Copper deposits are relatively abundant in Mauritania where there are frequent traces of ancient mining and smelting of copper ore. Thus, for example, copper may have come from the copper mines around Akjoujt (western Mauritania), although present thoughts are that around the end of the first millennium A.D. mining activities may have been suspended at that place for a time (see Grébenart 1988:130–136). Closer copper deposits are known in the area of Tajalt Oumou Kadiar to the east of the Tagant (Vanacker 1983:102); more precise data on their exploitation are, however, still awaited. Other ancient copper deposits in the southern Mauritania–northern Mali region

(Nioro-Sirakoro deposits) are also potential sources. These last deposits may be identified with the mines of copper described by al-'Umari in the early part of the fourteenth century: the time period of the Empire of Mali (see Herbert 1984:17). This implies that copper deposits were worked at the time of the full expansion of the trans-Saharan trade (if not earlier)—the time of massive imports of copper-based material from North Africa—confirming the diversity of the potential sources of metal at the time of the trans-Saharan trade.

If one considers the amount of income which the taxes on copper transactions may have represented for the king of Ghana—more than double those on salt (Vanacker 1983; Robert-Chaleix 1989:246)—it becomes apparent that it may have been lucrative to manufacture secondary brass products by mixing northern imported brass with local copper. Such tax considerations would augment the normal incentive to minimize the consumption of a valuable imported material. In terms of metal quality, this procedure is not likely to have been detrimental to the basic properties or value of the final brass product. Concerning the presence of lead in the final product one may also wonder whether lead was not deliberately added to the melt to improve its fluidity or to further lower the cost; lead was found on the site of Tegdaoust in the shape of small threads with thickened ends. These when analyzed have proven to be highly leaded copper, containing around 25% lead (Bourhis 1983:134). This may be related to the presence of 20% lead in one of the Tegdaoust brass ingots.

To explain the disparities between the metals of Sintiou Bara and Tegdaoust, one may call upon the Arab texts. Al-Bakri in the mid-eleventh century A.D. writes about Silla (which has been, as mentioned above, identified with the site of Sintiou Bara) as competing with Ghana in the trade of gold (Levtzion and Hopkins 1981). In the itineraries of the merchants in the "lands of the blacks," as described by al-Bakri, Tegdaoust (Audaghust) does not seem to be related to the Senegal localities, which are described in a separate itinerary. Al-Idrissi, a century later, refers to a trans-Saharan route which directly links Sidjilmasa in the north with the towns of Takrur and Silla on the Senegal River (see Devisse 1990:436). Although fewer in comparison with Tegdaoust, some foreign objects (enameled pottery, glass beads, and cowries) have been found at Sintiou Bara. Some form of exchange was certainly occurring between the areas of Hodh (around Tegdaoust) and the Senegal River, as shown by the occurrence of bracelets and bells with close affinities (Thilmans and Ravisé 1980). But the role of Tegdaoust as a redistributing center of northern imported goods (and metal) may have been restricted to the Empire of Ghana. In this context, it is of interest that the high leaded copper threads with thickened ends were not only found at the site of Tegdaoust but also at the site of Kumbi Saleh (identified with the capital city of the Empire of Ghana). There they are present in all of the habitation units excavated (Berthier 1983) and the fact that they were found mainly in groups and sometimes tied in bundles suggests a possible monetary use. These threads were not found associated with the metallic material of Sintiou Bara, a possible indication of their restricted use within the kingdom of Ghana and further evidence supporting a distinction between the metallurgy of Tegdaoust and that of Sintiou Bara.

At Sintiou Bara, pure copper, found in the form of a small ingot, was used as well as brass. Also found was a ternary alloy of copper-zinc-silver (possibly from the alloying of silver with brass) which if not manufactured on the site was certainly further manipulated there, since a small ingot and droplets of this alloy were found. Thus there is evidence of local secondary copper working and even though copper and its alloys were undoubtedly traded to the south not only in the form of ingots such as the Ma'den Ijâfen brass but also as finished items (Herbert 1984), there is similarly no doubt that metal artifacts were produced locally.

At Sintiou Bara the possibility of modification of the imported brass must be considered. Of the eight brass artifacts analyzed here, two have zinc contents comparable with the Ma'den Ijâfen material, while the other six are consistent with dilution by a factor of two to three. The low levels of zinc in the latter artifacts could be explained either by a deliberate modification of the composition of the metal or by accidental occurrences such as the loss of zinc that can occur during remelting. Conservation of a valuable import would certainly provide a motivation for dilution of the imported brass, but one should not exclude a possible concern for the appearance of the final material; the golden color of brass is deeper and redder around 10% zinc than around 18% where it is more yellow. Either dilution with copper or controlled loss of zinc in remelting processes could be alternative ways to deliberately lower the zinc content. Unlike the situation at Tegdaoust, where high levels of iron are significant, there are no clues to what was going on at Sintiou Bara. We can only discuss the possible scenarios and note that if dilution has occurred at Sintiou Bara, as has been proposed for Tegdaoust, the diluent copper must have been different from the copper used at Tegdaoust, for the iron contents of the northern brass and the Sintiou Bara brass are comparable and lower than the material from Tegdaoust. At this stage of the research, however, we can only underline this major difference between the metals industries of Sintiou Bara and Tegdaoust and also note their chronological difference (some decades) in addition to, as noted above, their different political and economic settings.

The elemental compositions of the Sintiou Bara bells and bars are consistent among themselves and are thus suggestive of a general trend in the brass composition of the funerary material.[4] For this reason, the presence of the ternary copper-zinc-tin alloy, in the form of the fully decorated previously published bell, is all the more surprising. Such a composition is not seen in the Tegdaoust material, and the only known copper-based artifacts from Senegal that contain intentionally added tin are two kettles found in a tumulus, of more recent date and of evident Moroccan style. Until recently, contemporaneous bronzes in other parts of West Africa had only been reported from Igbo Ukwu, in Nigeria (Craddock and Picton 1986). New analyses, however, are providing growing evidence of a tradition of bronze metallurgy in West Africa, not only in Nigeria but also in Niger (Bourhis 1983:131–132) and perhaps in Mali at Jenne-Jeno (McIntosh and McIntosh 1988:121). Even if the chronological and geographical relations between the two metallurgical traditions are not yet ascertained this tends to show that there was in West Africa at the end of the first millennium a diversity of metallic materials and more than a single source of supply. Thus brass from the north, best illustrated by the massive volume of the Ma'den Ijâfen ingots, can no longer be considered as the only source of the copper-based alloy material used south of the Sahara.

The anklet and bracelets from Dioron Boumak, Sine Ngayen, and Rao-Nguiguela are markedly different from the Sintiou Bara material in both composition and microstructure. Furthermore the four artifacts differ significantly among themselves. None of the four bracelets/anklet can be considered to be a brass, as their zinc contents are well below 1% except for the case of the anklet DB01, which contains only 2% zinc. The bracelet DB02 is a copper of quite high purity, while the other three artifacts contain 1–4% total of zinc, arsenic, and lead. The markedly pure copper of DB02 is of particular interest. For example, its iron content is very low in comparison with other artifacts analyzed here but it contains significantly less lead and silver than the Igbo Ukwu coppers that are believed to have been locally smelted. Although there is no conclusive evidence, it is not inconceivable that this bracelet is made from remelted native (naturally occurring) copper, traces of which have been found at Akjoujt (Herbert 1984:17). Native copper is generally of higher purity than smelted copper. The trace element contents of the other three artifacts are not dramatically different from those of the Sintiou Bara material, however their zinc contents set them clearly apart.

The microstructures of these artifacts are also different from those of the Sintiou Bara brasses. In particular, the non-metallic inclusions are different in each of the four objects and all differ from the inclusions in the Sintiou Bara material. Bracelet DB02, the markedly high purity copper, is much cleaner than the others in terms of nonmetallic inclusions and has clearly been forged to shape, rather than directly cast. The other three artifacts are castings which have subsequently been shaped either by hot or warm working or by cold working and annealing, like the Sintiou Bara material but with a greater amount of working so that they are fully recrystallized throughout their volumes. Some post-anneal working was carried out on the objects. The bracelet DB02, being a relatively pure, easily workable copper, has had any microstructural evidence for an original ingot structure removed by the subsequent mechanical and thermal treatment. The other three artifacts retain some of the ingot structure despite being fully recrystallized throughout.

There is little in the results of the elemental analysis (Table 1) which could shed light on the source or sources of the copper in these four objects. It should be noted, however, that the two bracelets from Sine Ngayen and Rao-Nguiguela have higher arsenic and silver and very low zinc contents and thus conceivably may be West African smelted products. In the future, lead isotope studies will have great potential for addressing such questions of origin; however, a complete data base of lead isotope data on sources must first become available.

There remains a lack of comparative metallographic analysis of techniques used on contemporary metal artifacts from West Africa, with the notable exception of the major work on the Nigerian "bronzes" (Igbo Ukwu, Ife, and Benin) which give a good picture of metalworking traditions and their developments (Craddock 1985; Craddock and Picton 1986). One interesting characteristic of the Igbo Ukwu material is that its technology is largely confined to lost wax casting; it has been suggested that some of the extremely intricate casting may have been forced on the Igbo smiths through lack of an alternative method. No true soldering is seen on the Igbo Ukwu artifacts; rather, in the case of large pieces, parts were joined together by casting-on or "burning in" more bronze into the space between them.[5] Craddock and Picton (1986:3) note that "much of the integral cast detail decoration on the Igbo bronzes that is part of the original casting would elsewhere have been cast separately and riveted on or soldered in place." In contrast, at Sintiou Bara riveting is commonly used as a side element of an industry that may be of a different metallurgical tradition. Sheet working is used in parallel with casting, and bi-metallic artifacts are numerous. It is also possible that soldering may not have been unknown at Sintiou Bara. For example a copper-zinc-silver (silver brass) pendant appears to have been soldered to its suspension tube. Furthermore, of the metal droplets which have been found at the site, one has a composition consistent with tin and lead added to the copper-zinc-silver alloy.

The subject of soldering of objects at Sintiou Bara is of particular interest because one of the stimuli for the present work has been the results of a previous analysis of a single small copper-based alloy bell from Sintiou Bara which was submitted for study by G. Thilmans and A. Ravisé. Spectrographic analysis of this bell showed a relatively high amount of tin (11.4%) (Bourhis 1983:139, table 5, no. 3485), a metal which, at the time of the discovery of the bell, was believed never to have been intentionally used as an alloying element at this time period in this part of West Africa (Thilmans and Ravisé 1980:89). The bell exhibits a decoration covering the entire body, a peculiarity which distinguishes it from the bulk of the other Sintiou Bara bells whose decoration is restricted to the rim and a band at the top of the body. Furthermore, the results of metallographic examination of this bell were interpreted (Ravisé and Thilmans 1978) as indicating the use of a special technique in the realization of the decoration: according to this interpretation, elements of decoration were soldered onto the body of the bell using a tin or tin-based solder and this tin was then apparently diffused throughout the object by reheating the entire piece. The excavators concluded that fragments of clay molds recovered on the site may have been related to this practice; it was suggested that in the reheating stage the bell may have been encased in clay. This is thus far—apart from one other questionable case discussed in the Appendix—the unique recorded example of the application of such a technique in West Africa. The results of the analysis of this bell, if confirmed, would provide another illustration of the wide range of techniques used for the manufacture of copper artifacts along the Senegal River, and would give additional proof of the presence in these areas of sophisticated skills usually ascribed to more "advanced" northern neighbors. The use of this decidedly unorthodox technique, however, required corroboration by further research since the bell is unique in terms of patterns of decoration even among similar artifacts and could well have been imported.

The question of the local manufacture of this artifact is not yet resolved. In terms of manufacturing techniques, all the other Sintiou Bara artifacts considered in this study are consistent among themselves; no evidence was obtained which would indicate that the decoration was applied by any unorthodox technique such as the solder-annealing process suggested for the bell. It is difficult to see proof of any soldering techniques in the small fragments of ceramic molds recovered at the site, which were interpreted by the excavators as related to the annealing process. These molds have shown no traces of metal when submitted to elemental analysis (pers. comm., J. R. Bourhis, who noted, however, that residues of metal may not be found if the mold is coated with soot). Furthermore, these fragments present a criss-cross pattern of imprints of intertwined ropes both on the inside and the outside, difficult to ascribe to any metal decoration. Nevertheless, even if the motif and the pattern of decoration of the body of the bell are unique among artifacts from the site, some details do link this particular bell to the bulk of the Sintiou Bara bells. Most interesting in this regard is the presence on the handle of a decoration pattern (a braided motif with a bead on the topmost part) identical to handle patterns on most of the other bells. Less decisive is the fact that the bell clapper is of iron as in all of the other bells and is suspended with the same attachment technique. Finally the metal, with the exception of its tin content, has a composition in line with that of the other artifacts from Sintiou Bara.

In addition to the problem of the origin of the artifact—local or imported—there remain questions about the peculiar solder-annealing technique. The results of a re-examination of the metallographic sample originally taken from this bell, presented in the Appendix, are inconclusive. On balance, bearing in mind the unusual nature of such a process and the lack of supporting evidence in this study, any further consideration should await additional reports of the use of this technique.

Conclusions

Bearing in mind the limitations caused by the analysis of small areas of larger objects, the following conclusions can be drawn from this study.

1. The Sintiou Bara brasses, bells and end-looped bars, are of similar composition, as determined by PIXE analysis, and similar microstructure as determined by optical and electron metallography. The only difference relates to the sulfide inclusion pattern, which differs between the bells and the bars.

2. It was possible to reconstruct the technology used in the production of these artifacts, bearing in mind the limitations mentioned above. All were cast, then worked to a greater or lesser extent (at the sections studied), showing that the casting process had not produced the precise shapes, and/or conceivably the properties, desired. The worked objects were then annealed at a temperature which is estimated to be in the 350–800°C range, which recrystallized the worked areas. Finally, in some cases, a further working was carried out; this ranged from a very minor retouching or polishing by abrasion, to more extensive deformation by forging or engraving.

3. Differences noticed among the microstructures can be related to differences in the amounts of mechanical working prior to the anneal, the annealing time/temperature conditions, and the amount of post-anneal working among the artifacts examined. In all cases only the surface seemed to have been worked, with no deformed or recrystallized structure seen deep in the samples.

4. The Sintiou Bara brasses are similar in their elemental makeup and in the character of their sulphide inclusions to the brass which was at that time being imported from the north, as typified by that found at Ma'den Ijâfen. The observed range of zinc contents could be the result of the northern brass being diluted with copper (possibly of West African origin but more likely imported) in a remelting operation prior to manufacture of the artifacts for reasons of conservation or to achieve a desired color. Alternatively, zinc loss during the remelting operation, either inadvertently or intentionally in order to control the color, might be responsible for the range of zinc contents.

5. Differences are apparent between the metallurgical industries of Sintiou Bara and Tegdaoust. These differences are probably related to the political and economic environments of the two trading cities and the rise during the eleventh century of direct trading relations between the Senegal River cities and the north.

6. No evidence was found which would corroborate the previously suggested solder-diffusion technique for applying decoration to metalwork. No structure of tin-soldered decoration was found on any of the artifacts of this study, which were monolithic castings in the sections examined.

7. The three bracelets and the anklet from other Senegal sites contemporary with Sintiou Bara are markedly different copper-based materials, with much lower contents of zinc. In all cases their fabrication involved more extensive forging than the Sintiou Bara brasses.

8. Our picture of the African past has considerably changed over recent years; no longer is sub-Saharan Africa seen as a desert of resources and techniques prior to initial contacts with more advanced areas. At the time of the trans-Saharan trade period, the texts mention the importation of copper from the north. However, local West African responses to these northern imports, in regard to local metallurgical traditions, are not yet fully understood. This present work adds to the corpus of knowledge on copper metal working techniques in Senegal, and broadly, in West Africa, at the end of the first millennium and the early second millennium A.D.

Acknowledgments

We wish to thank Dr. Guy Thilmans and Ms. Annie Ravisé for permitting the study and analysis of the artifacts from Sintiou Bara. Preliminary sample preparation was done in Dakar, Senegal, at the Ecole Nationale Superieure Universitaire de Technologie (E.N.S.U.T.), with the kind assistance of Mr. Marc Dubreuil, Chef de l'Atelier Mécanique, E.N.S.U.T. Further work was done at MASCA with major help from Katherine Moreau, and at the University of Alberta with the assistance of Christina Barker and Robert Konzuk. We are also grateful to Dr. Stuart Fleming, Scientific Director of MASCA, and Dr. Charles Swann of the Bartol Research Institute of the University of Delaware, who carried out the PIXE analyses. Finally, we wish to include in our thanks Mr. Jean-Roger Bourhis, Université de Rennes, who provided much useful information and Dr.

P. T. Craddock, British Museum Research Laboratory, for his helpful comments. Many thanks also to Dr. Susan McIntosh for her advice and communication with regard to research in progress at Sintiou Bara and to M. Claude Forrières, Directeur du Laboratoire d'archeologie des métaux, Jarville (Nancy), for his very kind assistance in providing all information possible about former research at the Laboratory at Jarville.

Notes

1. "Sudan" is used here in the medieval sense of the expression. Major gold fields lie in the upper Niger and Senegal River areas, deep in the forest.

2. Because they are small relative to the smallest volume of material which can be analyzed at a single "spot" using the SEM-EDA system, the brass matrix makes an indeterminate contribution to the analyzed copper and zinc contents of the inclusion. Larger sulfide inclusions could be seen to have higher Zn/Cu ratios as a result of this effect. It is not possible to be certain therefore whether these inclusions are zinc sulfides or zinc-copper sulfides, but all contain zinc, and in the largest particles analyzed the Zn/Cu ratio is as high as 3/1.

3. This is strictly true only if zinc oxide or carbonate were the source of zinc. If the zinc ore was a sulfide it would have become purified during the calcination which is a necessary prerequisite to the use of zinc sulfide as a source of zinc in brass production.

4. This is further confirmed by other elemental analyses of Sintiou Bara copper-based material (see Garenne-Marot 1993).

5. A similar casting-on technique was used for the application of decoration to an armlet (?) found at the Senegal River site of Podor (see Fig. 1) (Thilmans 1977).

References

ASM. 1990. *Metals Handbook*, Vol. 2, 10th ed. ASM International, Materials Park, OH.

Berthier, S. 1983. *Etude archéologique d'un secteur d'habitat à Koumbi Saleh (Mauritanie)*. Thèse de 3e cycle, Université de Lyon 2, Sciences historiques et géographiques—études et civilisations islamiques, 2 vols.

Bocoum, H., S. K. McIntosh, and R. J. McIntosh. 1992. L'âge du fer dans la moyenne vallée du Fleuve Sénégal: chronologie et intégration. *West African Archaeological Association, Vth colloquium.* Ouagadougou, Burkina-Faso, August 26–September 2, 1992. See also McIntosh, S. K., R. J. McIntosh, and H. Bocoum. 1992. The Middle Senegal Valley Project: Preliminary Results from the 1990–91 Field Season. *Nyame Akuma* 38:47–61.

Bourhis, J. R. 1983. Résultats des analyses d'objets en cuivre, bronze et laiton et des résidus de métallurgie antique d'Afrique. In *Métallurgies africaines, nouvelles contributions*, ed. N. Echard, pp. 127–152. Mémoire Société des Africanistes 9. Paris.

Castro, R. 1974. Examen métallographique d'un fragment de baguette de laiton coulé provenant d'une épave caravanière 'Ma'den Ijâfen'. *Bulletin de l'Institut Fondamental d'Afrique Noire*, B, 36(3):497–510.

Chikwendu, V. E., P. T. Craddock, R. M. Farquhar, T. Shaw, and A. C. Umeji. 1989. Nigerian Sources of Copper, Lead and Tin for the Igbo Ukwu Bronzes. *Archaeometry* 31:27–36.

Craddock, P. T. 1985. Medieval Copper Alloy Production and West African Bronze Analyses, Part I. *Archaeometry* 27:17–41.

Craddock, P. T., S. C. La Niece, and D. Hook. 1990. Brass in the Medieval Islamic World. In *2000 Years of Zinc and Brass*, ed. P. T. Craddock, pp. 73–101. British Museum Occasional Paper No. 50. British Museum Publications, London.

Craddock, P. T., and J. Picton. 1986. Medieval Copper Alloy Production and West African Bronze Analyses, Part II. *Archaeometry* 28:3–32.

Devisse, J. 1990. Commerce et routes du trafic en Afrique occidentale. In *Histoire Générale de l'Afrique*. III: *L'Afrique du VIIème au XIème siècle*, ch. 14, pp. 397–464. Unesco/Nouvelles Editions Africaines (NEA).

Devisse, J., and D. Robert-Chaleix. 1982. *Tegdaoust III: Recherches sur Aoudaghost. Campagnes 1960/65: Enquêtes Générales.* Memoire de l'Institut Mauritanien de la Recherche Scientifique No. 3. Nouakchott.

Fleming, S. J., C. P. Swann, P. E. McGovern, and L. Horne. 1990. Characterization of Ancient Materials using PIXE Spectrometry. *Nuclear Instruments and Methods in Physics Research* B49:293–299.

Garenne-Marot, L. 1993. *Archéologie d'un métal: le cuivre en Sénégambie (Afrique de l'Ouest) entre le Xe et le XIVe siècle*. Thèse de doctorat, Université de Paris I, Panthéon-Sorbonne, 2 vols.

Grébenart, D. 1988. *Les premiers métallurgistes en Afrique occidentale. Les origines de la métallurgie en Afrique occidentale.* Errance/Nouvelles Editions Africaines (NEA), Paris.

Herbert, E. W. 1984. *Red Gold of Africa: Copper in Precolonial History and Culture.* University of Wisconsin Press, Madison.

Joire, J. 1955. Découvertes archéologiques dans la région de Rao (Bas-Sénégal). *Bulletin de l'Institut Fondamental d'Afrique Noire*, B, 18(3):249–333.

Levtzion, N., and J. F. P. Hopkins (eds.). 1981. *Corpus of Early Arabic Sources for West African History*, transl. J. F. P. Hopkins. Cambridge University Press,

Cambridge.

McIntosh, S. K., and R. J. McIntosh. 1986. Recent Archaeological Research and Dates from West Africa. *Journal of African History* 27:413–442.

——— 1988. From Stone to Metal: New Perspectives on the Later Prehistory of West Africa. *Journal of World Prehistory* 2:89–133.

Monod, T. 1969. Le Ma'den Ijâfen: Une épave caravanière ancienne dans la Majâbat al-Koubrâ. In *Actes du première colloque international d'archéologie africaine (Fort Lamy)*, pp. 286–320.

Ravisé, A., and G. Thilmans. 1978. A propos d'une clochette trouvée à Sintiou Bara (Fleuve Sénégal). *Notes Africaines* (Dakar) 159:57–59.

Robert-Chaleix, D. 1989. *Tegdaoust V: Recherches sur Aoudaghost. Une concession médiévale à Tegdaoust: implantation, évolution d'une unité d'habitation.* Mémoire No. 82. Editions recherches sur les civilisations, Paris.

Thilmans, G. 1977. Sur des objets de parure trouvés à Podor (Sénégal) en 1958. *Bulletin de l'Institut Fondamental d'Afrique Noire*, B, 39(4):669–694.

Thilmans, G., and C. Descamps. 1982. In *Amas et tumulus coquilliers du delta du Saloum*, pp. 31–50. Mémoires de l'Institut Fondamental d'Afrique Noire (IFAN), No. 92. Dakar.

Thilmans, G., C. Descamps, and B. Khayat. 1980. *Protohistoire du Sénégal.* I: *Les sites mégalithiques.* Mémoires de l'Institut Fondamental d'Afrique Noire (IFAN), No. 91. Dakar.

Thilmans, G., and A. Ravisé. 1980. *Protohistoire du Sénégal.* II: *Sintiou Bara et les sites du Fleuve.* Mémoires de l'Institut Fondamental d'Afrique Noire (IFAN), No. 91. Dakar.

Vanacker, C. 1979. *Tegdaoust II: Recherches sur Aoudaghost. Fouilles d'un quartier artisanal.* Memoire de l'Institut Mauritanien de la Recherche Scientifique No. 2. Nouakchott.

——— 1983. Cuivre et métallurgie du cuivre à Tegdaoust (Mauretanie Orientale). In *Métallurgies africaines, nouvelles contributions*, ed. N. Echard, pp. 89–107. Mémoire Société des Africanistes 9. Paris.

Werner, O., and F. Willett. 1975. The Composition of Brasses from Ife and Benin. *Archaeometry* 17:141–156.

Appendix: Examination of the decorated Sintiou Bara bell

The original examination of this decorated bell, carried out in 1973 in the Laboratoire d'archeologie des métaux, Jarville (Nancy), led the examiners to propose that rather than having been cast by the lost wax method, the bell had been fabricated from sheet copper (or brass), followed by the attachment of decoration by an unorthodox technique (Ravisé and Thilmans 1978). The suggestion was that the decoration in the form of small copper (or brass) wires had been soldered with tin onto the surface of the sheet, followed by the encasing of the bell in a envelope of clay. The assembly was then, according to the suggestion, heated to allow the tin from the solder to diffuse throughout the object. A diffusion temperature of 700–800°C was suggested as being sufficient to achieve homogenization, and it was noted that if hot enough, a dendritic structure could be produced (i.e., the object would melt inside its envelope of clay and then resolidify upon cooling). A dendritic structure was indeed observed in the artifact. This proposed technique was supported by replication experiments which successfully reproduced the microstructure of the bell.

However, because the metal inside its clay shell mold melted and resolidified during the solder-diffusion treatment, the microstructure obtained would have been substantially the same as if the bell had been produced by lost wax casting. Hence the observations which led the investigators to the proposed technique were not microstructural. They stated that "toute trace de soudure a disparu sauf en un endroit ou des scories conservent la courbure du fil soudé sur la tole" ("all trace of welding has disappeared except in one location where slag has preserved the curvature of the wire welded onto the sheet").

The same solder-diffusion technique was subsequently suggested by the same analysts to explain the decoration on a bracelet from La Séguié, in Ivory Coast, but in this case the only evidence was the argument that it is not likely that the object could have been successfully cast integrally with its decoration by the lost wax method because of its thinness.

Because of the importance of the use of such a technique in this context, it was felt desirable to confirm the interpretation. It was hoped that improvements in analytical instrumentation in the decades since this work was carried out, especially in microbeam analysis techniques, could have permitted the corroboration of this technique on a stronger basis than was originally the case. Through the kind co-operation of M. C. Forrières, Directeur du Laboratoire d'archeologie des métaux, Jarville (Nancy), we have been able to re-examine the metallographic sample originally taken from the decorated Sintiou Bara bell. This sample is a section through both the decorative wire and the underlying base sheet. Unfortunately, due to the understandably degraded condition of the surface of the sample, which was first polished nearly two decades ago, it was necessary to lightly repolish the surface. Following this, examination was unable to confirm the presence of the slag layer following the original surface of the wire. Hence other evidence was sought for or against the proposed technique.

The microstructural examination confirmed that the entire cross-section, including both the decorative bead and the underlying body of the bell, had been liquid and had solidified together from the liquid state. The bell had either been cooled slowly from the liquid state or else had subsequently been annealed at a high temperature for a long time, since all traces of solute coring have disappeared. Nothing was observed in the microstructure which could have helped to distinguish between the solder-diffusion and the lost wax casting techniques; in fact, however, the only possible distinguishing observations would have been the presence of concentration gradients in the material, these being more likely in the case of the solder-diffusion technique than in a lost wax casting. The analyses, by x-ray fluorescence and also by SEM-EDA, showed that the composition is the same in all parts of the sample, approximately 9–10% tin, 5.5% zinc and 0.5% lead, with no concentration gradients. Hence there is nothing to suggest that the proposed solder-diffusion process was in fact used for the application of decoration to this bell.

INDIGENOUS AND IMPORTED METALS AT SWAHILI SITES ON THE COAST OF KENYA

Chapurukha M. Kusimba

The Field Museum of Natural History, Roosevelt Road, Chicago, IL 60605-2496

David J. Killick

Department of Anthropology/Department of Materials Science and Engineering, University of Arizona, Tucson, AZ 85721

Richard G. Cresswell

IsoTrace Laboratory, Department of Physics, University of Toronto, Toronto, Ontario M5S 1A7*

ABSTRACT This paper examines the roles of long-distance trade, regional exchange, and local craft production in forming the assemblages of metals recovered from five Swahili archaeological sites (eighth–sixteenth centuries A.D.). All non-ferrous alloys appear to have been imported, although some were locally recast. There is, however, much evidence for the local smelting of iron and steel by the bloomery process. One interesting result of this work has been the identification of several samples of crucible steel, presumably imported from the Indian subcontinent or the Islamic world. Several of these samples were directly dated by accelerator mass spectrometer and yielded calibrated ages between the seventh and the sixteenth centuries.

Introduction

This paper is a progress report on a long-term study, initiated by C.M.K. in 1988, on the production and consumption of metals on the coast of present-day Kenya from the early first millennium A.D. to the present day. We are concerned here with metals excavated from Swahili sites dating between the eighth and sixteenth centuries, the period that saw the founding, florescence, and decline of most of the Swahili coastal towns. Early interpretations of the Swahili tended to portray them as a colonizing elite almost entirely engaged in long-distance maritime trade, and to stress their economic and cultural isolation from the non-Swahili peoples of the interior. Historians and anthropologists have begun to rethink this picture, but archaeologists have not yet paid much attention to reconstructing local economic activity or to studying interaction between the Swahili towns and the hinterland. It occurred to us that a study of the metals in Swahili sites might contribute useful data to the current reassessment of the place of the Swahili in the history of East Africa.

The Swahili and their past

The Swahili are Muslims who inhabit the coast of East Africa. Their language and culture are a unique synthesis of African and Arabian elements (Middleton 1992). Archaeologists have traced the origins of Swahili culture to the eighth century A.D. (Chittick 1974, 1984; Horton 1984, 1987, 1988). There are a few written descriptions of Swahili towns in Arabic from the tenth through the sixteenth centuries, and more numerous accounts by European, Arab, and Swahili observers thereafter (Freeman-Grenville 1962; Lewicki 1969). These records show that the Swahili towns played a prominent role in the triangular maritime trade linking India, the Persian Gulf, and East Africa.

The major exports from East Africa between the twelfth and sixteenth centuries were ivory, gold, and mangrove poles. Of these, only the mangrove poles (used for construction in the treeless Persian Gulf) were a local resource. Gold was purchased by Swahili and Indian agents in the region of present Zimbabwe, while ivory was obtained from the inhabitants of the savanna woodlands that cover vast areas of southern and southeastern Africa. Archaeological evidence from South Africa and Mozambique (reviewed in Hall 1991) indicates that long-distance trade between the East African coast and the interior of southern Africa began by the ninth century. Swahili elites grew wealthy from their access to the sources of gold and ivory, which were resold to Islamic and Indian merchants who sailed to the East African coast on the annual monsoon. The Swahili elites transformed some of this wealth into fine buildings in coral masonry and into imported luxuries. These include fine Chinese and Near Eastern ceramics, Near Eastern glass, and Indian textiles, glass beads, and metalwork (Freeman-Grenville 1962; Middleton 1992).

Professional archaeological research in Swahili towns began in 1948, but was focused almost exclusively on the standing ruins and their contents until the 1980s. The portrait of the Swahili that emerged from these studies was of an alien mercantile society, perched on the rim of Africa but with little cultural connection to it (Kirkman 1964:22; Trimingham 1964:7–9; Chittick 1974, vol. 2:345). The Swahili elites themselves tend to emphasize their historical links to the Persian Gulf and their differences from their African neighbors, as can be seen in the written chronicles of the coastal towns (Freeman-Grenville 1962).

This is undoubtedly an unbalanced portrait of Swahili society as a whole (Nurse and Spear 1985). Systematic archaeological survey of the Kenyan coast by Tom Wilson (1978, 1980) and George Abungu (1990) during the last 15 years has shown that there is great variation in the amount and quality of masonry buildings within Swahili walled towns. This suggests much variation in the wealth of these towns, and therefore in the extent of their participation in long-distance maritime trade. The trading elite appear also to have been a minority even in the richest towns, where humble mud huts appear to have greatly outnumbered stone houses (Kusimba 1993).

Little effort has been directed to studying the role of agriculture, fishing, or herding in Swahili towns, while the products of indigenous crafts have received much less attention than those of Arabian, Indian, or Chinese craftspeople. Assertions that Swahili towns had little or no interaction with the non-Swahili peoples of the immediate hinterland should also be treated with skepticism, since almost no archaeological excavation has been done on non-Swahili sites near the coast. One of us has noted elsewhere that the image of the Swahili as parasitic colonists has had unfortunate consequences since Kenya became independent in 1963. These include appropriation of Swahili lands and seeming indifference by non-Swahili officials to the destruction of Swahili archaeological sites and monuments (Kusimba forthcoming).

Archaeologists have begun to correct this bias (Stiles 1982; Wilson 1982; Chittick 1984; Nurse and Spear 1985; Horton 1987; Abungu 1990; Fawcett and LaViolette 1990), but a more balanced assessment of the place of the Swahili in East African history requires that all aspects of Swahili economy and society be investigated, not just those that relate to long-distance trade. This study is a contribution to that end.

Expectations derived from history and archaeology

The earliest historical record of maritime trade along the East African coast long predates the Swahili era. This is the *Periplus of the Erythraean Sea*, an anonymous guidebook for mariners written in Greek in the mid-first century A.D. (Casson 1989). The author referred briefly to the demand in East Africa for metal goods manufactured in Muza (near present-day Aden on the Red Sea) and, in particular, for spears, axes, knives, and awls. Archaeologists have not yet located sites of comparable age on or near the Kenyan coast. Evidence of extensive iron smelting has been reported, however, from the coastal hinterland south of Dar es Salaam in Tanzania (Fawcett and LaViolette 1990). Radiocarbon dates of 2000±60 B.P. and 2010±90 B.P. for the lower levels of the smelting site span (when calibrated into calendar years) the date of the *Periplus*. There are few other pertinent archaeological data for the period, but these facts alert us to look for both indigenous and imported metals in pre-Swahili sites on the coast.

The next historical reference to metals on the coast is not until A.D. 915, when al-Masudi noted that the inhabitants of the East African coast wore iron and copper ornaments, were skilled workers in metal, and collected ivory for the maritime trade (Freeman-Grenville 1962). Al-Idrisi (A.D. 1100–1166) reported that the inhabitants of Malindi and Mombasa produced large quantities of iron, that the main exports of the East African coast were iron and leopard skins, and that there was substantial demand for East African iron in south India (Freeman-Grenville 1962; Radimilahy 1993).

Evidence for the working of iron, in the form of iron slag, has been reported on several Swahili sites. These include Manda (Chittick 1984:209), Shanga (Horton 1984, 1988), Ungwana (Abungu 1990), and Kilwa (Chittick 1974, vol. 2:441). We do not yet know whether the slag was produced by smelting iron ore or by forging metal smelted elsewhere. Chittick claims to have found iron-smelting furnaces at both Manda (Chittick 1984:210–211) and Kilwa (Chittick 1974, vol. 2:439–459), but the published descriptions and plans look more like forge firepits than smelting furnaces. Evidence of iron smelting at the sites of Ungwana and Galu is discussed below.

The geological mapping of Kenya has been quite thorough, but no deposits of copper, lead, or tin are reported near the coast of Kenya, nor has any copper ore or copper slag been reported from an archaeological context on Swahili sites. Crucibles encrusted with green corrosion product have been recovered, however, at Manda (Chittick

1984:207), Kilwa (Chittick 1974, vol. 2:331), Shanga (Horton 1984:259), Ungwana (Abungu 1990), and Mafia (Chittick 1961). These have not yet been studied, but we tentatively accept them as evidence for the casting of copper or copper alloys.

From these records, and from our wider knowledge of regional geology and the history of metallurgy, we derive the following sets of expectations:

1. Non-ferrous metals appear to have been cast on Swahili sites, but we presume that the metals were smelted elsewhere. The principal source of gold in Swahili sites was presumably southern Africa, for reasons noted above. Much of the silver recovered from Swahili sites is in the form of coins, many of which have legible inscriptions. Some were struck in locations as far distant as Sicily (Horton 1988). Many locally struck silver coins are also known, but the sources of the metal are unknown. Silver is listed in historical documents as an export from the Swahili coast, and may possibly have come from Chicoa in the Zambesi valley or from Madagascar (Axelson 1973:passim). Copper could have reached the East African coast from many sources, the most probable of which are Oman, India, Central and Southern Africa, and (after the sixteenth century) Europe. The potential sources of tin are rather limited; the nearest are in Afghanistan, India, and South Africa. Only two radiocarbon dates are available for prehistoric tin mining in South Africa, but both fall (after calibration) in the thirteenth or fourteenth centuries A.D., when the Swahili trade to southern Africa was at its zenith (Killick 1990). Nor is there as yet any record of the smelting of lead in Eastern or Southern Africa.

   Metallic zinc in Swahili sites would presumably have been imported from India, the only known source of that metal until the sixteenth century. Brass could have been prepared in East Africa by alloying imported zinc with African or imported copper. An account in 1648 of such an alloying strategy employed in what is today Zimbabwe is cited by Craddock et al. (1990:57). The alternative method of making brass—by heating metallic copper and zinc carbonate (calamine) in a sealed crucible—was practiced throughout most of the Old World except, based on present knowledge, in sub-Saharan Africa. Thus, we expect at least the zinc in any brass found on Swahili sites to have been imported through long-distance maritime trade.

2. Iron artifacts found on Swahili sites were probably locally smelted by some variant of the bloomery process. We cannot prove, however, whether a given piece of bloomery iron was locally manufactured or imported. The bloomery process was in use throughout Africa, India, and the Near East during this time, but there are no scientific techniques that can distinguish between the thousands of possible sources. It is possible, of course, to demonstrate that iron was produced locally from the presence of iron-smelting slag left on the site, and to make a rough estimate of the scale of production from its quantity.

The blast furnace had been employed to smelt iron in China for more than five hundred years by the time that the *Periplus of the Erythraean Sea* was written, and appears to have reached the Islamic world from the Far East by A.D. 1050 (al-Hassan and Hill 1986:252–253). It did not reach Europe until the twelfth or thirteenth century, and was not employed in sub-Saharan Africa until European colonial settlers introduced it in the nineteenth century. Cast iron is often produced, however, in small quantities in bloomery furnaces, and there are several records of this in sub-Saharan Africa (Killick in press). In all known cases, the cast iron was either discarded or decarburized to steel before being used. We presume, therefore, that any iron castings found in Swahili sites would have been imported from outside the continent. Small lumps or pellets of cast iron, on the other hand, may be the product of a local bloomery furnace.

The temperatures required to cast steel are much higher than those required to pour cast iron, and, until the nineteenth century, could only be attained by melting small batches in sealed crucibles. Crucible steel appears to have been first made in south India or Sri Lanka, but its early history is as yet unknown (Bronson 1986). The only sample directly dated by radiocarbon before this study is from Sri Lanka and dates in the eleventh century cal A.D. (Cresswell 1991:83). The technology had diffused to the Near East by this time (al-Hassan and Hill 1986:254), but crucible steel was not made known in Europe until independently invented by Huntsman in England around 1740. A special type of crucible steel was the famous *wootz*, produced in India and the Near East, which was much prized for the richly textured surfaces that it exhibited after skillful forging and etching (Smith 1988; Bronson 1986; al-Hassan and Hill 1986:255–256). There is no evidence as yet that *wootz* (or crucible steel in general) was ever made in sub-Saharan Africa, so any finds of these in Swahili sites presumably were imported.

Sample selection

We have examined 179 artifacts to date from five sites (Table 1). Note, however, that the samples do not necessarily cover the whole range of metals or of metal artifact types from each site. We have not sought to examine artifacts of gold or silver, nor have we had access to the larger and better-preserved metal artifacts that are suitable for museum display. The samples were mostly selected from the "small things forgotten" on museum shelves that appeared to be shapeless masses of rust.

The five sites are (Fig. 1):

Mtwapa (site HhJx4 in the SASES registry of African archaeological sites). The ruins of this walled town, some eight hectares in area, are 15 km north of Mombasa. The imported ceramics recovered from the ruins suggest that the site was occupied from the fifteenth to the eighteenth centuries. Among the features excavated is an ironworking area near the north end of the town from which eleven iron objects were selected (Kusimba 1993).

Shanga (site HaKe9). This is located on the southern side of Pate Island in the Lamu Archipelago and is the most thoroughly studied of all the Swahili towns (Horton 1984, 1988). The chronology of the town, as reconstructed from imported ceramics, radiocarbon dating, oral history, and an indigenous written history (the Pate Chronicle), spans the period from ca. A.D. 800 to 1425 (Horton 1988). Twenty-one objects of iron and one of copper alloy were selected for this study, and span the whole occupation.

Ungwana (site HcKc1). The ruins of Ungwana are situated some 30 km south of Lamu. The site has been excavated by Kirkman (1966) and more extensively by Abungu (1990). The span of occupation proposed by Abungu, on the basis of imported Chinese and Islamic ceramics and glasswares, is ca. A.D. 950–1600. His excavations in a large midden outside the town wall produced copious quantities of slag, crucibles, and metallic artifacts. Several of the crucibles contain green residues that suggest the melting of copper or copper alloys. We examined 79 iron artifacts, nine copper or copper alloy artifacts, and one tin/lead artifact from Ungwana, together with several samples of slag.

Mwana (site HcKc5). Mwana is a large Swahili settlement in the Tana River delta about 60 km southwest of the Lamu archipelago. The imported ceramics recovered in small test excavations show that the site was occupied in the fifteenth century, but its full span of occupation is not yet known. It is currently under excavation by Athman Lali Omar of the University of Florida. Three objects from his excavations were included in this study.

Galu (site HjJw4). Galu is situated in the Kwale District on the south coast of Kenya. The remains of coral walls form a rectangular enclosure of about two and one-half hectares with gates at the eastern and western ends and a well in the center. The imported ceramics from the site suggest that it was occupied from the fifteenth through the eighteenth centuries. C.M.K. excavated a metallurgical workshop near the west gate in 1991 and found a shallow circular pit with fire-hardened surfaces, associated with much ash, abundant slag, scraps of iron, and fragments of tuyéres (Kusimba 1993). This area is bisected by the town wall, and a single radiocarbon date (see below) confirms that it predates the main occupation of the site. Fifty-three samples of iron and one sample of a copper alloy from this area of

Table 1. Metallurgical samples from the Kenya Coast examined in this study

Artifact type	Galu	Mtwapa	Mwana	Shanga	Ungwana
Iron/steel					
Arrowheads	-	1	-	-	5
Axes	-	-	-	1	-
Bells	-	1	-	-	-
Blooms	6	-	-	-	1
Chisels	-	-	-	-	1
Hooks	1	-	-	-	3
Knives	6	-	-	9	12
Rods	-	-	-	1	-
Pellets	-	1	-	-	2
Points/nails	8	2	-	7	34
Scythe blades	1	-	-	-	-
Iron sheet	-	1	-	-	1
Unclassifiable	31	5	2	3	20
Subtotal	**53**	**11**	**2**	**21**	**79**
Copper alloys					
Kohl sticks	-	-	-	-	4
Bells	-	-	-	-	1
Blades	-	-	1	1	-
Bracelets	-	-	-	-	1
Coins	-	-	-	-	1
Rings	-	-	-	-	1
Unclassifiable	1	-	-	-	1
Subtotal	**1**	**0**	**1**	**1**	**9**
Tin/lead alloy					
Bar	-	-	-	-	1
Site totals	**54**	**11**	**3**	**22**	**89**

the site are included in this study. Studies of the smelting and forging slags will be reported elsewhere.

Methods

The metal samples were sectioned longitudinally with a diamond-rim saw, mounted in epoxy, and ground and polished by conventional metallographic techniques. The slag samples were prepared as polished thin sections. The chemical composition of the non-ferrous metals was estimated with an energy-dispersive x-ray spectrometer mounted on a JEOL scanning electron microscope. The results reported in Table 2 are averages of analyses made on four to six regions per sample, each of which was 800 by 600 μm in size. The analyses were calculated by a standardless ZAF routine and were normalized to 100%. The lower limit of detection for the elements analyzed is ca. 0.5% wt. These analyses must be regarded as approximate, because the energy-dispersive x-ray detector does not discriminate well among lead, arsenic, and sulfur.

Fig. 1:
Map of the Kenya coast, showing the location of sites discussed in the text.

Table 2. Composition of non-ferrous artifacts (wt. %)

Site and no.	Artifact type	Microstructure	Copper	Zinc	Tin	Lead	Chlorine
Ungwana 3216	*Kohl* stick	Forged, annealed	76.6	21.7	nd*	1.1	nd
Ungwana 2405	*Kohl* stick	As cast	63.8	3.4	7.1	27.8	0.7
Ungwana 1400	*Kohl* stick	Forged, annealed	90.3	0.5	8.5	0.7	nd
Ungwana 2069a	Nose/ear ring	Forged, annealed	85.3	13.4	nd	1.0	nd
Ungwana 2069b	as above	As cast	81.0	5.8	11.8	0.9	nd
Ungwana 1457	Bracelet	Forged, annealed	86.5	12.5	nd	0.8	nd
Ungwana 2721	Bell	As cast	87.7	5.3	0.5	6.2	nd
Ungwana 401	Small bar	As cast	nd	nd	80.1	19.9	nd

* nd = below limit of detection

The individual analyses for each sample were in fair agreement for all elements but lead and chlorine. Where lead globules are large and unevenly distributed in the specimen, the lead content may vary significantly from one analysis to the next. In sample 2405 (the worst case), the lead content varied between 22 and 34% in four analyses. Chlorine occurs only in areas that are affected by corrosion.

Dating

Since all of these sites have deep stratigraphy, it would be relatively easy for errors of stratigraphic association to arise, especially where small finds are concerned. Small objects such as these may also be moved from one level to another by burrowing animals. Direct radiocarbon dates were obtained, therefore, from several of the more interesting steel samples. The crucial assumption here is that the fuel used (the source of the carbon in the steel) was derived from wood or other vegetable matter that was taking in radiocarbon from the atmosphere shortly before the steel was made. Since charcoal was the fuel usually used in metal smelting before the eighteenth century, most preindustrial steel samples can be dated by radiocarbon. Errors may still arise if the wood from which the charcoal was made had ceased to incorporate radiocarbon from the atmosphere long before the steel was made, as for example when the charcoal fuel was prepared from the heartwood of long-lived trees. Such cases can only be detected where some independent method of dating flags the radiocarbon date as anomalously old.

The dating of steel was pioneered by van der Merwe (1969) using decay-counting techniques, but recently has been revolutionized by Accelerator Mass Spectrometry (AMS) which requires only a few milligrams of carbon. Six samples of steel and one of cast iron were dated by R.G.C. in the IsoTrace AMS laboratory at the University of Toronto. Four of these were from Ungwana and three from Galu. The methods used to extract the carbon from the samples and to measure the radiocarbon content are described in Cresswell (1991, 1992). The sample size and measured carbon content for each specimen are listed in Table 5. The radiocarbon ages were calibrated to ranges of calendar ages at 2σ with the computer program CALIB 3.03 (Stuiver and Reimer 1993).

Results

Non-ferrous metals

The non-ferrous metals were in a fair state of preservation and could be classified with confidence by artifact type. Table 1 shows that only two of the eleven identifiable artifacts are tools (pieces of knife blade), the remainder being small items of jewelry, toiletries, a much worn coin without legible inscription, and a slender bar of a tin/lead

alloy that is probably unworked metal stock. Four cylindrical or square-sectioned rods are identified as *kohl* sticks because of their strong resemblance to the rods still used by Swahili women to apply *kohl* (antimony sulfide) as eye shadow. These have been recovered from most Swahili sites. There are also two bracelets, a small clapperless bell, and one delicate nose or ear ring.

Ten of the thirteen samples retain some metal within their jacket of corrosion. Eight have been studied to date. All are from Ungwana and were found in levels containing Islamic and Chinese ceramics that are cross-dated to between A.D. 1400 and 1600. Table 2 provides approximate chemical compositions for these artifacts. This shows that the compositions vary widely, but almost all contain a substantial amount (>3% wt.) of zinc, which implies that the metals were imported from outside sub-Saharan Africa. Two samples (3216 and 1457) are true brasses with minor lead, one (2721) a low zinc leaded brass, one (2405) a gunmetal heavily adulterated with lead, one (1400) a tin bronze, and one (2069) a finely laminated structure of brass and gunmetal. The bar of tin/lead alloy (sample 401) has a square cross-section, about 8 mm on a side, and is 80% tin and 20% lead. It may be classified as a pewter, therefore. There are as yet no reported artifacts of pewter from Swahili sites, so perhaps this was intended for some other purpose, such as a solder or a master alloy to make a leaded bronze when melted with copper.

The level of manufacturing skill represented by these artifacts is very variable. The most sophisticated piece is the nose/ear ring which consists of fine wire bent into an open circular loop (diameter ca. 15 mm) subtending about 270° of arc. Although the diameter of the section is barely 1.5 mm, the polished cross-section (Fig. 2) shows it to be composed of alternating layers, two of wrought brass (2069a in Table 2) and three of cast gunmetal (2069b in Table 2). The gunmetal layers display a barely distorted cast structure and, therefore, cannot have been subjected to much forging or drawing. Given that the two brass laminae have the same composition, and that the three cast gunmetal layers are also identical to each other, it appears that this unusual structure was made by folding a narrow strip of brass and casting gunmetal around it. A narrow strip was then cut from this composite plate, rounded by light forging or grinding, and bent into a loop. We cannot explain why the artisan should have gone to such trouble, for the banding is on a scale barely visible to the unaided eye.

A small clapperless bell (maximum diameter 17 mm), which is asymmetrical and very porous (resembling a sponge in some areas), is at the opposite extreme of skill. Its porosity and quantity of oxide inclusions indicate that an excessive amount of oxygen was present in the molten copper alloy, and that the artisan failed to remove it before casting.[1] Both the form and the microstructure of this piece reflect extremely poor craftsmanship. The remaining pieces

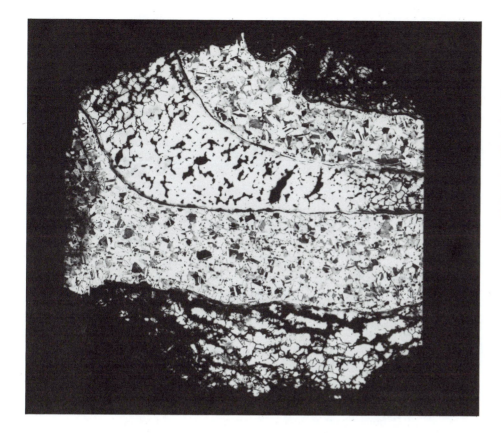

Fig. 2:
A partial cross-section of nose/ear ring from Ungwana (specimen 2069), etched with hydrogen peroxide and ammonia. Three cast gunmetal layers (the outer two of which are extensively corroded) alternate with two wrought brass layers. Magnification 75×.

are of sound quality, although the large amount of lead in one of the *kohl* sticks (sample 2405) marks this as low quality adulterated metal.

Ferrous samples

Most of the ferrous samples were very badly corroded. Many were amorphous lumps of rust, although the original shape of the object could in all cases be clearly discerned in polished section. The classification of ferrous samples by artifact type in Table 1 is tentative. Many of the objects classified as "points," for example, could equally well be nails or the tangs from arrows that have lost their heads to corrosion. The category of "unclassifiable" in Table 1 includes pieces too corroded to classify and pieces of partially worked or scrap iron.

In spite of the uncertainty about function, there is a clear difference in the range of artifact types between the non-ferrous and the ferrous metal assemblages at Ungwana, the only site for which we can yet make such a comparison. The non-ferrous metals are mostly toilet items or jewelry, whereas the classifiable ferrous samples are tools, partially processed metal (bloom, pellets, sheet), or forged scrap. All of these are small pieces less than 30 mm in maximum length that weigh less than 80 g.

Table 3 shows how few of the ferrous artifacts sampled had any metal preserved. All of the samples from Mtwapa, Mwana, and Shanga were entirely corroded, as were most of those from Galu and Ungwana. In a few of the fully corroded samples, relict structures were visible that are pseudomorphs of iron carbides or of slag stringers, but, in the great majority of these samples, no trace of the original microstructure appears to remain.

The 25 ferrous samples that have some remnant metal include examples of forged and unforged bloomery iron

Table 3. The problem of corrosion: survival rate of metal artifacts by site

	Galu	Mtwapa	Mwana	Shanga	Ungwana
Sample of ferrous artifacts	53	11	2	21	79
Number with any metal remaining	15	0	0	0	10
Sample of non-ferrous artifacts	1	0	1	1	10
Number with any metal remaining	1	0	1	1	8

Table 4. Ferrous metals

Site	Sample no.	Unit/ level	Microstructure	Comments
Galu	26/001	1B/1	>1.5% C, spheroidized, badly corroded	Crucible steel (?)
Galu	28/004	1C/3	<0.05% C, much slag	Bloomery iron
Galu	29/002a	1B/3	>1.5% C, homogeneous, normalized, no slag	Crucible steel
Galu	29/002b	1B/3	ca. 0.7% C, normalized, much slag	Bloomery steel
Galu	31/005a	2B/2	<0.1% C, much slag	Forged bloomery scrap
Galu	31/005b	2B/2	<0.05% C, normalized, much slag	Forged bloomery iron
Galu	32/007a	2C/2	>2% C, white cast iron, slag	Unforged bloom
Galu	32/007b	2C/2	<0.05% C., much slag	Bloomery iron scrap
Galu	33/006b	2B/2	>1.5% C, homogeneous, badly corroded	Crucible steel
Galu	34/013a	3C/1	0.15% C, normalized, cold worked, little slag	Forged bloomery scrap
Galu	35/052a	2C/1	<0.05% C, ferrite colonies and slag	Unforged iron bloom
Galu	35/052b	2C/1	<0.05% C, equiaxed ferrite, slag stringers	Bloomery iron
Galu	36/009	2B/?	0.1–0.6% C, normalized slag stringers	Bloomery iron & steel
Galu	36/005b	2B/2	0.8–1.0% C, slag stringers	Bloomery steel
Galu	37/011a	3B/1	0.2% C, slag stringers, copper coating	Bloomery iron
Ungwana	193	1C/3	>1% C, homogeneous, spheroidized, no slag	Crucible steel
Ungwana	194	1C/3	>1% C, homogeneous, spheroidized, no slag	Crucible steel
Ungwana	2408	4/7	Two pieces, 0.8% and 0.1% C, welded	Bloomery steel & iron
Ungwana	2/2966a	4/12	ca. 1% C, homogeneous, normalized, no slag	Crucible steel
Ungwana	11/2660b	4/11	Two pieces, >1.0% and ca. 0.5% C, welded	Crucible & bloomery steel
Ungwana	15/3061a	4/13	ca. 0.2% C, homogeneous, low slag content	Bloomery steel
Ungwana	15/3061c	4/13	>1.2% C, homogeneous, spheroidized, no slag	Crucible steel
Ungwana	15/3061d	4/13	>1.2% C, homogeneous, spheroidized, no slag	Crucible steel
Ungwana	17/2692b	3/9	Banded, 0.1% C/0.8% C/0.1% C, much slag	Welded bloomery
Ungwana	17/2692c	3/9	0.8% C, homogeneous, no slag	Crucible steel

and steel, eight (possibly nine) pieces of what we believe to be crucible steel, and a single nodule of white cast iron. The distribution of these by site is shown in Table 4.

Bloomery iron

The criteria that we employ to identify samples as bloomery iron or steel are: (1) the presence of iron silicate slag stringers; and (2) inhomogeneous distribution of carbon within the section, arising from variation in the carbon content of the bloom (Fig. 3).

Bloomery iron was locally manufactured at Galu, where excavations uncovered both smelting and forging slag and the base of a smelting furnace with three tuyére ports (Kusimba 1993). There was evidently a forge nearby, for many of the specimens recovered from the excavations in this area of the site are encased in a jacket of tabular fragments of hammer scale, tiny spheres of slag (expelled as liquid from the bloom and air chilled), and charcoal fragments, all cemented together by corrosion products. These specimens were clearly discarded on the floor of a forge.

The ferrous objects recovered at Galu run the gamut from wrought iron to cast iron. The amount of slag retained in the metal also varies widely. Such extreme variation is typical of the bloomery process and may even be seen within a single run of a furnace (e.g., David et al. 1989). Two fragments of unworked bloom were noted. One of these (sample 35/052a) is essentially carbon-free iron, while the other (32/007a) is an egg-shaped lump of white cast iron (ca. 2.0% C) about 25 mm long. The latter is inhomogeneous, contains abundant slag inclusions, and, therefore, is the product of a bloomery rather than a blast furnace (Fig. 4). The cast iron nodule was directly dated by AMS to 740±70 B.P., corresponding to a calendar age between A.D. 1170–1400 (Table 5), while a forged piece of bloomery steel from this area returned a date of 1400±240 B.P. The large standard error of the latter (a reflection of inadequate sample size) makes it essentially useless for archaeological interpretation.

We cannot prove that most of the metal forged here was smelted on site, but the presence of a smelting furnace and abundant smelting slag makes this seem likely. There are several pieces from the site that may have originated elsewhere, however. Two of these are bimetallic. One (no. 37/011a) is a thin plate of bloomery iron of good quality, plated on both sides with a thin layer of copper alloy. The other is a shapeless lump of iron coated with brass. The function cannot be inferred for either piece. There are also several pieces of crucible steel, to be discussed below.

70

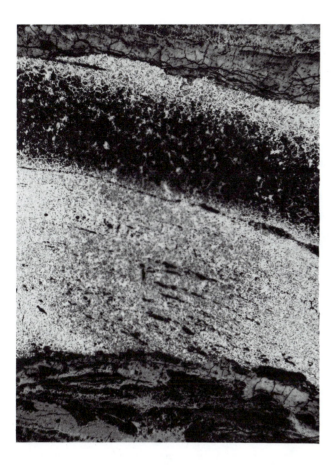

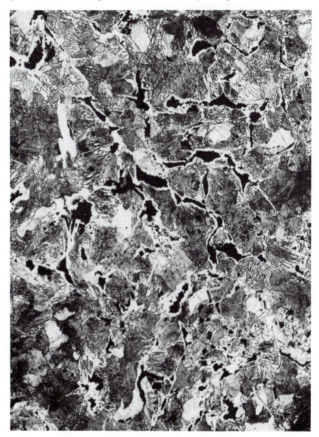

Fig. 3:
Forged bloomery iron from Ungwana (specimen 17/2692b), etched with 3% nital. An obvious weld line separates a strip of near-eutectoid steel from a piece of bloomery iron of irregular carbon content. The elongated black inclusions are slag stringers, and the grey borders are corrosion product. Magnification 18.8×.

Fig. 4:
Microstructure of an unworked nodule of white cast iron (ca. 2.0% C) from Galu (specimen 37/007a), etched with 3% nital. The grey areas are pearlite, the white areas are cementite, and the areas of black tone are entrapped slag (most enclosed by a rim of cementite). Magnification 375×.

All the surviving bloomery iron and steel from Ungwana is in the form of finished artifacts, and is very variable in both carbon content and in the volume and distribution of entrapped slag. Several pieces are of good quality, and two contain well-executed forge welds. No evidence for quenching and tempering was found.[2] In several cases, the pearlite in the steel has been extensively spheroidized; the implications of this for forging technology are discussed below.

One piece of low-carbon steel from Ungwana was dated by radiocarbon, returning a date of 1210±140 B.P. or cal A.D. 595–1030. This falls within the known range of occupation of the site, but the high standard deviation on this date makes it of little use in archaeological interpretation.

Crucible steel

The most interesting finds in this sample are eight pieces of what we believe to be crucible steel. Six of these are from Ungwana and two from Galu. A third sample from Galu may also be crucible steel, but is too badly corroded to be sure (Table 4). All are small; the largest mounted and polished surface is about 35 by 10 mm, but in most cases only cores of metal remain. The metal differs from that of the bloomery irons and steels in two respects. Slag stringers are absent (Fig. 5), except in one case where a piece of this material is welded to bloomery iron containing much

slag. The carbon content is invariably hypereutectoid (> 0.8% C) and the distribution of carbon is absolutely homogeneous within the specimen (Fig. 6). Both characteristics suggest that this is crucible steel rather than bloomery steel.

The microstructures of these pieces are variable. Two samples have been air-cooled (normalized) from the austenite range and, therefore, display a network of proeutectoid cementite (usually with Widmanstatten morphology) around the former austenite grains, now transformed to pearlite. The remaining six specimens have microstructures that resemble those of forged crucible steel (for which see Verhoeven and Jones 1987; Peterson et al. 1990; Verhoeven et al. 1990). Each has a microstructure of

Fig. 5:
Unetched longitudinal section of the best-preserved specimen of crucible steel from Ungwana (specimen 15/3061d). Note the lack of slag stringers. The dark longitudinal bands are caused by chains of tiny, circular, glassy slag inclusions. The larger rounded black areas are corrosion product. Magnification 7.5×.

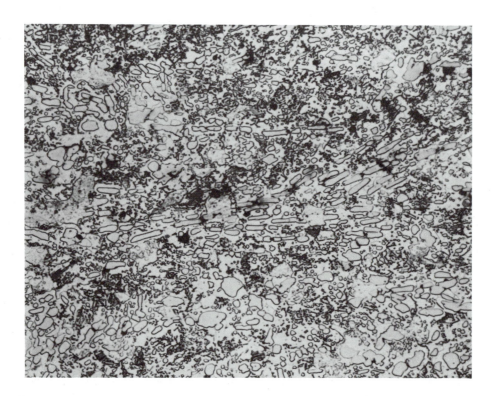

Fig. 6:
Microstructure of crucible steel from Ungwana (specimen 15/3061d), etched with 3% nital. Large blocks and rectangular laths of cementite are present in a matrix of almost completely spheroidized pearlite. The small circular black areas are non-metallic inclusions. Magnification 750×.

subrectangular blocks of cementite, usually 5–20 μm long by 1–10 μm wide, in a matrix of heavily spheroidized pearlite (Fig. 6).

The larger subrectangular grains of cementite are invariably aligned in rows with their longer dimension parallel to the length of the artifact (i.e., perpendicular to the plane of motion of the blacksmith's hammer). In no case did we note the very regular parallel spacing of cementite bands that has been reported in fine Damascus blades (e.g., Peterson et al. 1990). The primary cementite blocks in these specimens are coarser than those reported in fine Damascus blades, which are reported in the range of 4–9 μm (Verhoeven et al. 1990:210). The experiments of Verhoeven and his colleagues with heat treatment and forging of simulated *wootz* ingots suggest that the cementite blocks in the Kenyan specimens originated as either divorced eutectic carbide during solidification from the molten state (mechanism Ia of Verhoeven and Jones 1987), or as grain-boundary allotriomorphs (GBA) around austenite grains formed by lengthy heat treatment of the as-cast microstructure (their mechanism II).

The fully spheroidized pearlitic matrix seen in several of these specimens can only have been produced by prolonged heat treatment below the A_1 temperature (727°C for plain carbon steel) (Samuels 1980:225–246). It is necessary to anneal a 1.4% C steel for between 16 and 32 hours at 700°C to produce a degree of spheroidization comparable to that seen in these artifacts (Samuels 1980:fig. 57). Heavy mechanical work (forging) speeds this transformation considerably, but several hours of such treatment are still required to produce a comparable microstructure. The fact that the primary cementite blocks in our specimens are still subangular, while the matrix is largely or completely spheroidized, strongly suggests that the forging of these pieces was done entirely below A_1. Since this would have taken considerable time, the most likely explanation is that these pieces have been recycled, possibly several times, at forge temperatures not exceeding around 730°C. The two pieces of very clean normalized high carbon steel noted above are probably pieces of cast steel that were heated above the A_{cm} temperature, thereby dissolving the cementite blocks into austenite. A rapid air cooling then produced a structure of Widmanstatten cementite around and within the former austenite grains.

Since only small cores of metal remain in most of these specimens, the skeptic may legitimately ask whether these are not just small areas of unusually clean hypereutectoid bloomery steel. Each of these pieces was originally homogeneous throughout, as proeutectoid cementite laths are preserved in the corrosion product of each of these specimens, and their distribution, shape and orientation correspond exactly to those in the surviving metal (Fig. 7).[3]

The second reason that these pieces are probably crucible steel is the lack of comparable material among samples known to have been produced by the bloomery process. One of us (D.J.K.) has studied more than three hundred samples of bloomery iron and steel from Africa, Europe, and America in the last decade without encountering any samples that are as homogeneous and as clean as these, nor any that have the distinctive subrectangular blocks of cementite seen here. Nor is there, to our knowledge, any published description of comparable material that is known to have been produced by the bloomery process. Lastly, the microstructures of the Kenyan specimens are strikingly similar to published photomicrographs of forged *wootz*, except for the greater degree of spheroidization in the former.

Even if these samples are crucible steels, as we believe, there still remains the possibility that they are intrusive from later levels of the sites. The crucible steel process was independently invented in England around A.D. 1740 and, by the late eighteenth century, crucible steel was the preferred material in Europe for making files. These would certainly have been in the tool-kit of European mariners voyaging to the East Coast of Africa. Some files might have been traded to local blacksmiths and reforged into

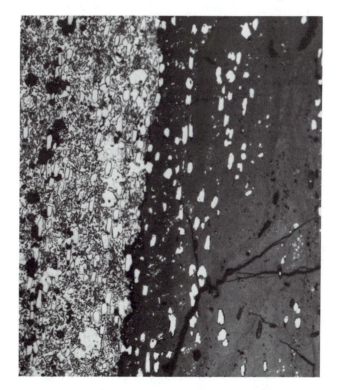

Fig. 7:
Microstructure of a crucible steel artifact from Ungwana (specimen SF 193), etched with 3% nital. The surviving metal consists of aligned subrectangular laths of cementite in a matrix of spheroidized pearlite; the black areas are voids caused by corrosion. Note how the cementite laths survive in the corroded areas, showing that these once had the same microstructure as the surviving metal. Magnification 1000×.

Table 5. AMS radiocarbon dates for steel samples

Site	Sample no.	Material	Lab sample no.	Sample size (mg)	Carbon content (wt. %)	^{14}C age (yrs. B.P.)	Calibrated age range, 2σ (probability)
Ungwana	11/2660b	Crucible & bloomery steel	TO-3889	347	0.9	870±100	A.D. 990–1300 (1.00)
Ungwana	15/3061d	Crucible steel	TO-3890	529	1.4	530±90	A.D. 1290–1520 (0.97)
Ungwana	17/2692b	Bloomery steel	TO-3891	623	0.4	1210±140	A.D. 595–1030 (0.97)
Ungwana	17/2692c	Crucible steel	TO-3892	368	0.3	1360±650	785 B.C.–A.D.1685 (0.99)
Galu	29/002b	Bloomery steel	TO-3893	556	0.3	1400±240	A.D. 125–1050 (0.98)
Galu	32/007a	White cast iron	TO-3894	284	2.0	740±70	A.D. 1170–1400 (1.00)
Galu	33/006b	Crucible steel	TO-3895	355	1.7	1300±70	A.D. 630–890 (1.00)

other items, as they were on the Northwest Coast of North America in the late eighteenth and nineteenth centuries (Wayman 1993).

To make sure that these samples were not intrusive from later levels, four samples were dated directly by radiocarbon at the IsoTrace AMS laboratory. The results are reassuring (Table 5). Two samples from Ungwana returned dates of 530±90 B.P. and 870±100 B.P., corresponding to calendar ranges of A.D. 1290–1520 and A.D. 990–1300, respectively. Both are in agreement with the ages of the strata from which they were excavated, as inferred from imported Islamic and Chinese ceramics. A third sample returned an unusable date of 1360±650 B.P. Its very large standard deviation reflects an unexpectedly low yield of carbon from the sample, probably because the portion used for dating was more severely corroded than that used for metallography.

The fourth sample of crucible steel was from Galu and was dated to 1300±70 B.P., calibrating to a calendar range of A.D. 630–890. The possible implications of this date are discussed below.

Discussion

The picture that emerges from our work on the non-ferrous metals conforms to our prior expectations. Almost all of the copper alloys described here are brasses or gunmetals of low tin and zinc content. Thus, they were either imported from outside sub-Saharan Africa or alloyed in Africa using imported zinc. The former explanation seems more probable, since no metallic zinc has yet been reported on Swahili sites. As there is no counterpart to the tin/lead alloy (Ungwana sample 401) among analyzed samples from the tin-producing areas of southern Africa (Friede and Steel 1976; Killick 1991), this too is probably an import from the north.

The analyzed pieces are mostly petty luxuries, such as jewelry and toilet items, but a broader range of copper objects has been recovered from Swahili sites. At Kilwa

and Manda, for example, the artifact inventory in copper alloys includes door fittings, keys, handles, sewing needles, fine chain, a belt buckle, a tiny vessel with lid, and ornaments of cut and incised sheet that were presumably once attached to cloth or wood (Chittick 1974, vol. 2:448–457; Chittick 1984:203–207). Several fragments of metal mirrors were also recovered by Chittick at Kilwa. One of these was analyzed by Nikolaas van der Merwe (pers. comm.) and proved to be a high-tin bronze mirror similar to published Chinese examples of the period. Thus, copper alloys appear to have been employed by the Swahili primarily for personal adornment and public display, rather than for such mundane purposes as knives, spears, or tableware. This is a pattern that was almost universal in precolonial Africa (Herbert 1984). Copper alloys, in contrast, were widely used for utilitarian purposes in the Islamic world and India, while gold and silver were the metals most valued for adornment and display. Gold jewelry is an essential part of the dowry of elite Swahili women today (Middleton 1992:129), and a few pieces of gold and silver jewelry have been recovered from Swahili archaeological sites. An interesting question for future research is whether the beginning of the use of gold and silver reflects the adoption of Islamic and Arabian social norms among the elites.

There is definite evidence of the forging of bloomery iron at Galu, and iron smelting at Galu and Ungwana. We cannot at present make estimates of the quantity of bloomery iron production at these or any other Swahili sites, although such estimates can be made by using the weight or volume of slag as a proxy measure (e.g., Killick 1990:164–167). One question that we hope to investigate further is whether the coastal sites were self-sufficient in iron, or whether they imported blooms from the mainland. Iron ores are abundant along the northern Kenyan coast in the form of black beach sands, largely composed of magnetite (Fe_3O_4) and ilmenite ($FeTiO_3$). If the Swahili were smelting these ores, then one would expect to find high levels of titania in the slag inclusions within the iron objects smelted from them. No instances of this have yet been found. Chittick (1984:212) had two slag samples from Manda tested for the presence of titania, but neither contained more than a trace. We intend to make a more thorough investigation along these lines, and to investigate the composition of other potential sources of iron ore on the mainland.

The bloomery ironworking technology seen in this sample is no different from that noted elsewhere in sub-Saharan Africa. The absence of evidence for the hardening of steel in this sample conforms to a pattern noted throughout precolonial sub-Saharan Africa. This technique was widely employed in India and the Islamic world, however. Its absence in this sample suggests that there was little transfer of metallurgical technology from these areas to the Swahili coast.

The presence of crucible steel in these sites is not altogether unexpected, for the deposits from which these specimens were excavated contain fine ceramics, glass, beads, and other imports from the Islamic world, the Indian subcontinent, and China. The one major surprise is the early radiocarbon date (cal A.D. 630–890) for a specimen of crucible steel from Galu. There is no technical reason to reject this date, but a radiocarbon date on a bloom from the same deposit is much later (cal A.D. 1170–1400). Possible explanations are that: (1) the crucible steel was curated for at least two centuries before being discarded, or (2) the date reflects the use of old wood, or of a mixture of contemporary and fossil carbon (e.g., coal) by the makers of the crucible steel. If the date is accurate, then it is presently the oldest known specimen of crucible steel; nothing of comparable age is yet known from the Indian subcontinent, where this technology is thought to have been developed (Thelma Lowe, pers. comm.). It is worth noting in this connection that the *Periplus* of the first century A.D. specifically mentions the export of both iron and steel from India to the Axumite port of Adulis in the Red Sea (Casson 1989). If Indian crucible steel was part of this cargo in pre-Islamic times, then it is likely that some of it might have been re-exported to the East African coast.

Crucible steel was historically an expensive material (Bronson 1986), so it is curious that the objects of crucible steel described above are simple items like nails or arrow tangs. These may have been originally imported as somewhat grander objects, such as edged weapons, and were recycled as they broke or wore out (hence the heavily spheroidized microstructures). This reconstruction assumes that the technology for making crucible steel had not itself been transferred to the Swahili coast. Although unlikely, this possibility needs to be investigated. We intend to do so by making a thorough study of the crucibles and other refractory ceramics from Swahili sites.

Eight (and possibly nine) of the 25 iron or steel samples listed in Table 4 are identified as crucible steel, but we do not take this to mean that crucible steel was a common material in Swahili towns. It is probably over-represented in this sample because it is more resistant to corrosion than bloomery iron. This can be seen quite clearly when the state of preservation of the six crucible steel fragments from Ungwana is compared to that of the bloomery iron from the same excavation units. The inferior corrosion resistance of the bloomery iron is clearly related to the presence of slag in the structure and to weld lines. Where either of these intersect the surface of the artifact, corrosion spreads rapidly along them into the interior. This is somewhat ironic, for there is a widespread folk belief among modern metallurgists that bloomery or wrought iron has superior corrosion resistance to plain carbon steel. In this case at least, the reverse is true.

Conclusion

Our studies have been limited by the severe state of corrosion of the iron artifacts, but some interesting findings have emerged. The evidence for indigenous iron working in Swahili sites confirms the observations made by contemporary writers like al-Idrisi. The iron-smelting and blacksmithing technology of the Swahili appears thus far to be entirely African; we see no evidence of technology transfer from Arabia or India. The same conclusion holds thus far for the non-ferrous metallurgy.[4] The apparent lack of technology transfer in metallurgy contrasts strikingly with the transfer of stone-working, architectural, and boat-building technologies from Arabia to the Swahili coast. The reasons for such disparities in technology transfer need to be identified.

We hope that this article has shown that archaeometallurgy can contribute something of value to the ongoing reassessment of Swahili history. We are now extending our study to characterize Swahili iron-smelting technology through analysis of the slags and refractory ceramics. A thorough examination of any excavated ceramic materials that might have been part of a metallurgical process will also be made in the future, particularly crucibles and pieces of casting molds. We also intend to make an inventory of potential ore sources and examine the slags recovered to date from all Swahili sites. We shall distinguish smelting slags from smithing slags on these sites, and hope eventually to be able to decide whether some Swahili towns were, as we suspect, dependent upon supplies of bloom smelted elsewhere.

Acknowledgments

C.M.K. thanks Dr. George Abungu, Dr. Mark Horton, and Mr. Athman Lali Omar for samples of metals from their excavations, and Dr. Vincent Pigott, Professor Nikolaas van der Merwe, and Professor Michael Schiffer for access to laboratory facilities at various times. C.M.K.'s doctoral fieldwork in Kenya, of which this is a part, was supported by a Dissertation Improvement Grant from the National Science Foundation, and by research grants from the Royal Anthropological Institute of Great Britain and Ireland, the National Museums of Kenya, and the Wenner-Gren Foundation for Anthropological Research. We thank Dr. Roelf Beukens of the IsoTrace Laboratory of the University of Toronto for the AMS dating of the steel samples. The AMS dating, sample preparation, and chemical analysis were supported by a grant from the Swedish Agency for Research and Economic Cooperation (S.A.R.E.C.), for which we thank Professor Paul Sinclair. AMS dating was also supported in part by grants to the IsoTrace Laboratory from the Natural Science and Engineering Research Council of Canada. We thank Buehler Ltd. for their generous support of the University of Arizona sample preparation facility, and Suzanne Young and Anthony Ciulla for technical assistance. D.J.K. is most grateful to Thelma Lowe for allowing him to examine her unpublished microsections of unforged and forged Indian *wootz*. Lastly, we thank the two anonymous reviewers for their exceptionally helpful criticism of an earlier draft.

Notes
* Current affiliation/address for this author is as follows: Department of Nuclear Physics, Research School of Physics and Engineering, Australian National University, Canberra, ACT 0200, Australia.

1. The usual method is to stir the molten metal with a green twig.

2. The sections are thin, so one would expect to see evidence of quenching even in the core of the object.

3. For this reason, corrosion product should never be removed from ancient iron before metallographic examination.

4. There is, for example, no present evidence that Swahili metalworkers were acquainted with techniques for soldering non-ferrous metals.

References
Abungu, G. H. O. 1990. *Communities on the River Tana, Kenya: An Archaeological Study of Relations between the Delta and the River Basin, 700–1890 A.D.* Ph.D. dissertation, Cambridge University.

Axelson, E. 1973. *Portuguese in South-East Africa 1488–1600.* C. Struik, Cape Town.

Bronson, B. 1986. The Making and Selling of Wootz, a Crucible Steel of India. *Archaeomaterials* 1:13–51.

Casson, L. 1989. *The Periplus Maris Erythraei.* Princeton University Press, Princeton.

Chittick, N. 1961. *Kisimani Mafia: Excavations at an Islamic Settlement on the East African Coast.* Government Printer, Dar es Salaam.

_____ 1974. *Kilwa: An Islamic Trading City on the East African Coast,* 2 vols. Memoir 5. British Institute in East Africa, Nairobi.

_____ 1984. *Manda: Excavations at an Island Port on the Kenya Coast.* Memoir 9. British Institute in East Africa, Nairobi.

Craddock, P., I. C. Freestone, L. K. Gurjar, A. Middleton, and L. Willies. 1990. Zinc in India. In *2000 Years of Zinc and Brass,* ed. P. Craddock, pp. 29–72. British Museum Occasional Paper 50. London.

Cresswell, R. G. 1991. The Radiocarbon Dating of Iron Artifacts Using Accelerator Mass Spectrometry. *Journal of the Historical Metallurgy Society* 25:76–85.

_____ 1992. Radiocarbon Dating of Iron Artifacts. *Radiocarbon* 34:898–905.

David, N., R. Heimann, D. Killick, and M. Wayman. 1989. Between Bloomery and Blast Furnace: Mafa Iron-smelting Technology in North Cameroon. *The African Archaeological Review* 7:185–210.

Fawcett, W. B., and A. LaViolette. 1990. Iron Age Settlement Around Mkiu, South-Eastern Tanzania. *Azania* 25:19–25.

Freeman-Grenville, G. S. P. 1962. *The East African Coast: Select Documents from the First to the Earlier Nineteenth Century.* Oxford University Press, Oxford.

Friede, H. M., and R. H. Steel. 1976. Tin Mining and Smelting in the Transvaal during the Iron Age. *Journal of the South African Institute of Mining and Metallurgy* 76:461–470.

Hall, M. 1991. *Farmers, Kings and Traders: The Peoples of Southern Africa, 200–1860.* Chicago University Press, Chicago.

al-Hassan, A., and D. R. Hill. 1986. *Islamic Technology.* Cambridge University Press/UNESCO, Cambridge/Paris.

Herbert, E. W. 1984. *Red Gold of Africa.* University of Wisconsin Press, Madison.

Horton, M. 1984. *The Early Settlement of the Northern Kenya Coast.* Ph.D. dissertation, Cambridge University.

_____ 1987. The Swahili Corridor. *Scientific American* 257:86–93.

_____ 1988. Early Muslim Trading Settlements on the East African Coast: New Evidence from Shanga. *The Antiquaries Journal* 68:290–325.

Killick, D. 1990. *Technology in its Social Setting: Bloomery Iron-working at Kasungu, Malawi, 1860–1940.* Ph.D. dissertation, Yale University.

_____ 1991. A Tin Lerale From the Soutpansberg,

Northern Transvaal, South Africa. *South African Archaeological Bulletin* 46:137–141.

_____ in press. On Claims for "Advanced" Ironworking Technology in Precolonial Africa. In *The Culture of African Iron Production*, ed. P. Schmidt. University of Florida Press, Gainesville.

Kirkman, J. 1964. *Men and Monuments on the East African Coast*. Lutterworth Press, London.

_____ 1966. *Ungwana on the Tana*. Mouton, The Hague.

Kusimba, C. M. 1993. *The Archaeology and Ethnography of Iron Metallurgy on the Kenya Coast*. Ph.D. dissertation, Bryn Mawr College.

_____ forthcoming. Kenya's Destruction of the Swahili Cultural Heritage. In *Africa's Disappearing Past: The Erasure of Cultural Patrimony*, ed. P. R. Schmidt and R. J. McIntosh. University of Florida Press, Gainesville.

Lewicki, T. 1969. Arabic External Sources for the History of Africa to the South of the Sahara. *Oddzial Krakowie Prace Komisji Orientalistycznej* 9. Polska Akademia Nauk, Wroclaw.

Middleton, J. 1992. *The World of the Swahili: An African Mercantile Civilization*. Yale University Press, New Haven.

Nurse, D., and T. Spear. 1985. *The Swahili: Reconstructing the History and Language of an African Society, 800–1500*. University of Pennsylvania Press, Philadelphia.

Peterson, D. T., H. H. Baker, and J. D. Verhoeven. 1990. Damascus Steel, Characterization of One Damascus Steel Sword. *Materials Characterization* 24:355–374.

Radimilahy, C. 1993. Ancient Iron Working in Madagascar. In *The Archaeology of Africa: Food, Metals and Towns*, ed. T. Shaw, P. Sinclair, B. Andah, and A. Okpoko, pp. 478–483. Routledge, London and New York.

Samuels, L. E. 1980. *Optical Metallography of Carbon Steels*. American Society for Metals, Metals Park, OH.

Smith, C. S. 1988. *A History of Metallography*, 2nd ed. M.I.T. Press, Cambridge, MA.

Stiles, D. 1982. A History of the Hunting Peoples of the Northern East African Coast. *Paideuma* 28:165–174.

Stuiver, M., and P. J. Reimer. 1993. Extended ^{14}C Data Base and Revised Calib 3.0 ^{14}C Age Calibration Program. *Radiocarbon* 35:215–230.

Trimingham, S. 1964. *Islam in East Africa*. Oxford University Press, Oxford.

van der Merwe, N. J. 1969. *The Radiocarbon Dating of Iron*. University of Chicago Press, Chicago.

Verhoeven, J. D., and L. L. Jones. 1987. Damascus Steel. Part II: Origin of the Damask Pattern. *Metallography* 20:153–180.

Verhoeven, J. D., H. H. Baker, D. T. Peterson, H. F. Clark, and W. M. Yater. 1990. Damascus Steel. Part III: The Wadsworth-Sherby Mechanism. *Materials Characterization* 24:205–227.

Wayman, M. L. 1993. The Early Use of Metal by Native Americans of the Northwest Coast. *Journal of Metals* 45(6):60–64.

Wilson, T. H. 1978. *The Monumental Architecture and Archaeology of the North Kenya Coast*. National Museums of Nairobi, Kenya.

_____ 1980. *The Monumental Architecture and Archaeology of the Central and Southern Kenya Coast*. National Museums of Kenya, Nairobi.

_____ 1982. Spatial Analysis and Settlement on the East African Coast. *Paideuma* 28:201–220.

KAONDE COPPER SMELTING:

TECHNICAL VERSATILITY AND THE ETHNOGRAPHIC RECORD

Duncan Miller

Department of Archaeology, University of Cape Town, Rondebosch 7700, South Africa

ABSTRACT   A detailed eye-witness account of indigenous copper smelting re-enactments which took place in northern Zambia in 1961 is presented. In these demonstrations, copper was smelted from carbonate ore and currency crosses of two different sizes were cast as the product. The group responsible for these demonstrations had toured the country and various descriptions of their work exist. These accounts are summarized and compared with the descriptions presented here. Furnace design and operation differed significantly between the re-enactments. This variation has implications for the interpretation of ethnographic accounts and for archaeological reconstruction of indigenous African copper smelting technologies.

Introduction

In 1961, an elderly Kaonde man named Ndungu and his assistants performed a number of smelting re-enactments in Zambia, then Northern Rhodesia (Fig. 1). Some aspects of these have been described in a number of published accounts (Chaplin 1961; Horizon 1961; Dahn 1964; Wilson 1967; Herbert 1984) and have come to exemplify Kaonde smelting practice. A final demonstration ten years later was witnessed and described by Bisson (1976). In this paper, I present a further eye-witness account of two of Ndungu's copper smelting re-enactments not yet described in the literature. There appear to have been significant differences between Ndungu's various smelting re-enactments when they are all compared, illustrating a technological flexibility which is not apparent from the earlier accounts. This has implications for our conception of historical Kaonde smelting practice and, in general, for the reconstruction of smelting technologies from the description of isolated archaeological remains.

Ndungu originally came from the Kansanshi area, famous for its long history of copper mining (Bisson 1974, 1976, 1989; Bisson et al. 1978; Herbert 1984), and was familiar with the indigenous mining and copper smelting which took place there before European colonization in 1899 (Horizon 1961). Ndungu and a group of helpers, including another elderly man called Jelanda who had additional knowledge of indigenous iron smelting, staged several smelting re-enactments in various parts of the country. These were at the instigation of the Zambian

Provincial Administration, and were sponsored by the Rhodes-Livingstone Museum (Chaplin 1961). Ndungu's group visited the Roan Antelope copper mine at Luanshya in May and performed copper smelting demonstrations at the Seventh Commonwealth Mining and Metallurgical Congress (Horizon 1961) and later at the local Ndola agricultural show (H. Bellardie, pers. comm.).

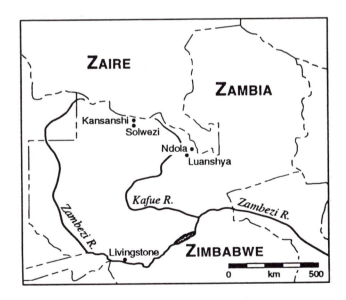

Fig. 1:
A map of Zambia showing the locations referred to in the text.

Mr. Harry Bellardie, a retired mining engineer who worked at the Luanshya Roan Antelope copper mine from January 1934 to March 1973, witnessed the demonstrations at the mine and at the Ndola show. Mr. Bellardie was the sectional engineer in charge of maintenance of the modern copper smelting plant at the mine and therefore was in a particularly good position to appreciate the technical details and intricacies of the reconstructed indigenous smelting operation. He is a highly informed witness so his descriptions of the smelting re-enactments are worth recording in detail. His account differs in some ways from the published accounts of the other smelting re-enactments performed by the same group of people (Horizon 1961; Dahn 1964). There are numerous descriptions of indigenous African iron smelting but relatively few accounts of indigenous copper smelting (Herbert 1984), so Mr. Bellardie's account is in itself a valuable addition to the record.

Description of the Luanshya demonstration

This description is based on my notes and the tape recordings made of our conversation, and is illustrated by diagrams based on the sketches drawn by Mr. Bellardie.

The smelting team consisted of three men from near Mwinilunga in northwestern Zambia. A fairly young man operated the bellows and an older man was in charge of loading the furnace with charcoal and ore. The old smelt master, who was perhaps 90 years old, controlled the operation.

The ore and charcoal used in the smelt were apparently local. The unidentified charcoal was bought, presumably from roadside vendors who still manufacture charcoal by indigenous methods. For instance, when the area around the mines was originally cleared for pine plantations, the felled trees were stacked in two cord heaps, fired from the underside with very dry wood, and covered with inverted sods and earth creating the appearance of huge grave mounds. An acrid smoke was emitted by these smoldering heaps, which burned for about two weeks. The sods had the effect of smothering the flames and the wood became charcoal without burning to ash. This charcoal was bagged and sold at the roadside, as still takes place.

The ore was pure crushed malachite, some of it of gem quality, and presumably was supplied by the mine because the smelting team had not mined it locally. Any inclusions of silica must have been minute because the malachite ore was visually very clean, and there was no deliberate addition of flux. The ore had been trimmed into pieces each about the size of a hen's egg.

The furnace consisted of a hollowed out termite hill—about 60 cm in internal diameter at the base, 45 cm to 50 cm high, and conical with a diameter of about 25 cm at the top (Figs. 2 and 3). The termite hill was hollowed out with steel spikes and spear-type rods like long chisels. These tools were hand-held, and probably were made originally from iron ore smelted locally. The furnace was conical with walls about 8 cm to 10 cm thick and a slight waist on the inside (Fig. 2). This waist may have helped support the charge in the furnace while the reduction took place. The furnace was set onto a slightly concave base of smoothed clay forming a floor about 5 cm thick.

The two clay tuyeres were attached to a pair of hand-operated bag bellows consisting of animal bladders supported on a clay base. The bladders were intact except for

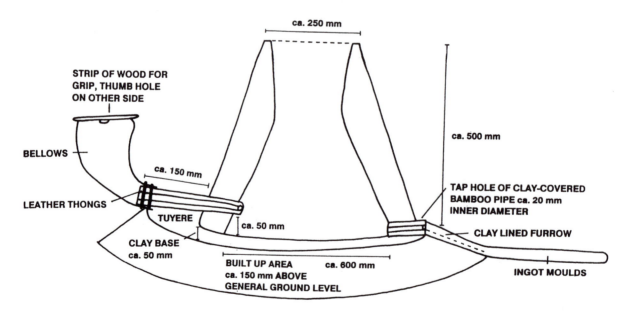

Fig. 2:
A vertical section through one of the furnaces constructed at the Roan Antelope mine.

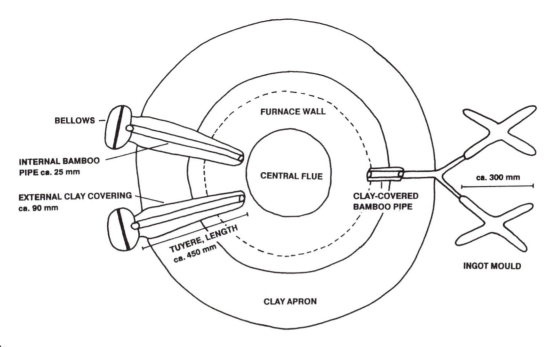

Fig. 3:
A plan drawing of one of the furnaces constructed at the Roan Antelope mine.

a slit at the top which had a thumb hole on one side and a flat slat of wood as a grip on the other. These features enabled the slit to be operated manually as an inlet valve. The tuyeres, consisting of clay-covered bamboo pipes, were made before the smelt; the clay covering was dried but not fired before use. The tuyeres were inserted through the furnace wall on one side and entered the furnace at a shallowly inclined angle that pointed downwards, but above the estimated level of the molten copper product. They were cemented in place with wet clay. The internal bamboo pipes were about 2.5 cm in diameter and the outer clay created an external diameter of 8–9 cm. The lower openings of the bellows were tied to the tuyeres with leather thongs.

On the opposite side of the furnace, there was a tap hole consisting of a clay-covered bamboo pipe, approximately 2 cm in internal diameter, that was set in the base of the furnace wall. It protruded about 15 cm from the furnace wall and led to a channel that sloped slightly downward to the prepared molds. This pipe was plugged on the outside with a damp clay plug at the beginning of the smelt. The inner ends of the bamboo pipes in the tuyeres and tapping pipe charred during the course of the smelt.

The two ingot molds were prepared before the smelt began. Each mold was about 45 cm to 60 cm away from the actual furnace and was formed in the ground. The molds were made by scraping two symmetrical crosses into the earth, cutting them with a steel blade, and shaping them so that they tapered slightly towards the bottom. They were level and the molten copper could be led into one arm of one cross by blocking the access to the other cross with a

clay dam in the feeder channel. The molds were smoothed out with clay and then dried. They had to be absolutely dry because molten copper explodes violently on contact with wet sand or soil. The clay-lined molds were baked in position by placing burning charcoal in them just before use which heated the molds so that the copper could run into them without freezing prematurely.

The smelting started with charging the furnace with charcoal and then lighting it. The bellows man, who was obviously well trained, pumped continuously throughout the process, about three quarters of an hour. Seated between the tuyeres, he worked both bellows alternately to maintain an almost continuous air supply.

The second man started introducing the ore charge when the furnace was hot and the charcoal burned freely. Lumps of charcoal and malachite ore were added alternately at that time, and a handful (about half a dozen pieces) of ore was added intermittently throughout the subsequent duration of the smelt. More charcoal than malachite was added and there was no addition of silica or other materials to act as a flux. The appearance of green smoke and flame slightly tinged with purple from the furnace flue indicated the onset of the actual smelting reaction. At this stage, the bellows man speeded up his operation while the old man started an incantation. The rhythm of the chanting was taken up by the bellows man and all three participants chanted while more charcoal was added. The flames remained green from this point until the furnace was tapped.

After about three quarters of an hour of continuous pumping, the clay plug was removed from the tap hole by wiggling a sharp iron spike around in it. The copper ran out forcefully because, at that stage, the molten metal had built up quite high in the furnace. It squirted out of the tap hole into the feeder and ran down the slope into one of the preheated molds swept clear of charcoal. Some residual ash and charcoal fragments floated to the top when the molten copper was introduced. Only one large ingot was cast at the Luanshya demonstration. The smelters were apparently very good at judging how much copper ore to load so that the metal just filled the mold of the large copper cross. The large H-shaped ingot weighed about 9 kg.[1]

The furnace was only used once for this demonstration and then abandoned. The entire process, from hollowing out the termite hill to producing the cast ingot took about two days, excluding the time taken to produce the charcoal and trim the ore.

Description of the demonstration at the Ndola show

The smelters produced several small X-shaped ingots to sell as souvenirs at a subsequent series of demonstrations at the Ndola show. A parallel series of molds were used to cast the small ones. In one demonstration, they were fed from several different feeder channels. The flow to each channel could be blocked off with a clay cone rammed into place with an iron plate attached to a rod. In another demonstration at the Ndola show, an earthenware bowl was loosely built into the floor of the furnace and the molten copper collected in the bowl during the smelt. The furnace wall was broken down and the bowl was removed by hand with suitable protection provided by wads of grass, clay, and bark. The molten copper was then poured by hand into each small mold, producing a series of ingots about 25 cm long. All of these small ingots were shaped like the small cross-shaped *handa* ingots from northwestern Zambia.[2]

Published descriptions of the other smelting re-enactments

Chaplin (1961)

Chaplin's account describes three smelts: Lungu iron smelting at Chibote Mission, 50 km northwest of Luwingu in the Northern Province; Kaonde copper smelting at Solwezi, about 16 km from Kansanshi; and Kaonde iron smelting, also at Solwezi. Malachite ore was recovered for the copper smelt from the Kansanshi outcrops and trimmed to about a cubic centimeter in size. The furnace, about 40 cm high, was built of termite hill fragments bound with clay and the single tuyere, about 15 cm long, also consisted of a perforated termite hill. The nozzles of the bag bellows, made out of an inverted *sitatunga* (*Tragelaphus spekei*) skin, were inserted into the tuyere pipe and were held in place with small stakes.

The fired furnace was charged with charcoal and ore and, after three hours, a stick poked through the central flue

revealed the presence of molten copper. This was tapped through a vent produced by breaking down a section of the furnace. This "crude copper" was then melted in a second furnace and the molten metal collected on a bed of ash inside an open clay pot embedded in the floor of the furnace. The furnace was broken down to remove the pot, but attempts to decant the molten copper into a mold cut into a piece of termite hill were unsuccessful because the pot was too hot. The illustrations to this paper include a characteristically buttressed iron smelting furnace and a smaller copper smelting furnace (Chaplin 1961:pl. IIA, B). Ritual was apparently unimportant in this copper smelting demonstration. "No medicines were used, and orientation of the kiln was not significant. The only prohibition was for ritually 'impure' people to refrain from touching the ore, or crude copper" (Chaplin 1961:57).

Horizon (1961)

This paper records that "for a month the group demonstrated the copper and iron smelting methods at the African craft village at the Victoria Falls, and then in May visited Roan Antelope, where they intrigued hundreds of visitors to the Seventh Commonwealth Mining and Metallurgical Congress with their demonstrations" (Horizon 1961:31). The photographic illustrations of furnaces were taken at Roan Antelope and include a copper furnace and another example of a buttressed iron smelting furnace (Horizon 1961:31, 32). The copper furnace was built out of pieces of termite hill and had a double tuyere and *sitatunga* skin bag bellows. An ash-filled clay pot was built into the base of the furnace. The charcoal was lit through the tuyere and, once it was burning well, the ore was added slowly. After about 40 minutes of pumping a green stick was used to test for the presence of molten copper. The furnace was broken down and the blast directed onto the top of the clay pot to concentrate the molten copper onto the ash surface. Then the pot was removed, using wads of dried grass for insulation, and the copper was poured into molds cut into builders' bricks or pieces of termite hill.

Dahn (1964)

This paper, illustrated with a reproduction of the photograph of the bellows operator from Horizon (1961:31), does not describe the technical process but repeats that Ndungu was a Kaonde from Solwezi and was familiar with copper mining and smelting at Kansanshi (Dahn 1964:6).

Wilson (1967)

This paper reproduces four of the photographs from Horizon (1961), failing to distinguish the characteristically buttressed Kaonde iron furnace from a copper smelting furnace. A generalized account of copper smelting and casting is presented that is an anecdotal conflation of descriptions from a variety of sources.

Bisson (1976)

Bisson witnessed a smelting re-enactment performed by the same team in 1971. He noted discrepancies between Chaplin's account of the 1961 smelts and those he witnessed ten years later, but ascribed these to "the result of the declining strength of these last Kaonde copper smelters" (Bisson 1976:49). The major difference was the absence of the initial smelting stage and the copper was caught directly in an ash-filled pot set into the furnace base. Water soaked grass pads bound with bark ropes were used to remove the pot from the furnace by hand, but three attempts to pour the molten copper to fill a mold were frustrated by slag obstructing the free flow of the copper.

Herbert (1984)

Herbert provides an extremely faithful transliteration of Chaplin's 1961 account of the Kaonde copper smelting re-enactment at Solwezi.

Discussion and concluding remarks

The previously published accounts of Kaonde copper smelting summarized above depend entirely on three descriptions (Chaplin 1961; Horizon 1961; Bisson 1976). They describe three different but superficially similar enactments that took place in northern Zambia. All three describe the building of the relatively small furnace out of pieces of termite hill bound together with clay.[3] Two of them involve a two-stage process with the initial production of "crude" copper and its subsequent refinement by melting it in an ash-filled bowl. The latter acted as a casting crucible. These steps were completely separated in one case, while they took place sequentially in the same furnace structure in the other case. This two-step process appears to have been the one demonstrated in 1961 at Livingstone and later also at Roan Antelope (Horizon 1961), as well as at the Ndola show (H. Bellardie, pers. comm.). The 1971 re-enactment seen by Bisson was a one-step process producing molten copper directly in the crucible bowl. The Luanshya re-enactment also used a one-step process to produce enough copper to tap molten metal directly from the furnace.

The construction of the tuyeres differed significantly between the re-enactments reported by Chaplin (and Bisson) and Bellardie. The single tuyere consisted of the hollowed out tip of a conical termite hill in the former, while the two tuyeres for the larger furnace consisted of clay-covered bamboo tubes in the latter. There is no record of whether a specially selected clay was used for this purpose, as is known to have been the case elsewhere in central Africa (Childs 1989).

A detailed comparison of these smelting re-enactment accounts reveals that the re-enactments all differed from each other, sometimes very considerably. In the first re-enactment at Solwezi (Chaplin 1961), the furnace was small, manufactured from pieces of termite hill, and operated with one tuyere. The copper was tapped before subsequent remelting in a second furnace and was collected in an ash-lined bowl for pouring into a mold cut from an termite hill. The process was similar in the Livingstone re-enactment(s), but there the molten copper was collected in a ceramic bowl built into the smelting furnace (Horizon 1961). Apparently, this was also the case for at least one of the Roan Antelope re-enactments (Horizon 1961)—the one at the Ndola show (H. Bellardie, pers. comm.)—and the 1971 attempts (Bisson 1976). The other two re-enactments described by Mr. Bellardie, one at Roan Antelope and the other also at the Ndola show, involved tapping molten copper directly from the furnace and allowing it to run into preheated molds of two different sizes. The double tuyere furnaces in these latter cases were much larger and were built from whole, hollowed-out termite hills. The attachment of the bellows to the tuyeres by thongs also differed from the other accounts—the bellows nozzles, made from a variety of materials, were inserted directly into the tuyere(s) and were held in place with stakes.

What are we to make of these differences, particularly the record of tapping molten metal at Luanshya? Mr. Bellardie's account cannot be dismissed as a fabrication. It is lucid and detailed, and describes well the differences between the various re-enactments which took place at Roan Antelope and at the Ndola show. Clearly, the Kaonde copper smelting re-enactments embodied a variety of techniques, and the range of knowledge of the smelting team was not evident from the observations made of any single performance. The team was capable of successful copper production by using a variety of techniques. In several demonstrations, they cast traditionally shaped ingots of different shapes and sizes by tapping molten copper and by pouring from a crucible.

We have no way of knowing to what extent these smelting re-enactments may have been affected by the practitioners' experience with modern copper technology, but there is no recorded evidence that the smelters received advice from modern mining technologists. If these re-enactments can be taken to represent Kaonde copper smelting technology, then it was far more diverse technically than is evident from the previously published accounts (Chaplin 1961; Horizon 1961; Bisson 1976; Herbert 1984).

Given the demonstrated technical versatility of the Kaonde smelters, ethnographic accounts which purport to describe the typical metals production technology of any particular group must be read with caution. Not only can re-enactments be affected in unpredictable ways by the presence and inadvertent input of observers, but the full spectrum of possible production techniques may not be evident in a single demonstration.

This finding, in turn, has implications for the archaeological reconstruction of metal technologies in general.

The bewildering diversity of furnace shapes, sizes, and layouts encountered in Africa may not only reflect regional and temporal diversity, but also diverse smelting practices within any one community. Inspection of a single furnace alone, like inspection of a single metal artifact, cannot support the reconstruction of an entire production technology.

There are potentially significant elements missing from all the ethnographic accounts described above. The chanting observed by Mr. Bellardie indicates that in Kaonde copper smelting ritual was probably not as insignificant as stated by Chaplin (1961). Ritual may have been played down in these re-enactments, but the fact that Mr. Bellardie noted that the bellows operator took up the rhythm shows that this chant was an integral part of the smelting operation. The distinction between ritual and technique is seldom (if ever) made by indigenous African metalworkers (van der Merwe and Avery 1987).

No explanation was offered in the recorded accounts for the diversity of techniques employed by Ndungu's smelting team. The volume of copper required may have decided the furnace size and whether copper would be caught in a bowl or tapped directly from the furnace. The recovery of smaller amounts of copper using a bowl, either in a secondary furnace or built into the floor of a small primary smelting furnace, is more probable, whereas a larger amount of copper may have made the use of the bowl impractical and unnecessary. Larger amounts could be tapped directly from the larger furnaces by exploiting the pressure of the pool of molten copper and slag inside.[4] It is tempting to speculate that, historically, the production requirements could have determined the smelting techniques used. Particular craftsmen may have used a variety of smelting and casting techniques to produce differently shaped or sized products in response to market demand. If this was the case, then the archaeological record could be far more complex than generally thought, with a diversity of coeval styles and techniques used for copper production.[5]

Ndungu's 1961 re-enactments of Kaonde copper smelting are a series of demonstrations of the technical versatility of one group of indigenous metalworkers. They show that significant differences can exist between successive re-enactments by one group of smelters. These re-enactments took place 40 years after the routine production of copper using these methods had ceased, which makes the largely successful application of this diversity of techniques all the more remarkable.

Acknowledgments

I wish to thank Judith Sealy, Terry Childs, Petar Glumac, and Michael Bisson for their helpful comments on drafts of this paper, and Mr. and Mrs. Bellardie most warmly for the time and effort they spent speaking to me, corresponding with me, tracking down references, and commenting on the figures and drafts of this paper. Financial support from Anglo-American De Beers Chairman's Fund Educational Trust and the Foundation for Research Development (CSIR, South Africa) for research at the University of Cape Town into early mining and metallurgy is acknowledged with thanks.

Notes

1. From Mr Bellardie's description, it appears to have been similar to the H-shaped ingot, like those from Ingombe Ilede and illustrated by Bisson (1975:fig. 8E), but he described the molds as "cross-shaped."

2. A similar one is also illustrated by Bisson (1975:fig. 8D).

3. I am indebted to Michael Bisson for pointing out that this form of construction appears to be similar to that used for smelting furnaces at Kansanshi and Kipushi (Bisson 1976) and at Luano near Lubumbashi (Anciaux de Faveaux and Maret 1980, 1984; Maret 1981). This would suggest that the furnace design has a history of at least 600 to 700 years.

4. Unfortunately, there is no record of collection, preservation, or analysis of slag samples from these re-enactments.

5. It has been suggested that trace element or lead isotope studies might identify ingots of different size and design that originated from the same or different sources (S. Terry Childs, pers. comm.). Obviously, the potential success of such an enterprise would depend on the distinct geochemical characterization of the various known sources of copper in south-central Africa. This has been initiated (Bisson et al. 1978). The analysis of ingots, which presumably represent primary material and hence would be good candidates for sourcing studies, could verify if the crosses cast in the Zambian/Katanga copper belt were traded primarily northwards into Zaire, as is believed to be the case (Bisson 1975; Childs 1991).

References

Anciaux de Faveaux, E., and P. de Maret. 1980. Vestiges de l'âge du fer dans les environs de Lubumbashi. *Africa-Tervuren* 23:13–19.

_____ 1984. Premières datations pour la fonte du cuivre au Shaba (Zaïre). *Bulletin Société Royale Belge d'Anthropologie et de Préhistoire* 95:5–20.

Anon. 1961. An Ancient Smelting Craft Revived. *Horizon* 3(8):30–32.

Bisson, M. S. 1974. Prehistoric Copper Mining in Northwestern Zambia. *Archaeology* 27(4):242–248.

_____ 1975. Copper Currency in Central Africa. *World Archaeology* 6:272–292.

_____ 1976. *The Prehistoric Coppermines of Zambia.* Unpublished Ph.D. dissertation, Department of Anthropology, University of California, Santa Barbara.

_____ 1989. Continuity and Discontinuity in Copperbelt and North-western Province Ceramic Sequences. *Nyame Akuma* 31:43–46.

Bisson, M. S., F. T. Hedgecock, G. G. Kennedy, and D. F. Wolford. 1978. Trace Element Analysis of Prehistoric Copper Samples from Kansanshi and Kipushi Mines. *Nyame Akuma* 12:49–51.

Chaplin, J. H. 1961. Notes on Traditional Smelting in Northern Rhodesia. *South African Archaeological Bulletin* 16:53–60.

Childs, S. T. 1989. Petrographic Analysis of Archaeological Ceramics. *Materials Research Society Bulletin* 14:24–29.

_____ 1991. Transformations: Iron and Copper Production in Central Africa. In *Recent Advances in Archaeometallurgical Research*, ed. P. Glumac, pp. 33–46. MASCA Research Papers in Science and Archaeology 8, part 1. University of Pennsylvania Museum, Philadelphia.

Dahn, J. 1964. The Dying Race of Craftsmen. *Horizon* 6(12):4–9.

Herbert, E. W. 1984. *Red Gold of Africa*. University of Wisconsin Press, Madison.

Maret, P. de. 1981. L'évolution monétaire du Shaba central entre le 7e et le 18e siècle. *African Economic History* 10:117–149.

van der Merwe, N. J., and D. H. Avery. 1987. Science and Magic in African Technology: Traditional Iron Smelting in Malawi. *Africa* 57(2):143–172.

Wilson, J. A. R. 1967. Ancient Copper Production in Central Africa. *Horizon* 9(4):26–29.

Fig. 1:
The Jenne mosque, from the northeast corner. Photograph by B. E. Frank, 1983.

MASONS OF MALI:

A MILLENNIUM OF DESIGN AND TECHNOLOGY IN EARTHEN MATERIALS

Adria LaViolette

Department of Anthropology, University of Virginia, Charlottesville, VA 22903

ABSTRACT The earthen buildings of the West African sudanic region have come to world attention over the last twenty years as part of a broader fascination with "indigeneous" architecture. In the West African Sudan, life-long specialist masons design and build rectilinear, often multi-story structures of sunbaked brick that use a minimum of timber and are held together with mud mortar. Masons plaster their constructions inside and out with specialized mixtures of mud and other natural materials tailored to each surface, which function to maintain the integrity of the brick underneath. These coatings and recoatings lend to the structures both a massiveness and a sensual plasticity of form for which Sudanese architecture has gained its renown.

This paper examines select aspects of Sudanese buildings and their builders, as they occur in Jenne, Mali: a multi-ethnic town of about 12,000 people considered one of the historical headquarters of the master masons of the Sudan. Jenne is the site of the single most famous example of Sudanese architecture, the Jenne mosque, and is considered a center of this building style. This paper does not focus on the design of the buildings, but on the "impermanent" substances that comprise material culture *per se*—in this case, unbaked brick, sandy plaster, glutinous mud mixtures—and their linkages to the archaeology of complex society in Africa. I also contextualize the building materials with the people responsible for their use and the broader sociohistorical setting in which they have been developed and used.

Introduction

The earthen buildings of the West African sudanic region have come to world attention over the last twenty years as part of a broader fascination with "indigenous" architecture (the American Southwest, North Africa, and the Middle East are other areas of interest; see, e.g., Bourgeois et al. 1989; Iowa 1985; Leslie 1991; Werner 1992). In the West African Sudan, life-long specialist masons design and build rectilinear, often multi-story, structures of sunbaked brick that use a minimum of timber and are held together with mud mortar. Masons plaster their constructions inside and out with specialized mixtures of mud and other natural materials tailored to each surface, which function to maintain the integrity of the brick under-neath. These coatings and recoatings lend to the structures both a massiveness and a sensual plasticity of form for which Sudanese architecture has gained its renown.

This paper examines selected aspects of Sudanese buildings and their builders in Jenne, Mali: a multi-ethnic town of about 12,000 people considered one of the histori-cal headquarters of the master masons of the Sudan. These masons, called the Jenne *bari* (all foreign terms herein are Sonhray), are one of several groups of artisans among whom I conducted a total of six part-time and 12 full-time months of research in 1981 and 1983, respectively (LaViolette 1987). I conducted much of the research with masons in French, and when this was not possible, with the aid of interpreters speaking Sonhray in Jenne, and Bambara or Bozo in area villages. Jenne is the site of the single most famous example of Sudanese architecture, the Jenne mosque (see Fig. 1), and is on the world heritage list due principally to its spectacular array of Sudanese buildings (see Figs. 2 and 3). Indeed, the "look" of the town has been under the protection of the Malian government for over a decade. My purpose is not to focus on the design of the buildings themselves, which has been done thoroughly in other venues (see below). Rather, I want to draw attention to "impermanent" substances as comprising material culture

Fig. 2:
The Monday regional market in Jenne, taken from the roof of the mosque, facing east. Photograph by B. E. Frank, 1983.

per se—in this case unbaked brick, sandy plaster, glutinous mud mixtures—and these substances' linkages to the archaeology of complex society in Africa. Also, I wish to contextualize the building materials with the people responsible for their use, and briefly, with the broader sociohistorical setting in which they have been developed and used.

Jenne's architecture in a research context

Masterful "Sudanese" architecture has long been acknowledged in the Western Sudan's own patrimony: in its historical chronicles (e.g., es-Sa'di 1981; Kati 1981), and in conceptions of the powerful and of Islam. Early European travelers were struck by the urban and religious architecture (e.g., Caillie 1830; Park 1799), and it was documented during the French colonial administration in historically weighty locales such as Jenne (especially Monteil 1903, 1932) and Timbuktu (Dubois 1897). Western interest in Sudanese building was restimulated particularly by Prussin's appreciative architectural-historical research (e.g., 1970, 1974, 1977, 1986) which focused in its early phase on Jenne (related studies concerning West African architecture include Blier 1987; Bourdier and Minh-ha

1985; Brasseur 1968; Denyer 1978; Devisse 1983; Engstrom 1955, 1957, 1959; and R. Gardi 1974). Jenne has remained in the scholastic limelight due to the nexus of several fields of fruitful study. These include archaeology, through which we know that within sight of Jenne is the locale of the earliest urban system to evolve in sub-Saharan Africa known to date, Jenne-jeno (e.g., R. McIntosh and S. McIntosh 1981, 1988; S. McIntosh and R. McIntosh 1980, 1984; also Bedaux et al. 1978). Ongoing research at Jenne-jeno has provided us with literally volumes about the deep cultural, socioeconomic, and geomorphological history of this area.

Excavations at Jenne-jeno have also revealed much about the evolution of building techniques here, beginning ca. 300 B.C.: from seasonal wattle-and-daub encampments; to permanent, round, honeycombed structures of coursed mud, or *banco*, and later, small cylindrical bricks (*jennefrey*); to rectilinear structures of these bricks (S. McIntosh and R. McIntosh 1980). *Jennefrey* remained in use until the early twentieth century, when colonialists introduced larger rectangular molded bricks (*tubabufrey*; see below). Such archaeologically documented changes provide insight into broader socioeconomic and political change in the region—from the early Iron Age seasonal habitation of mixed farmers, fishers, and herders through the evolution of a densely populated urban settlement system that spread across the floodplain by the eighth century A.D. We are also quite probably seeing, in the evolution of building style and the growing demands of first an urban and then a Muslim elite, the emergence of specialists in earthen masonry.

My ethnoarchaeological study (LaViolette 1987, 1995) focused on artisans (primarily masons, potters, and blacksmiths), the technology of their arts, and the social and economic systems in which the artisans were articulated (see also the encyclopedic studies of the region's human geography by Gallais 1967, 1984; and see B. Gardi 1981, 1983 for related work on artisans in nearby Mopti). Research on the anatomy of Jenne's architecture continues, and has resulted in a spate of scholarly and photographic publications (e.g., Bourgeois 1987; Maas 1986; van Gijn 1983; van Rangelrooy 1984; Snelder 1984; van der Velden 1989) including the recent comprehensive architectural-historical study of Jenne by Maas and Mommersteeg (1992).

The Jenne *bari*

The masons with permanent residences in Jenne numbered about 100 in late 1983, although their skills were in such demand that many were employed in other parts of Mali, and in other West African countries. While the Jenne *bari* are the most highly reputed participants in West Africa's huge industry of earthen masonry, centuries of apprenticeship, population shifts, and building campaigns have resulted in active masons' groups in many regions of West Africa. Jenne's hinterland villages are often home to their own masons, some of whom have apprenticed with Jenne *bari*, but who exercise their own micro-traditions, teach others, and often find work far afield. It is appropriate, then, to think of at least the nineteenth and twentieth century sudanic building style about which we know the most as a Jenne school of architecture, which has evolved with different regional characteristics within an extensive and deep tradition in the Western Sudan.

Fig. 3:
Examples of Sudanese domestic architecture. The house at right, which dates to the later nineteenth century at the latest, is considered the oldest one still standing in the town. Only the front has been replastered recently; rain and wind have eroded the sides and rear of the house. Photograph by A. LaViolette, 1983.

Contemporary masons do not articulate closely with specialists of the *nyamakalaw*: the usually endogamous, socially distinct, lineage-based professional groups such as blacksmiths, potters, leather workers, and bards found throughout the Mande-speaking region of West Africa (see, e.g., Bird and Kendall 1980; Camara 1976; Conrad and Frank forthcoming; Gallais 1967; McNaughton 1988; N'Diayé 1970; Tamari 1991). For example, unlike the majority of *nyamakalaw*, the *bari* are fully intermarried with "noble," undifferentiated farmer/fisher populations, frequently accept young men from diverse origins—except *nyamakalaw*—as apprentices, and have what would appear to be a social status more akin to that of elite businessmen, say, than any other of the prominent Jenne artisans. This extra-*nyamakala* status need not be ancient, but it does not appear to be recent (LaViolette 1990).

Tamari's (1991) review and historiographic analysis of "casted" specialists in West Africa, drawing from the majority of informative African, Arabic, and European historical accounts, does not consider masons; it focuses instead, as the sources themselves do, on bards, blacksmiths, goldsmiths, weavers, woodworkers, and leatherworkers (e.g., Caillié 1830; es-Sa'di 1981; Kati 1981). However, one mention of builders to receive attention is in an early nineteenth century addendum to the seventeenth century chronicle, *Tarikh el-Fettach* (Kati 1981). This addendum, meant to be read as contemporary with the original version, contains an allusion to large groups of state-controlled builders (and other artisans) which supposedly existed under Sonhray ruler Askia Mohammed in the fifteenth century. This reference to the political arrangements of an earlier state, from which the later state wished to draw political analogies about its own jurisdiction over artisan labor, including masons, suggests that state-sponsored building campaigns using state-controlled specialist labor was desirable (Levtzion 1971), if probably not achieved (Tamari 1991:235). Nonetheless, the nineteenth century effort to control the labor of the *bari* or groups like them is not at all surprising, given that the deployment of their impressive knowledge had fabulous potential for the assertion of power.

Without more specific historical references to early masons' activities or their status vis-à-vis other artisans and/or the halls of power, we are limited to archaeological evidence for the early presence and role of masons. While we tend to associate the masons' activities with Islam, their origins predate Muslim influence and conversion in the region (S. McIntosh and R. McIntosh 1980; Denyer 1978:162). Signature building techniques existed prior to the adoption of Islamic architectural forms into the local repertoire. It is highly likely that groups of masons worked in the area of Jenne from at least the eighth century A.D., when a massive 3 km brick wall—of the cylindrical *jennefrey* bricks the *bari* claim as one of their trademarks—was built around the full circumference of the urban mound of Jenne-jeno (S. McIntosh and R. McIntosh 1980). It has been suggested that peripatetic Manding traders and religious leaders diffused the building style (Prussin 1974:171ff.). Alternatively, Denyer (1978:161–162) has suggested that building in bricks was autochthonously developed as densely populated urban centers grew in the Sudan of the first centuries A.D., as a strategy to deal with drought, heat, and fire. The "millennium" in this paper's title is clearly conservative. Whatever the early nature of their organizational structure, which due to the demands and logistics of building—and the organization of society around them—would probably have included hierarchically arranged teamwork, the masons have certainly gone through numerous transformations. The *bari* maintain their own traditions (see, e.g., Bourgeois 1987; Prussin 1974:appendix D), which focus on watershed building projects and major personality dynamics, and even relations with authority, but which are chronologically too shallow to shed light on origins.

The contemporary Jenne masons constitute a guild-like structure, called the *bari ton*, of about twelve major lineages, with a single head, by-laws, fixed wages for lower-level masons, formal apprenticeships, meetings, and dues. They are more explicitly organized than the strictly lineage-based groups of the *nyamakalaw* (LaViolette 1990) In their lifetimes, masons pass through four professional strata according to age, experience, and achievements, from apprentice to master. The vertical relationships are kin-based, although the apprenticeship structure is open to non-family members and young men of other ethnic groups (see below), a phenomenon seen more in the villages than in Jenne, where there is no shortage of family members committed to becoming masons.

The Jenne *bari* are, in the twentieth century, predominantly from two ethnic groups which are seemingly unlikely partners: the Bozo (or Sorko), and the Sonhray. The former are primarily fishers but also cultivate, and in Jenne culture they are accepted as the autochthones, who have the mixed legacy of first inhabitants, on the one hand, and being the conquered, the ones to have lost political control, on the other. Nor do the Bozo have symbolic power within the masons, although this does not speak to their wealth or individual status, which equals that of Sonhray, or to their number, which is greater. The Sonhray are the most urban of the Middle Niger groups, engaging in farming and commerce and no other major specialization except masonry. The head of the Jenne *bari* has come from a single Sonhray lineage for over a century. Diverse masons claim that this Sonhray/Bozo partnership is rooted in building campaigns, when the Sonhray, who were the original masons, drafted the help of lower-status Bozo men as a workforce (LaViolette 1987). Although this tradition may shed light on the evolution of what we see today, the nature of changing ethnic identities and relations would warn us against placing too much historical depth on recent constructs. Despite whatever transformations have taken place, the presence of specialized building technology in the Jenne region by the eighth century at the latest (S. McIntosh and R. McIntosh 1980) speaks to the long and complicated history of building here, of which we have but scratched the surface.

Tools and techniques of the trade

The engineering, design, and chemical knowledge behind Sudanese architecture is the real treasure of the *bari*. Visually, what makes the architecture work is the choice of design elements from a fairly large but well-defined repertoire which includes façades incorporating mass, open spaces, small pillars, and projections; arches; verandas; courtyards; balustrades; decorative and functional internal niches; indoor latrines and water management systems; and metal-studded windows and doors. Despite the "traditional" feel of Jenne, style has, of course, changed over time (see Maas and Mommersteeg 1992), and certainly not every client can afford to incorporate all or even any of the most favored features. The talents of the masons include the ability to scale their structures to the wants of the client, to think through the often complex architectural plan without resorting to paper, and to work with particular clients to individualize structures within the aesthetic vocabulary of Jenne. Masons and their clients innovate all the time.

The work is carried out with the most basic tools, and never with a formal blueprint (see Maas and Mommersteeg 1992:184 and back cover for masons' drawings in the sand). The toolkit in the Jenne region comprises about a dozen objects, most of which are locally developed and made, with some tools synthesizing characteristics of imported ones (see Fig. 4). The tools are: a round iron bar about a meter long and 2–2.5 cm in section, resembling a crowbar, with one flared and sharpened end; a trowel; an ax; a sturdy basket of woven rushes; a flat piece of wood about 20 cm square and 1–2 cm thick with a handle affixed to one side; another length of wood resembling a two-by-four; copious amounts of string and rope; a line level; a plumb bob; a sponge; a measuring tool such as a tape or folding rule; and, for those who work often with cement, a roller for roughening cemented floor surfaces.

At the core of the kit are four all-purpose tools: the iron bar, the trowel, the stick of wood, and string or rope, the first two of which are made locally by blacksmiths (the trowel is sometimes an import). The bar is a standard measure, to double, triple, and so on; the flared end is a chisel to score and break bricks, to push things into place, and to dig. The wood is used to align bricks and to measure out door and window openings. Masons use the trowel as a worker would anywhere, to scoop and spread mud

between bricks and on surfaces, and to smooth wall plaster. String and rope are used in place of surveying instruments, no matter how large the building is to be. The wood square and the sponge are for applying interior wall and ceiling plaster with finesse.

The raw materials for construction are also few: mudbricks; several kinds of mud plaster; wooden poles for roof beams; architectural pottery; sometimes, nowadays, a small amount of cement; and window and door elements in wood or metal (see Maas and Mommersteeg 1992 for detailed drawings of all architectural elements). Children and adolescents make bricks during much of the year, but especially when the water which encircles Jenne (when the Niger and Bani rivers flood annually) slowly recedes and leaves a rim of clayey mud ideal for brickmaking. The brickmakers capture water on the edge of town in pools, each a few meters in diameter, add grass, and leave the mixture to sit for several days. The brickmakers press the

Fig. 4:
Tools of Jenne master mason Be Sau. From top left: roller for cement floors; long and short multipurpose iron rods; industrial level; tape; square; basket for carrying *banco*; plumb bob; trowel; tape; wooden square for smoothing interior walls. The rods, basket, trowel, and pieces of string and wood are the only tools used by most village masons. Photograph by A. LaViolette, 1983.

mud into wooden frames (ca. 40 by 20 by 10 cm), removed after a few minutes. The bricks dry in the sun until sold to the proprietor of the construction. The architectural pottery is made by one of the two groups of local potters, those women (*numumusow*) married to Jenne's blacksmiths (the *numu*). They make rain spouts, columnar latrine elements, ceiling/roof vent covers, and forms over which the rounded tops (*sarafar dyutu*) on points (*sarafar idye*) in the Sudanese façade are shaped (Maas and Mommersteeg 1992:220). The window shutters and doors are made or imported by local carpenters.

The molded bricks or *tubabufrey* ("foreigners' bricks") came into common use in the 1930s or '40s (LaViolette 1987:296; Bourgeois 1987 suggests a slightly earlier date) and are now the dominant mode of building in this area. *Jennefrey* can still be seen throughout Jenne and the region's villages (Fig. 5) and dominate the later building phases at Jenne-jeno (after ca. eleventh century) (S. McIntosh and R. McIntosh 1980). Masons made them by cupping their hands around a small amount of the clay mixture, which they say differed from the present mix in having rice and millet chaff blended into it instead of grass. The mixture was prepared as it is now, but with water added to it on two subsequent mornings before it was ready to use

on the third day. The masons unanimously consider *jennefrey* construction sturdier than its replacement, but acknowledge that it is easier to make straight, even walls (not always part of the aesthetic) with the latter.

The clayey mixtures found inside, between, and over mudbricks are known collectively as *banco*, but by individual terms as well. This *banco* today is clayey mud, water, and grass; when *jennefrey* were in use, the plaster reportedly contained no added grass or chaff. Because the water encircling Jenne is a repository of large amounts of organic material, however, the mud dredged from its bed is already heavily mixed.

The *banco* used to face and reface outside walls, the roof, and the ceiling is similar to the substance of the bricks (new homes of the wealthy are sometimes faced with a mixture including a modicum of cement, which obviates refacing; this is permitted by the government as long as the look of *banco* is maintained). It is clayey sediment mixed with cereal chaff, sheep/goat feces, and water, and is made in a small steep-sided pool, 1–2 m in diameter, dug into the street by the house under construction. The organic material decomposes, giving the mix a glutinous consistency desirable for application and durability. It is left standing for about a week before application, an event whose timing

Fig. 5:
Eroded house wall with *jennefrey* at bottom left and *tubabufrey* above and to right. Photograph by A. LaViolette, 1983.

Fig. 6:
Detail of central minaret of Jenne mosque; the minaret contains the interior *mihrab*, the niche that faces Mecca. The sticks of palm at left mark the line of ceiling beams; the *toronw* jutting from the minarets are unique to religious architecture. Ostrich eggs, symbolizing the unity of Islam, are mounted atop each minaret; due to the disappearance of ostriches in the Sahel, potters now make white ceramic replicas. A single light bulb is mounted below the eggs; in 1983 this was lit by a generator in a nearby shop. Photograph by A. LaViolette, 1983.

is signaled by the strong odor of the mixture before it dries.

The favored interior wall plaster (*dow labu*; Maas and Mommersteeg 1992:220) has a lower clay content than the mixtures already described and a higher sand content, leaving an uncracked finished surface. The reddish sand base (the sand comes from the Bani river bed 7 km away from Jenne) is mixed with a small amount of premixed, soaked *banco* with a low debris content, the *banco* in a quantity just sufficient to hold the sand together. Brushing against an interior wall with this surface results in a minor sand shower, a situation sometimes remedied by adding a small amount of cement to the sandy mud in the final application, which strengthens it without changing its appearance. Decorative washes are made for the walls by using clay with high kaolin content steeped in water, a technique yielding shades from white to deep grey, the latter used at the foot of the wall. The addition of crushed pebbles high in iron oxide, such as those used in pottery paint, yields a gold pigment for detailing the grey and white. Occasionally, bright industrial paints are used, especially bright pink, blue, and green.

The wood used in the layered ceiling designs, roof beams, and protruding *toronw* is predominantly palm imported from areas to the south, around Matombo. No wood is used in construction of the walls except in the case of mosque architecture, which is characterized by *toronw* sticking out perpendicularly from the tower elements (Figs. 1 and 6). An effort is made to keep any ceiling plaster (often ceilings remain unplastered) free from large potsherds, bones, bits of cloth, and other debris commonly present in the exterior wall and roof plaster. Because the ceilings are not exposed to the heat of the outside, they tend not to crack as much as do the building exteriors. The ceiling is ideally faced two times with this plaster, and the third time with a plaster usually containing a higher concentration of sand for a smooth but slightly textured look.

The laying of a foundation begins with the excavation of a trench in the rough shape of the proposed building. In Jenne and in every village situated on a settlement mound, this involves digging into cultural deposits with unequal densities. Soft deposits are excavated completely, so that the resulting foundation trench may be quite deep and irregular in some places, and filled in with bricks. The same molded bricks used in the walls of the house are then placed in the trench. Most walls are two to three bricks thick (the bricks are placed parallel to the lines of the wall), and the normal foundation width would be the same as the wall it supports. Under normal circumstances a foundation would be about five bricks deep, but may be as many as 10 deep. Any foundation that can bear the weight of one story can bear the weight of a second (making the archaeological determination of building heights at sites such as Jenne-jeno, and therefore population density estimates, difficult). Because normal beam and *banco* rooftops are made to be used as verandas, the weight of a second story usually does not create more stress than the roof itself was designed to take. The weight of the upper stories rests directly on the walls of the house, as described above. Therefore, a building that has existed for years with a single story can be made into a taller building with only minor alterations.

The importance of repeated external plastering to the integrity and design of the architecture cannot be overstated. Replastering also accounts for a large portion of the commissions a mason receives in a year; he may work on the construction of four or five new buildings or additions, but do 30 replasterings (homeowners replaster their own houses not infrequently, but the best quality work is done by masons). The intense downpours of the March and April rainy season can bring immediate damage to the unfired brick structure unless there is at least a centimeter of *banco* on the exterior. Much of this will wash off the building each year, so that annual applications are ideal. The only building assured of this continued care, in Jenne and most towns, is the mosque.

The mosque as centerpiece

The mosque standing now in Jenne is the third to have stood in this town. The earliest was built in the thirteenth century and stood for 600 years (Bourgeois 1987). The new mosque was built in 1907 by Jenne *bari* under the sponsorship of the French colonial administration, on the site of the ruined thirteenth century mosque. Bourgeois (1987) has convincingly overturned the position held by a number of scholars (e.g., Prussin 1974, 1986) and many *bari* themselves—that the structure's design shows significant French cultural influence as well as Sudanese architectural elements. It is clearly indigenous, perhaps influenced by the French only in their encouragement and financial support of its building, as a public relations gesture, and in the desire of the people of Jenne to make the most of this offer by building on a massive scale.

The mosque is greater than the sum of its parts, though the parts are masterfully executed (see Prussin 1974 and Maas and Mommersteeg 1992 for the most comprehensive documentation of the mosque). It is immense, and can be seen many kilometers from Jenne jutting above the skyline

Fig. 7:
Interior of the mosque, showing columns, the sand floor, a lamp niche in the rear wall, and fluorescent light, lit by a generator in a nearby shop. Photograph by B. E. Frank, 1983.

of the town. The mosque is built on a platform roughly 75 m square (Maas and Mommersteeg 1982:111), and its central minaret (Fig. 6) which marks the location of the niche inside facing Mecca (the *mihrab*, in Arabic) stands nearly 20 meters above the surface of the market square before it, topped by two ostrich eggs. The mosque's façade, which projects above the roof proper, comprises a total of three minarets and corner buttresses, numerous *toronw* (wooden projections), small towers, and tiny windows, and is a mass of alternating shadow and light throughout the day. The same is true of the two sides of the building, though simpler in design. Behind the mosque proper is attached a large walled courtyard, nearly the size of the mosque itself, where women pray. The mosque's interior is dominated by a forest of 99 slightly uneven, rectangular clay columns, which extend to the roof, at a height of over 10 m (Fig. 7). The floor is not solid, but made of deep, cool sand, on which men walk barefoot and kneel to pray.

Every year thousands of able-bodied residents of Jenne reiterate the centrality of this earthen building to their lives

Fig. 8:
Annual replastering of the mosque. Photograph by A. LaViolette, 1983.

by helping to coat the enormous mass of the mosque with a new layer of *banco* (Fig. 8). On two consecutive weekends before the late spring rains, first one half of the town and then the other comes out to work: men bring the *banco*, prepared at the town's edge, by basketfuls on their heads, while women carry buckets of water needed to thin the mixture. The parades of people are accompanied by drumbeating and singing. Huge lashed-together ladders lean on the mosque, bearing the younger masons (Fig. 9), who direct what can only be described as carefully orchestrated commotion. Master masons and other elders, in their best starched white or blue gowns, sit on the surrounding walls holding their walking sticks, proprietarily overseeing the activities while the thousands of other participants become covered with mud.

Conclusion

When we ponder gifted craft specialists in the ancient world, we do not necessarily include those who are responsible for objects—or buildings—made of impermanent materials. Because of our reliance on the tangible, there is a rough correspondence between an object's durability and the value we attribute to it; western and scientific value systems grant prestige to material culture that stands the test of time and continues to look good.

In the instance of the Jenne *bari* and their Sudanese architecture, we do not have to make the case that the more recent, historically known impact of both the masons and their architecture is something we can project into deep history, although it would quite possibly be valid if we did. We can simply suggest that buildings, even "impermanent" ones, can be socially valued to the extent that great sophisti-

Fig. 9:
Young masons apply *banco* to the southern wall of the mosque, standing on ladders built for the occasion. Although this is a city-wide effort, only masons climb the ladders to apply the mixture. Photograph by R. Maassen, 1983.

cation of design and engineering technology can be invested in them. Further, we can suggest that in such a case, those responsible for holding and passing on the vast knowledge involved can acquire a status akin to that of other great artisans, artists, and highly valued members of society. In the architecture of these earthen towns, and in the ruined structures which lie in the archaeological deposits across the countryside, what is preserved is not permanent objects *per se*, but a medium in which creation, adaptation, reworking, repair, and function may be the enduring traditions.

This brings us to a larger point, concerning how we use material remains to construct ancient history, society, and culture in Africa. At the ground level, literally, we struggle archaeologically to be able to discern the remains of buildings—of unbaked mud or even less permanent materials—which once framed the human landscape (e.g., see R. McIntosh 1974, 1976, 1977). We expect to struggle with archaeological invisibility vis-à-vis, for example, early hominid sites and those of gatherers and hunters, but expect more and more substantive deposits as we study increasingly complex societies. Yet the nature of building in large expanses of Africa runs counter to these expectations. True, stone architecture of regions such as the Nile Valley, the Zimbabwe Plateau, Ethiopia, and the Swahili coast have drawn archaeologists to them and have led to the delineation of urbanism and/or statehood in these places. Yet in other areas we know from historical sources of great political centers—among them, states as recent as the nineteenth century—which have left tantalizingly little behind them, especially architecturally, from which one could discern the wealth and extent of the polity (see, e.g., Connah 1987:214–226). Indeed, the "invisibility" of these complex societies has meant their exclusion from narratives of social evolution, which go from the peripatetic to the "enduring," "solid" "achievements" of the "heights" of civilization.

Archaeologists have shown that the unbaked mud brick architecture of the Inland Niger Delta is not, as it turns out, invisible at all. Yet the high art of its design cannot be entirely reconstructed from archaeological remains, nor can we trace the streams of architectural influence in details that have melted away in the rains. What the Jenne *bari* and their architecture can lead us to is the possibility of truly great design in impermanent materials, and the suggestion of a correspondingly complex social and cultural milieu in which the space for such design and technology existed.

Acknowledgments

The field work upon which this paper was based was supported by the Wenner-Gren Foundation for Anthropological Research (Grant-in-Aid #4257), Sigma Xi, The Explorers Club, and the Graduate School of Washington University, St. Louis. It was ultimately made possible by the hospitality and cooperation of the people of Jenne. I thank Terry Childs, Barbara Frank, Richard Handler, and the anonymous reviewers for their comments in preparation of this paper, and Barbara Frank and Rémy Maassen for contributing photographs.

References

Bedaux, R. M. A., T. S. Constandse-Westermann, L. Hacquebord, A. G. Lange and J. D. van der Waals. 1978. Recherches archéologiques dans le delta intérieur du Niger. *Paleohistoria* 20:91–220.

Bird, C. S., and M. B. Kendall. 1980. The Mande Hero. In *Explorations in African Systems of Thought*, ed. I. Karp and C. S. Bird, pp. 13–26. Indiana University Press, Bloomington.

Blier, S. P. 1987. *The Anatomy of Architecture: Ontology and Metaphor in Batammaliba Architectural Expression*. Cambridge University Press, Cambridge.

Bourdier, J.-P., and T. Minh-ha. 1985. *African Spaces, Designs for Living in Upper-Volta*. Africana Publishing Company, New York.

Bourgeois, J.-L. 1987. The History of the Great Mosques of Djenné. *African Arts* 20(3):54–62, 90–92.

Bourgeois, J.-L., C. Pelos, and B. Davidson. 1989. *Spectacular Vernacular: The Adobe Tradition*. Aperture, New York.

Brasseur, G. 1968. *Les etablissements humains au Mali*. Memoire d'Institut Fondamental d'Afrique Noire, No. 83. IFAN, Dakar.

Caillié, R. 1830. *Journal d'un Voyage à Temboctou et à Jenne*. 3 vols. Imprimerie Royale, Paris.

Camara, S. 1976. *Gens de la parole: essai sur la condition et le role des griots dans la société malinké*. Mouton, The Hague.

Connah, G. 1987. *African Civilizations*. Cambridge University Press, Cambridge.

Conrad, D. C., and B. E. Frank (eds.). 1995. *Status and Identity in West Africa: Nyamakalaw of Mande*. Indiana University Press, Bloomington.

Denyer, S. 1978. *African Traditional Architecture*. Heinemann, London.

Devisse, J. 1983. Urban History and Tradition in the Sahel. In *Reading the Contemporary African City*, Proceedings of Seminar Seven in the Series Architectural Transformations in the Islamic World, Dakar, Nov. 2–5, 1982. Concept Media, Singapore.

Dubois, F. 1897. *Tombouctou la Mysterieuse*. Flammarion, Paris.

Engstrom, T. 1955. Contribution aux connaissance des styles de construction au Soudan Français. *Ethnos* 20:122–126.

———— 1957. *Notes sur les modes de construction au Soudan*. Statens Etnografiska Museum Memoir 26. Statens Etnografiska Museum, Stockholm.

_____ 1959. Origin of Pre-islamic Architecture in West Africa. *Ethnos* 24:64–69.

es-Sa'di, A.
_____ 1981 (1913–14). *Tarikh Es-Soudan*, transl. O. Houdas. Maisonneuve, Paris.

Gallais, J. 1967. *Le delta intérieur du Niger; étude de géographie régionale*. Memoire de l'Institut Fondamental d'Afrique Noire, No. 79. 2 vols. IFAN, Dakar.

_____ 1984. *Hommes du Sahel, espaces-temps et pouvoirs, le Delta Intérieur du Niger 1960–1980*. Flammarion, Paris.

Gardi, B. 1981. Der Nabel der Gesellschaft: Griots und Handwerker in Westafrika. *Ethnologica Helvetica* 5:1–24.

_____ 1983. *Ein Markt wie Mopti*. Ph.D. dissertation, University of Basel, Switzerland.

Gardi, R. 1974. *Indigenous African Architecture*. Van Nostrand Reinhold, New York.

Gijn, A. van. 1983. *Huisgebruik in Djenné, Mali*. Unpublished thesis (ethnology), University of Groningen.

Iowa, J. 1985. *Ageless Adobe: History and Preservation in Southwestern Architecture*. Sunstone, Santa Fe.

Kati, M. 1981 (1913–14). *Tarikh El-Fettach*, transl. O. Houdas and M. Delafosse. Maisonneuve, Paris.

LaViolette, A. 1987. *An Archeological Ethnography of Blacksmiths, Potters, and Masons in Jenne, Mali (West Africa)*. Ph.D. dissertation, Washington University. University Microfilms, Ann Arbor.

_____ 1990. The Jenne Bari: Islamic and Nyamakalaw Synthesis in Artisan Organization. Paper presented at the 33rd Annual Meeting of the African Studies Association, Baltimore.

_____ 1995. Women Craft Specialists in Jenne: The Manipulation of Mande Social Categories. In *Status and Identity in West Africa: Nyamakalaw of Mande*, ed. D. C. Conrad and B. E. Frank, pp. 170–181. Indiana University Press, Bloomington.

Leslie, J. 1991. Building with Earth in South Arabia. *Mimar* 38:60–67.

Levtzion, N. 1971. A Seventeenth-century Chronicle by Ibn-Mukhtar: A Critical Study of the Ta'rikh al-Fattash. *Bulletin of the Society of Oriental and African Studies* 34(3):571–593.

Maas, P. 1986. Djenné: Living Tradition. *Aramco World* 41(6):18–29.

Maas, P., and G. Mommersteeg. 1992. *Djenné: chef-d'oeuvre architectural*. Institut des Sciences Humaines, Bamako and Université de Technologie, Eindhoven; and Institut Royal des Tropiques, Amsterdam.

McIntosh, R. J. 1974. Archaeology and Mud Wall Decay in a West African Village. *World Archaeology* 6:154–171.

_____ 1976. Square Huts in Round Concepts. *Archaeology* 29(2):92–101.

_____ 1977. The Excavation of Mud Structures: An Experiment from West Africa. *World Archaeology* 9(2):185–199.

McIntosh, R. J., and S. K. McIntosh. 1981. The Inland Niger Delta before the Empire of Mali: Evidence from Jenne-jeno. *Journal of African History* 22:1–22.

_____ 1988. From Siècles Obscurs to Revolutionary Centuries on the Middle Niger. *World Archaeology* 20(1):141–165.

McIntosh, S. K., and R. J. McIntosh 1980. *Prehistoric Investigations at Jenne, Mali*, 2 parts. Cambridge Monographs in African Archaeology 2. BAR International Series 89 (ii). British Archaeological Reports, Cambridge.

_____ 1984. The Early City in West Africa: Towards an Understanding. *African Archaeological Review* 2:73–98.

McNaughton, P. R. 1988. *The Mande Blacksmiths: Knowledge, Power and Art in West Africa*. Indiana University Press, Bloomington.

Monteil, C. 1903. *Monographie de Djenné, cercle et ville*. Jean Mazeyrie, Tulle.

_____ 1932. *Djenné: une cité soudanaise. Metropole du Delta Central du Niger*. Société d'Editions Géographiques, Maritimes et Coloniales, Paris.

N'Diayé, B. 1970. *Les Castes au Mali*. Editions Populaires, Bamako.

Park, M. 1799. *Travels in the Interior Districts of Africa*. W. Bulmer and Co., London.

Prussin, L. 1970. Sudanese Architecture and the Manding. *African Arts* 3(4):12–19, 64–67.

_____ 1974. *The Architecture of Djenné African Synthesis and Transformation*. Ph.D. dissertation, Yale University. University Microfilms, Ann Arbor.

_____ 1977. Pillars, Projections and Paradigms. *Architectura* 7(1):65–71.

_____ 1986. *Hatumere: Islamic Design in West Africa*. University of California Press, Berkeley.

Rangelrooy, A. van. 1984. *Toubabou ça va?: een Architectuuronderzoek in Djenné, Mali*. Unpublished thesis (architecture), Technological University, Eindhoven.

Snelder, R. 1984. The Great Mosque of Djenne: Its Impact Today as a Model. *Mimar* 12:66–74.

Tamari, T. 1991. The Development of Caste Systems in West Africa. *Journal of African History* 32:221–250.

Velden, R. van der. 1989. *Moskeen en Metselaars in de Regio van Djenne*. Unpublished thesis (architecture), Technological University, Eindhoven.

Werner, L. 1992. Rediscovering the Kasbahs. *Choices* 1:27–31.

SKIMMING THROUGH POTTERS' AGENDAS: AN ETHNOARCHAEOLOGICAL STUDY OF CLAY SELECTION STRATEGIES IN CAMEROON

Olivier P. Gosselain

Préhistoire, Musée Royal de l'Afrique Centrale, B-3080 Tervuren, Belgium

ABSTRACT Clay selection and processing are traditionally examined by archaeological scientists from a materialistic point of view, according to which each decision results directly from environmental, technical, and functional constraints. Potters' behavior is, however, much more complex as revealed by a recent study of pottery production in Cameroon.

Measurements of two clay properties that are directly perceivable by the potter (texture and plasticity/workability) and application of these data to technical and functional data reveal that material constraints are by no means the sole factors in clay selection and processing. Instead, cultural and economical concerns are decisive elements affecting decision making.

Introduction

The exploitation of raw materials is undoubtedly one of the most discussed topics in studies of pottery technology, but paradoxically, one of the least understood. Most studies have been carried out by archaeometrists who usually interpret archaeological pottery in the light of concepts and theories related to ceramic engineering. There has been therefore an increase in typically functionalist and determinist approaches to ceramics in which the characteristics of raw materials are conceived only in terms of adaptations to environmental, technical, and functional constraints (Stimmell et al. 1982; Braun 1983; Steponaitis 1984; Schiffer and Skibo 1987; Kaiser 1989; O'Brien et al. 1994). Without denying the relevance of such studies, I am afraid they yield a false picture of pottery making by unwittingly transforming partial realities into objective ones, especially since the ethnographic examples frequently cited probably apply only to rare or even extreme situations (Arnold 1971; DeBoer and Lathrap 1979). In fact, the so-called "archaeometry of pottery" is increasingly handicapped by fashionable research designs, new scientific gadgets, and an insatiable need to reach unambiguous results quickly. For example, when Braun (1983) showed how changes in vessel thickness and temper size distribution in Woodland period pottery could be interpreted in terms of heat conductivity and resistance to thermal shock, the latter notion became a real obsession for archaeologists (Woods 1986:169). Most researchers who used Braun's concepts, however, forgot that his work was only a case study and that his conclusions implied more than ceramic engineering.

One may indeed wonder whether the mechanical properties we consider are directly related to vessel or paste characteristics, whether these properties are the most relevant ones, whether prehistoric potters consciously manipulated them, and whether technical changes result only from functional changes. Some criticisms have already been heard regarding this purely materialistic approach to pottery (Plog 1980; Woods 1986; Feinman 1989; van der Leeuw et al. 1991), yet it seems that the more we focus on technical aspects, the more we forget to consider one of their most essential components—the cultural dimension.

Anthropologists interested in this matter have continuously shown us that technical systems are polydimensional and arbitrary, since they rely not only on choices determined by technical and functional factors, but by social, economic, and symbolic concerns as well (Mauss 1927; Lemonnier 1986, 1992; Pfaffenberger 1992). If there are indeed choices to be made, one can then speak of style when speaking of technique (Lechtman 1977; Childs 1986), at least if we accept the isochrestic definition of style as proposed by Sackett (1990).

It is evident that, in the field of clay selection, the cultural dimension has moved to the background and has often been implicitly denied (see some exceptions in Arnold [1985] and Nicklin [1979]). In order to avoid the continued

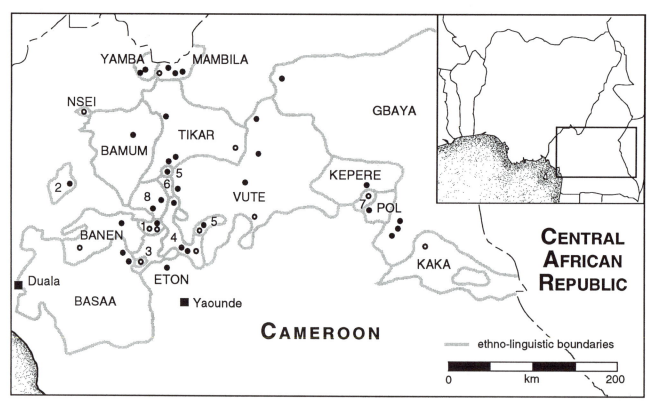

Fig. 1:
Location of potters (individuals or communities) indicated by circles. if circle is filled, clay samples were taken at those potter localities. Ethnolinguistic groups designated in caps, and as follows: (1) Bafia, (2) Bamileke fe'fe', (3) Yambassa, (4) Sanaga, (5) Bafeuk, (6) Djanti, (7) Kwakum, (8) Balom.

fragmentation of our approach to technical phenomena, we must consider all factors that influence the decision-making process and determine the mutual compatibility of these factors.

The first step in assessing the use of raw material is to determine the realm of choices that a potter can make in respect to his socioeconomic context, environment, technical tradition, and functional aims (as Childs [1986, 1989] has done in her study of refractory materials used in iron smelting). If clear choices are evident, the second step is to try to identify the reasons that led a potter to favor one alternative over another. This article proposes to use such an approach, based on the data on clay selection and processing collected during a recent ethnoarchaeological study in Cameroon (Gosselain 1993, 1995).

Fieldwork

Between 1990 and 1992, I observed the technical procedures of pottery production by 82 artisans of 21 ethnolinguistic groups south of the Adamawa Massif (Fig. 1). These 21 groups belong to 7 linguistic entities: Narrow Bantu, Ring Grassfields, Eastern Grassfields, Mambiloïd, Tikar, Oubanguian, and Adamawa (the first five are part of the Wide Bantu linguistic grouping; the other two are Oubangian-Adamawa). Despite the cultural diversity, the

socioeconomic context of pottery activity is almost identical in each group: (1) potters are primarily women, although men have the right to make pots; pottery is an exclusively male occupation among the Yamba for reasons that remain unclear; (2) only a few people have the skills to make pots; (3) pottery making is always subordinate to the primary professional concerns of the potter, such as farming and domestic tasks; (4) income derived from pottery is minimal; (5) the finished products are either used by the potter, sold, bartered, or offered in his/her immediate community, or sold in nearby markets (always within 15 km from the residential site of the artisan); and, (6) production is sporadic, usually restricted to the dry season; it occasionally occurs at other times depending on necessity or demand. One might expect that the present preference for plastic and metallic vessels would have a negative impact on the socioeconomic context of pottery production. As long as these potters can recall, however, the context of pottery making has not fundamentally changed except that there are many fewer artisans practicing today (this reduction in number paralleled a decrease in demand).

Two kinds of clay exploitation are used: (1) collective exploitation, where a number of potters use the same place and extract the clay individually or collectively; and, (2) individual exploitation where the potter is the only one to use a source. Anyone, however, can potentially exploit each place since there seems to be no exclusive rights to clay deposits. On the other hand, because potters never keep stocks of clay and clay is not a commercialized product, the technical process always begins with the extraction of clay. This task is carried out by the artisan him/herself or, less frequently, by a member of his/her family or friends.

Location of pottery clay sources

Precise information was usually available regarding the extraction sites, including distances from the manufacturing sites, economic situation, context of discovery, and relocalization, if required. Ninety-five percent of the exploited clay sources (n = 49) lie within a radius of 3 km. Only one source is situated at a distance exceeding 5 km, and this is the sole example involving the use of a vehicle. The pheric distance (Arnold 1985:33) rarely exceeds 30 to 45 minutes (15 minutes being the most representative value), despite the diversity of environments (savanna, forest, and mountainous regions). Beyond this threshold, potters consider clay extraction a problematic event. This is not because of the physical effort involved, but because of the limited time that can be devoted to pottery making, the need to perform other tasks at the same time, and the low income obtained through such work.

When comparing the distribution of clay-extraction sites to that of other activity areas, it is clear that all are situated in locations exploited primarily for other purposes (residential locations, farming and fishing sites, fields, hunting paths, and marketplaces). This situation is explained by both the context in which clay sources are discovered and the need to subordinate pottery making to primary subsistence activities. The identification of a clay source is never the result of systematic prospecting, but always arises from an accidental discovery (i.e., while ploughing fields, removing earth on riverbanks for the construction of fish barrages, observing soils brought up by crab burrowing activities, or observing embankment erosion by a living area and along roads or tracks). The potter or a member of his/her family or community may observe the presence of a possibly suitable clay in such situations, and either tests it or informs the potter of the location. This aspect of 'accidental discovery' is quite important because every potter knows that clay prospecting is both uncertain and time consuming. Even if a particular area is known to be a prime site for clay collection (i.e., riverbanks, marshlands, or swamps), the actual clay depth is extremely variable. One could dig testpits for months without any success. Clay is also sometimes attributed human-like qualities, and is considered a mobile material that may hide if it so chooses. It is useless to look for clay in such a case, because it may not want to be discovered. This notion, particularly explicit among Bafia potters (Gosselain 1992a), shows how symbolic conceptions can have an impact on selection strategies and, consequently, on the location of extraction sites.

The subordination of pottery making to other subsistence activities is especially explicit at the level of clay extraction. Many potters continue to exploit the same source as the person from whom they learned the technique, while others change sources once or more during their lifetime, or exploit several sources at the same time. The potters who have changed their extraction sites generally have done so because they relocated their residence or fields. Relocation of these sites by only a few kilometers is sufficient to momentarily stop pottery making until a new, nearby clay source is found.

Potters who exploit several sources at the same time are generally those who stay in their fields for a certain period of the year and in the village for the remaining part of the year (each clay source is situated near the residential site), or who take advantage of a different activity (i.e., fishing, hunting, fuel collection, market) while collecting clay. When asked the reasons for choosing a clay source near working or living areas, the potters explain that going far away would obviously be stupid. Also, the small income expected from pottery making can hardly make it a priority. There is no problem as long as pottery making can be done at the same time as other activities or does not interfere with them. The moment it calls for an independent investment of time and energy, a conflict arises which may result in abandoning the activity or restricting the pottery-making sessions.

Relationships between techniques, functions, and clay properties

After providing a rough outline of the socioeconomic context of pottery activity among the groups considered here, we must next consider how technical and functional aims define the properties of suitable clays, and assess the compatibility of those properties with the socioeconomic requirements of the activity.

I cannot fully estimate the range of sources that could have been exploited (Childs 1986, 1989), because I lack precise pedological information on the study area and have not had an opportunity to survey the environment of each potter systematically. A comparison between the technical procedures and functional aims of each potter and the characteristics of the exploited clays, however, allows us to determine the degree of flexibility in the selection of materials and see to what extent techniques and functions are interchangeable in the study area.

It is clear from an assessment of the functional aims of the potters that there is complete homogeneity among the groups under study. The methods of use and scope of products are nearly identical and each potter produces vessels for collecting, cooking, transport, and conservation. A comparison of the manufacturing processes, especially during the primary stages (clay processing, shaping, drying, and firing), however, reveals substantial technical variations. Each stage is discussed below.

Clay processing

Four procedures were observed of which the first is the most common: (1) simple pounding; (2) sand addition and pounding; (3) drying, grinding, sieving, moistening, and kneading; and, (4) grinding and kneading. The distribution of these techniques seems to correspond to the ethnolinguistic communities, yet a number of these communities also correspond to specific geographical areas. It, therefore, is premature to assign a purely cultural or functional origin to their distribution.

Shaping

Nine techniques were observed, although the differences among them are sometimes very subtle (i.e., the manner in which coils are placed or the methods for beginning or finishing a vessel). Here, I choose to group these techniques into six categories according to the manner in which the clay is shaped when constructing the body of the vessel (apparently the most delicate shaping operation). These six categories are: (1) superimposing thin coils; (2) crushing coils placed one against each other with the point of contact at half their diameter (see Gosselain 1992a); (3) superimposing large rings of clay which are drawn out; (4) hollowing and drawing a lump of clay with the addition of crushed coils to make the upper part; (5) hollowing and drawing a lump of clay; and, (6) pinching and drawing a loaf-shaped lump of clay and superimposing coils to make the upper part. The distribution of shaping techniques generally coincides with ethnolinguistic boundaries. Moreover, a series of technical groupings and affiliations also correspond to linguistic groupings and affiliations (Gosselain 1995).

Drying

Although different methods were observed that related to place, facility, and time-span, the processes are difficult to individualize because they depend on situational factors. These include the season in which work is carried out, the intensity of sun, the ambient moisture, the planning of firings as a function of markets, orders, or time available, and the manufacturing place at the time of observation.

Firing

Almost all the potters use the open firing technique. Only the Bamileke, the Bamum, and the Nsei use pits, but these are so shallow that they can be likened to open firings. The observed variations concern only the type of fuel utilized, the number of pots fired at once, the manner in which pots and fuel are placed, and the methods of starting the fire. Thermometric measurements taken in the field (see details and results in Gosselain 1992b, 1995) show that, despite these variations, temperatures reached, heating rates, the length of exposure to different temperature thresholds, and the duration of firings all fall within the same interval of variation for all potters. These firings are characterized by a fast heating rate (temperatures above 500°C are reached within the first 10 minutes), a tremendous thermic variability (differences between maximum temperatures in the same firing may be 500° to 600°C), and a short duration (potters start removing pots from the fire 15 to 30 minutes after it is set ablaze).

The technical point of view, then, reveals that only clay processing and shaping techniques show important variations. The goal of clay processing is to homogenize the extracted raw material, but one can also modify its granulometric composition by adding a certain fraction (here, for instance, sand) or by removing a certain fraction through grinding and sieving.

When asked why sand is added to the clay, potters explain that this increases the workability of the material and helps avoid cracking when pots are dried or fired. Most potters indicate that they have always added sand (since they continue to exploit the same clay source), although some received the recipe from other artisans when they changed clay sources. Those potters who grind and sieve the clay explain that it is impossible to shape a pot prior to these actions because sand and pebbles prevent the clay from 'sticking'. Even if they could fabricate a pot, it would automatically shatter when fired. A number of potters add that there is sometimes a much finer clay below the clay they exploit which could be used for pottery making. Its extraction would require more work, however, and it is always worthwhile to grind and sieve the material in order to assure good results.

The relationship between selected clays and the different shaping techniques is much more difficult to determine. First, almost all potters are familiar with only one shaping technique, so it is impossible for them to assess the suitability of a clay for all possible manipulations. Secondly, such relationships are extremely difficult to objectively assess for those not involved in the process of pottery making. All evidence indicates, however, that plasticity and workability are the decisive factors at this stage. Thus, it seems that the crucial problems that confront the potters concern the granulometry (range of grain size) and the plasticity/workability of the clays. I analyzed these two factors in the field and in the laboratory and then systematically compared all the clays to yield the results below.

Granulometry

Thirty-nine granulometric analyses were conducted on clays sampled at the time of extraction and then again after processing when their granulometric composition was altered by adding sand or by grinding and sieving. The analyses involved dry sieving the fraction above 63 μm, wet sieving the fraction between 63 and 32 μm, and decanting the fraction below 32 μm. The classification system I used considers gravel to be above 2000 μm, sand to be between 2000 and 63 μm, silt to be between 63 and 2 μm, and clay to be less than 2 μm. Granulometric fractions were broken down into three categories (clay, silt, and sand and gravel); the results are displayed on a tripolar graph to render comparisons easier (Fig. 2).

The graph shows that most of the clays used tend to concentrate in the range characterized by a large proportion of sand and gravel (40 to 80%), an intermediate proportion of silt (15 to 45%), and a low proportion of clay (3 to 30%). A number of particularities appear when this clay distribution is compared to the processing modes. For example, two of the four clays tempered with sand lie clearly out of the average range when analyzed in their raw state. They have a much higher proportion of clay content, and less sand and gravel. One of them falls into the group of clays described above after the sand is added, but the other remains outside the group. The two other samples are, at the time of their extraction, within this range; their granulometric composition changes either strongly or weakly with the addition of sand.

The granulometric composition of the three clays that are ground and sieved is much more ambiguous because they are hard to separate from all the others at the time of their extraction. Two of them fall well inside the overall cluster and remain there after having been processed, although they show a clear decrease in the coarser constituents. It also is evident that two potters may obtain completely different results when using the same clay and the same processing technique (note that the sample has two different trajectories and two different compositions after grinding and sieving). The third clay lies a little outside the concentration (although not outside all possible variation). While joining the cluster after having been processed, this clay remains beyond the range of the first two samples.

The distribution of clays that were only pounded or ground and kneaded is completely heterogeneous. They are found throughout the concentration range; two of them

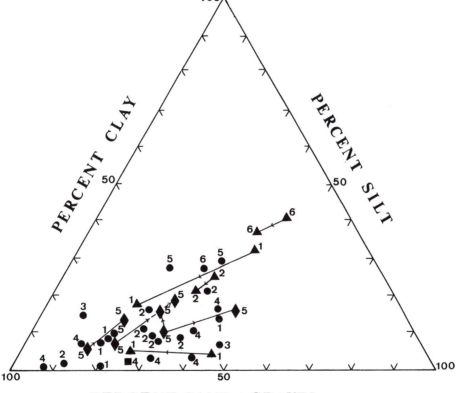

Fig. 2:
Granulometric distribution of clays exploited by potters. Numbers refer to shaping techniques (1: superimposing thin coils; 2: crushing coils; 3: superimposing large rings of clay; 4: hollowing and drawing a lump of clay plus crushed coils; 5: hollowing and drawing a lump of clay; 6: pinching and drawing a loaf-shaped lump of clay plus superimposing coils). Symbols refer to processing techniques (●: simple pounding; ■: grinding and kneading; ◆: grinding and sieving; ▲: addition of sand and pounding). For the latter two techniques, arrows indicate that it is the same clay, before and after processing.

are even outside the range where the proportion of sand and gravel exceeds eighty percent. These two clays mark the extreme limit of the variation and, consequently, seem to indicate that there is no threshold of coarseness beyond which grinding and sieving are compulsory. Finally, the distribution of clays as a function of shaping techniques reveals absolutely no correlation. Each clay is apparently suitable for any of the six identified techniques in regard to its granulometry.

In summary, neither shaping techniques nor most of the processing techniques appear to be directly influenced by the granulometric properties of the clays. Only two of the samples might require the addition of a coarse material (sand) because they are finer grained and contain more clay than the others. One of them, however, remains finer grained than all the other clays after processing. Tests carried out in the field and laboratory show that adding sand does not modify potential workability in any way, nor the drying and firing behavior. It cannot be precluded, however, that, in functional terms, fine-grained clays are less resistant to repeated heating and cooling than coarse-grained clays (Woods 1986:169–170).

Another experiment undertaken in the field was to exchange clays between potters. These exchanges have been only possible to date among those artisans who simply pound clay. Each time the potter was presented with an alternative clay, a number of complaints arose regarding its textural quality ("too coarse," "too fine," "impossible to shape," "impossible to fire"). Nevertheless, each artisan easily succeeded in shaping, drying, and firing a pot. These results confirm those of the granulometric analyses; the notion of "fine" and "coarse" is neither subject to consensus nor technical restrictions, but to individual appreciation.

Plasticity and workability

Identifying and measuring the plasticity of clay is quite difficult. This is not only because of the number of interfering factors (Bloor 1957; Rice 1987:60–61), but also because of the instruments required (i.e., Norton 1938). Workability is even more vague since one only perceives this quality manually and, hence, subjectively (Bronitsky 1982; Rice 1987:61). In order to make rapid and precise measurements in the field and overcome the subjectivity involved in using standard comparative means, I chose to retain only one aspect of plasticity: the yield point. I used a standard shear device (type Torvane, Soiltest Inc) commonly used in pedology and geomorphology. This is a small circular plate mounted on a calibrated spring with blades radiating toward the center. These blades are plunged into the clay until the clay reaches the plate. A rotating force then is applied to the spring until the clay offers no resistance to shearing. The threshold of resistance (or yield point) measured by the spring is expressed in grams per square centimeter and is an indicator of plasticity.

I measured the yield point of clays at the time of their extraction and after processing,[1] when the potter began the shaping process. Ten measurements were taken each time because of the heterogeneity of the clays (especially in their raw state); a mean value was then calculated. The results are grouped according to processing and shaping techniques (Fig. 3) and reveal that the yield point of a number of clays is extremely variable at the time of extraction. It falls between 66 and 683 gr/cm^2 regardless of the different techniques, an interval of 617 gr/cm^2. When broken down according to processing modes, it is clear that: (1) the clays which were simply pounded continue to have a very large interval (between 200 and 610 gr/cm^2); (2) clays to which sand was added prior to pounding may present a higher resistance to shearing than other clays (and this is probably related to their higher clay content), but may also occur within the same range as the first group of clays; (3) clays that have to be ground and sieved have a systematically lower resistance (between 66 and 100 gr/cm^2); and (4) the one sample of ground and kneaded clay has a lower resistance than those that were only pounded, yet has a higher resistance than those that were ground and sieved.

It thus seems that, in some instances, there may be a relationship between the initial plasticity and the processing technique. No relationship, on the other hand, can be demonstrated between the yield point and the shaping technique. There is a general overlap of measurement results here and, although technique by technique some intervals are smaller or slightly skewed to lower or higher values, this is essentially explained by the number of measurements recorded for each technique. Furthermore, after any kind of processing, the variation interval is strongly reduced to between 85 and 263 gr/cm^2. Here, the relationship between workability achieved and the processing technique cannot be proven because the overlap is somewhat generalized. Good workability can apparently be obtained by: (1) either reducing the plasticity through pounding, adding sand and pounding, or grinding and kneading, or (2) increasing plasticity through grinding and sieving. Field observations also indicate that the initial plasticity does not permit any predictions on later workability. Two potters processing the same clay also may obtain totally different results.

There is no relationship between workability and shaping technique; most measurements are between 100 and 200 gr/cm^2. The only occurrence of a possible interdependance between technique and plasticity/workability, then, should take place at the level of clay processing. The resulting implications would be that very plastic clays require the addition of sand and pounding to reach good workability, and non-plastic clays need to be ground and sieved to reach the same workability threshold. The question remains, however, whether or not this relationship is as simple as presented.

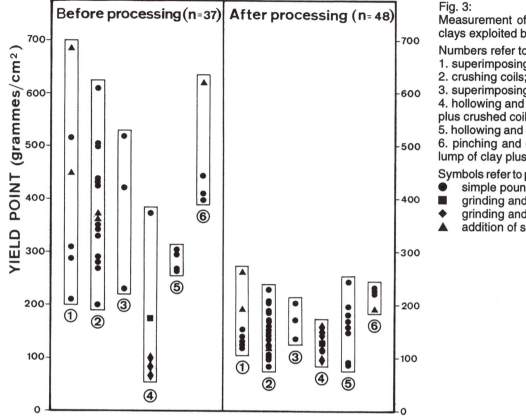

Fig. 3:
Measurement of the yield point of the clays exploited by potters.

Numbers refer to shaping techniques:
1. superimposing thin coils;
2. crushing coils;
3. superimposing large rings of clay;
4. hollowing and drawing a lump of clay plus crushed coils;
5. hollowing and drawing a lump of clay;
6. pinching and drawing a loaf-shaped lump of clay plus superimposing coils.

Symbols refer to processing techniques:
● simple pounding;
■ grinding and kneading;
◆ grinding and sieving;
▲ addition of sand and pounding.

Field and laboratory experiments indicate that, in the first case, simple pounding may yield the same workability threshold or even a lower one with or without the addition of sand. In the second case, the selected clays are systematically extracted closer to the soil surface than the other clays, and they are always more watery. The yield point rises in general from 100 to 200 gr/cm^2 when left to dry in the sun for one or two hours and simple pounding is then sufficient to reach the workability desired. Thus, all the plasticity and workability evidence indicates that we again are faced with deliberate choices and not material constraints.

Discussion and conclusion

We have seen the degree to which the socioeconomic context of pottery making forces the artisan to limit as much as possible his/her investment in time and energy. This situation results in very short geodesic and pheric distances (Arnold 1985) between the manufacturing place and the clay source as they relate to choices of raw materials, systematic exploitation of clays in locations already frequented for other activities, and deliberate choices to avoid clay prospecting. In comparison, Arnold's survey of the ethnographic literature indicates that the "preferred territory of exploitation . . . probably occurs at 1 km," while the upper limit of the maximum range of exploitation is 7 km (Arnold 1985:38, 50). His examples, however, come from different socioeconomic contexts. The Cameroonian potters also have a preferred territory of exploitation of 1 km, but their maximum range of exploitation is 3 km.

Generally speaking, such restrictions could leave the artisan with technical and functional problems that are impossible to solve. The more demanding a potter is in choosing a clay (as determined by its technical and functional suitability), the lower her/his chances are for finding it locally (Mason 1981:17–18) and/or the higher his/her labor input will be for processing it (Feinman et al. 1981:872). In order to systematically subordinate the location of clay extraction sites to other more imperative activities and to minimize the investment of time and energy, the potter must have technical and functional aims flexible enough to allow for a tremendous tolerence in clay selection.

What has field observation and laboratory analysis shown us regarding the selective flexibility of Cameroonian potters? First, the successfully exploited clays have an extreme granulometric and plastic variability for the same potting techniques and pot functions. Second, there is no clear correlation between the use of different techniques (e.g., processing and shaping) and the selected clays. The techno-functional advantage of adding sand must still be explored for some clays, yet for grinding and sieving no environmental, technical, or functional restrictions can be identified.

Thus, all evidence seems to suggest a number of technical and functional aims that enable considerable flexibility in the selection of raw materials. Very coarse clays and finer clays are equally suitable. This fact increases the ease and probability of locating a source near other activity areas, thereby meeting the socioeconomic demands of the potter. The capability of adapting methods to different clays is confirmed by the experimental clay-exchanges undertaken in the field, as well as by the artisans' explanations of their selection criteria. For example, a number of potters may assess the quality of the clay by its color, smell, texture, or plasticity, but all of them state that it is impossible to determine the suitability of a clay without having shaped and fired an experimental pot.

One must also bear in mind that, in the technical and functional context of the observed communities, the use of such coarse-grained clays probably helps the pots withstand open firing (Woods 1986) and allows them to be used for cooking (Cardew 1969).

The absence of similar studies prevents any immediate comparisons with other regions of Africa. Socioeconomic contexts (Drost 1968) and selection strategies of clays (Nicklin 1979) also vary considerably across Africa and may be quite different from those described in this paper. A more general comparison also seems impossible because, as far as I know, there are no precise data on the granulometry, plasticity, and workability of clays used by present or prehistoric potters. Some conclusions, however, can be roughly outlined.

Technical and functional constraints are by no account the only factors which bear on decision making, even at a level as important as clay selection. When interpreting paste compositional data, one must keep in mind the possibility that the potter's principal concern was to minimize his/her investment in time and energy. A change in raw materials can also result from a relocation of principal activity areas. In such a case, strictly materialistic interpretations may possibly conceal a mundane event, like the displacement of a field, or a much more fundamental event, such as a change in the local economy of production. Furthermore, if there are technical and functional constraints in pottery making, they may be more flexible than we have previously believed. The use of concepts related to ceramic engineering could lead archaeologists to label most of the exploited clay as functionally unsuitable in contexts similar to that of the Cameroonian potters studied.

The archaeologists then might attribute completely incorrect techno-functions to the pottery.

The apparent flexibility of constraints also shows that a stylistic approach to pottery techniques is inevitable. Potters make arbitrary choices at all levels of the technical process so that non-technical concerns are consistently introduced. This means that, far from having an independant existence, technical systems are completely embedded in culture in much the same way as decorative motifs, religious beliefs, or kinship systems.

More case studies which seek to understand the motivations behind potters' decisions are needed. Once scholars go beyond primary determinism, they undoubtedly will reach a more realistic level of analysis concerning the production of pottery. If culture is the archaeologist's first concern, why not begin by asking questions of cultural relevance?

Acknowledgments

My fieldwork, supervised by P. de Maret, was supported by a research grant from the University of Brussels. Granulometric analyses were conducted by H. Doutrelepont and interpreted by J. Moeyersons (both at the Royal Museum of Central Africa). I thank them and E. Cornelissen, K. Klieman, J. Renard, and G. Vendemmia for all the help they provided. Finally, I would like to thank the potters who kindly, patiently, and humorously supported my numerous inquiries.

Notes

1. Fewer measurements were taken before processing because they were sometimes impossible to conduct, and because some potters individually process a clay extracted collectively.

References

Arnold, D. E. 1971. Ethnomineralogy of Ticul, Yucatan Potters: Etics and Emics. *American Antiquity* 36(1):20–40.

_____ 1985. *Ceramic Theory and Cultural Process.* Cambridge University Press, Cambridge.

Bloor, E. C. 1957. Plasticity: A Critical Survey. *Transactions of the British Ceramic Society* 56:423–481.

Braun, D. P. 1983. Pots as Tools. In *Archaeological Hammers and Theories*, ed. J. A. Moore and A. S. Keene, pp. 107–134. Academic Press, New York.

Bronitsky, G. 1982. Clay Workability: A Pilot Study. *Archaeological Society of Virginia Quaterly Bulletin* 37(2):65–72.

Cardew, M. 1969. *Pioneer Pottery*. Longman, London.

Childs, S. T. 1986. *Style in Technology. A View of African Early Iron Age Iron Smelting Through its Refractory Ceramics*. Ph.D. dissertation, Department of Anthropology, Boston University.

_____ 1989. Clay to Artifacts: Resource Selection in

African Early Iron Age Iron-making Technologies. In *Pottery Technology: Ideas and Approaches,* ed. G. Bronitsky, pp. 139–164. Westview Press, Boulder, CO.

DeBoer, W. R., and D. W. Lathrap. 1979. The Making and Breaking of Shipibo-Conibo Ceramics. In *Ethnoarchaeology: Implications of Ethnography for Archaeology,* ed. C. Kramer, pp. 102–138. Columbia University Press, New York.

Drost, D. 1968. Töpferei in Afrika: Oekonomie und Soziologie. *Jahrbuch des Museums für Völkerkunde zu Leipzig* 25:131–270.

Feinman, G. M. 1989. Tinkering with Technology: Pitfalls and Prospects for Anthropological Archaeology. In *Pottery Technology: Ideas and Approaches,* ed. G. Bronitsky, pp. 217–220. Westview Press, Boulder, CO.

Feinman, G. M., S. Upham, and K. G. Lightfoot. 1981. The Production Step Measure: An Ordinal Index of Labor Input in Ceramic Manufacture. *American Antiquity* 46(4):871–884.

Gosselain, O. P. 1992a. Technology and Style: Potters and Pottery Among Bafia of Cameroon. *Man* 27(3):559–586.

_____ 1992b. Bonfire of the Enquiries. Pottery Firing Temperatures in Archaeology: What for? *Journal of Archaeological Science* 19(2):243–259.

_____ 1993. From Clay to Pottery, with Style. 1990–1992 Fieldwork in Cameroon. *Nyame Akuma* 39:2–7.

_____ 1995. *Identités Techniques. Le Travail de la Poterie au Cameroun Méridional.* Ph.D. dissertation, Faculté de Philosophie et Lettres, University of Brussels.

Kaiser, T. 1989. Steatite-tempered Pottery from Selevac, Yugoslavia: A Neolithic Experiment in Ceramic Design. *Archaeomaterials* 3(1):1–10.

Lechtman, H. 1977. Style in Technology. Some Early Thoughts. In *Material Culture. Styles, Organization, and Dynamics of Technology,* ed. H. Lechtman and R. S. Merrill, pp. 3–20. West Publishing Company, St Paul, MN.

Lemonnier, P. 1986. The Study of Material Culture Today: Toward an Anthropology of Technical Systems. *Journal of Anthropological Archaeology* 5:147–186.

_____ 1992. *Elements for an Anthropology of Technology.* Museum of Anthropology, University of Michigan, Ann Arbor.

Mason, R. 1981. *Native Clays and Glazes for North American Potters. A Manual for the Utilization of Local Clay and Glaze Materials.* Timber Press, Portland, OR.

Mauss, M. 1927. Divisions et proportions des divisions de la sociologie. *Année Sociologique* 2:98–176.

Nicklin, K. 1979. The Location of Pottery Manufacture. *Man* 14(3):436–458.

Norton, F. H. 1938. Instrument for Measuring Workability of Clays. *Journal of the American Ceramic Society* 21:33–36.

O'Brien, M. J., T. D. Holland, R. J. Hoard, and G. L. Fox. 1994. Evolutionary Implications of Design and Performance Characteristics of Prehistoric Pottery. *Journal of Archaeological Method and Theory* 1(3):259–304.

Pfaffenberger, B. 1992. Social Anthropology of Technology. *Annual Reviews of Anthropology* 21:491–516.

Plog, S. 1980. *Stylistic Variation in Prehistoric Ceramics.* Cambridge University Press, Cambridge.

Rice, P. M. 1987. *Pottery Analysis: A Sourcebook.* University of Chicago Press, Chicago.

Sackett, J. R. 1990. Style and Ethnicity in Archaeology: The Case for Isochrestism. In *The Uses of Style in Archaeology,* ed. M. W. Conkey and C. A. Hastorf, pp. 32–43. Cambridge University Press, Cambridge.

Schiffer, M. B., and J. M. Skibo. 1987. Theory and Experiment in the Study of Technological Change. *Current Anthropology* 28(5):595–622.

Steponaitis, V. P. 1984. Technological Studies of Prehistoric Pottery from Alabama: Physical Properties and Vessel Function. In *The Many Dimensions of Pottery,* ed. S. E. van der Leeuw and A. C. Pritchard, pp. 81–127. Universiteit van Amsterdam, Amsterdam.

Stimmell, C., R. B. Heimann, and R. G. V. Hancock. 1982. Indian Pottery from the Mississipi Valley: Coping with Bad Raw Materials. In *Archaeological Ceramics,* ed. J. S. Olin and A. D. Franklin, pp. 219–228. Smithsonian Institution Press, Washington, DC.

van der Leeuw, S. E., D. A. Papousek, and A. Coudart. 1991. Technical Traditions and Unquestioned Assumptions: The Case of Pottery in Michoacan. *Techniques et Culture* 17–18:145–173.

Woods, A. J. 1986. Form, Fabric, and Function: Some Observations on the Cooking Pots in Antiquity. In *Ceramic and Civilization.* Vol. 2: *Technology and Style,* ed. W. D. Kingery, pp. 157–172. The American Ceramic Society, Columbus, OH.

Research Papers in Science and Archaeology

Supplement to Volume 11, 1994

Series Editor
Kathleen Ryan

Production Editors
Helen Schenck
Jennifer Quick

Advisory Committee
Stuart Fleming, Chairman
Philip Chase
Patrick McGovern
Henry Michael
Naomi F. Miller
Vincent Pigott

Design and Layout
Helen Schenck

Graphics
Paul Zimmerman
Veronica Socha

The subscription price for *MASCA Research Papers in Science and Archaeology* is $20, payable in U.S. dollars. We also accept VISA/MASTERCARD. This price covers one main volume per year. In addition, we publish supplementary volumes which are offered to MASCA subscribers at a discounted price.

This is a refereed series. All material for publication and books for review should be sent to The Editor, *MASCA Research Papers in Science and Archaeology*. Subscription correspondence should be addressed to The Subscriptions Manager, MASCA, University of Pennsylvania Museum, 33rd and Spruce Streets, Philadelphia, PA 19104-6324.